BEYOND THE COVENANT CHAIN

Iroquois Books

BEYOND THE COVENANT CHAIN

The Iroquois and Their Neighbors in Indian North America, 1600–1800

Edited by

DANIEL K. RICHTER and JAMES H. MERRELL

Foreword by
WILCOMB E. WASHBURN

SYRACUSE UNIVERSITY PRESS

Copyright © 1987 by Syracuse University Press
Syracuse, New York 13244-5160

First published 1987

ALL RIGHTS RESERVED

First Edition

93 92 91 90 89 88 87   5 4 3 2 1

The paper used in this publication meets the minimum requirements of American National Standard for Information Sciences—Permanence of Paper for Printed Library Materials, ANSI Z39.48-1984. ∞™

Library of Congress Cataloging-in-Publication Data

Beyond the covenant chain.

(Iroquois books)
Bibliography: p.
Includes index.
1. Iroquois Indians. 2. Iroquois Indians—Government
relations. 3. Indians of North America—Government
relations. I. Richter, Daniel K. II. Merrell, James
Hart, 1953–   . III. Series.
E99.I7B37 1987   973'.0497   87-10226
ISBN 0-8156-2416-6 (alk. paper)

Manufactured in the United States of America

To **SHARON** and **LINDA**

CONTENTS

ACKNOWLEDGMENTS   *ix*

CONTRIBUTORS   *xi*

FOREWORD by WILCOMB E. WASHBURN   *xiii*

    The Iroquois and Their Neighbors in the Early 1670s (map)   2
    The Iroquois and Their Neighbors in the Early 1760s (map)   3

INTRODUCTION   5
    DANIEL K. RICHTER and JAMES H. MERRELL

I   PERSPECTIVES FROM IROQUOIA

    1   Ordeals of the Longhouse: The Five Nations in
       Early American History   *11*
       DANIEL K. RICHTER

    2   Linking Arms: The Structure of Iroquois Intertribal
       Diplomacy   *29*
       MARY A. DRUKE

    3   Covenant and Consensus: Iroquois and English,
       1676–1760   *41*
       RICHARD L. HAAN

II NEAR NEIGHBORS

    4   Toward the Covenant Chain: Iroquois and Southern
       New England Algonquians, 1637–1684   *61*
       NEAL SALISBURY

    5   "Pennsylvania Indians" and the Iroquois   *75*
       FRANCIS JENNINGS

    6   Peoples "In Between": The Iroquois and the Ohio
       Indians, 1720–1768   *93*
       MICHAEL N. MCCONNELL

III DISTANT FRIENDS AND FOES

    7 "Their Very Bones Shall Fight": The Catawba-
       Iroquois Wars   115
       JAMES H. MERRELL

    8 Cherokee Relations with the Iroquois in the Eighteenth
       Century   135
       THEDA PERDUE

    9 "As the Wind Scatters the Smoke": The Tuscaroras in
       the Eighteenth Century   151
       DOUGLAS W. BOYCE

NOTES   165

INDEX   203

ACKNOWLEDGMENTS

For advice and encouragement, the editors thank many friends and colleagues, in particular Francis Jennings, Philip Morgan, Thad Tate, and Stephen Saunders Webb. Gladys Cashman displayed great skill and greater patience in typing all of the notes for the volume, as did Linda Merrell in preparing the maps. The conference from which this book developed received financial support from the Institute of Early American History and Culture and the Wenner-Gren Foundation for Anthropological Research, Inc. Funding for the completion of the manuscript was provided by the Vassar College Committee on Research and by the Dickinson College Faculty Committee on Research and Development.

CONTRIBUTORS

DOUGLAS W. BOYCE, Dean of the Faculty at King College, is the author of several works on Tuscarora history and culture.

MARY A. DRUKE is a research consultant. She is Associate Editor of *The History and Culture of Iroquois Diplomacy: An Interdisciplinary Guide to the Treaties of the Six Nations and Their League.*

RICHARD L. HAAN, Associate Professor of History at Hartwick College, has written several articles on native American history. He is Book Review Editor for *Ethnohistory.*

FRANCIS JENNINGS is Director Emeritus of the Newberry Library's D'Arcy McNickle Center for the History of the American Indian. He is author of *The Invasion of America* and *The Ambiguous Iroquois Empire,* and he is editor of *The History and Culture of Iroquois Diplomacy.*

MICHAEL N. MCCONNELL is Assistant Professor of History at the University of Alabama, Birmingham. He has researched extensively on the eighteenth-century Indian peoples of the Ohio Country.

JAMES H. MERRELL is Assistant Professor of History at Vassar College. He has published a number of articles on Indian history during the colonial period and is completing a history of the Catawbas.

THEDA PERDUE, Professor of History at Clemson University, is the author of *Slavery and the Evolution of Cherokee Society, 1540–1866.*

DANIEL K. RICHTER, Assistant Professor of History at Dickinson College, has published several articles on Iroquois history and on early American Indian–European relations. He is Associate Editor of *Ethnohistory.*

NEAL SALISBURY is Professor of History at Smith College. Among his works is *Manitou and Providence: Indians, Europeans, and the Making of New England, 1500–1643.*

WILCOMB E. WASHBURN is Director of the Smithsonian Institution Office of American Studies. His contributions to American historiography include *The Governor and the Rebel: A History of Bacon's Rebellion in Virginia* and *The Indian in America.*

FOREWORD

WILCOMB E. WASHBURN

RARELY HAS so complex and powerful a myth — what has been called the "Myth of Iroquois Empire" — been so subtly and perceptively examined as in the essays in this book. While the Iroquois have long fascinated scholars, the products of that fascination have as often resulted in clouding as in clarifying the image of this powerful Indian people. The Iroquois were perceived by nineteenth-century American historians and writers as supermen of the wild frontier, fierce warriors who dominated their Indian neighbors and intimidated the French, Dutch, and English colonists. They were the stuff of myth and legend, in the fashion of the ancient Greeks. The American reader should always remember that myth incorporates truth and imagination as well as elements of the false and unknown. Because of their extraordinary accomplishments it was natural that the Iroquois were seen in a mythical context.

In recent years the mythical view of the Iroquois has given way to more careful analysis of the original data on which the nineteenth-century image rested. One of the results of that study has been a more perceptive understanding of the sophistication of Iroquois diplomacy. Recent works have paid particular attention to the role of the Covenant Chain, elevating it from the level of metaphor and imagery to an expression of a formal link between the Iroquois and various Indian and European nations.

This book examines in detail the extent and the significance of the Covenant Chain as it affected the friends and enemies of the Iroquois to the north, east, west, and south. In every direction, the Iroquois role has remained controversial if not puzzling; each of the essays in this volume sheds important new light on the nature of those relationships. The formal character of the Covenant Chain is challenged by several of the contributors: some see the Chain in more ambiguous, metaphorical terms; others argue that there was in fact a series of pacts linking individual nations, rather than a single comprehensive network among many nations.

xiii

Whatever their differences on the precise configuration of the Covenant Chain, the authors agree that the nature of Iroquois alliances was complex and dynamic, and each link reflected ongoing, ever-changing relationships.

Just as Iroquois foreign policy was dynamic, so were Iroquois internal politics. There was often confusion on the part of the Europeans in distinguishing between the Iroquois Great League of Peace as a cultural and ritual institution and the Iroquois Confederacy as a political and diplomatic entity. Early observers sometimes speculatively attributed state-like characteristics to the Great League of Peace and a common foreign policy to the Confederacy. But the authors here make it clear that the unity attributed to Indian confederacies such as the Iroquois and Cherokees tended to be a reflection of the objectives, desires, and minds of Europeans.

Beyond the Covenant Chain attempts to strip away the layers of myth and misinterpretation that have been applied to this remarkable people ever since Europeans encountered them. Not all the interpretations presented in this book will be accepted without question; controversy will continue to rage around the Iroquois, and this volume — a brilliant synthesis despite its varied authors and themes — will fuel the ongoing debate by setting forth views that all future scholars must contend with. Given the skill and erudition of the contributors, I venture to predict that it will become a landmark in Iroquois historical studies.

BEYOND THE COVENANT CHAIN

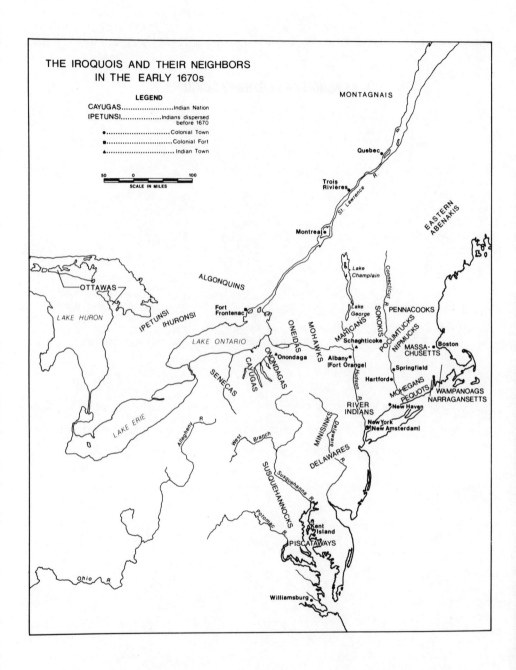

THE IROQUOIS AND THEIR NEIGHBORS
IN THE EARLY 1670s

LEGEND

CAYUGAS.....................Indian Nation
[PETUNS]..................Indians dispersed
                              before 1670
●..............................Colonial Town
■..............................Colonial Fort
▲..............................Indian Town

50   0   100
SCALE IN MILES

MONTAGNAIS

Quebec●

Trois
Rivières●

St. Lawrence R.

Montreal●

EASTERN
ABENAKIS

OTTAWAS

ALGONQUINS

Fort
Frontenac■

Lake
Champlain

Lake
George

PENNACOOKS

[PETUNS] [HURONS]

LAKE HURON

LAKE ONTARIO

ONEIDAS

MOHAWKS

MAHICANS

SOKOKIS

POCUMTUCKS

NIPMUCKS

MASSA-
CHUSETTS

Boston●

Schaghticoke▲

●Onondaga

ONONDAGAS

Albany●
[Fort Orange]

Springfield●

SENECAS

CAYUGAS

Hudson R.

Hartford●

MOHEGANS

PEQUOTS

WAMPANOAGS
NARRAGANSETTS

LAKE ERIE

RIVER
INDIANS

●New Haven

Allegheny R.

West   Branch

MINISINKS

Delaware R.

New York
●[New Amsterdam]

DELAWARES

Susquehanna R.

SUSQUEHANNOCKS

Potomac R.

Kent
Island

PISCATAWAYS

Ohio R.

Williamsburg●

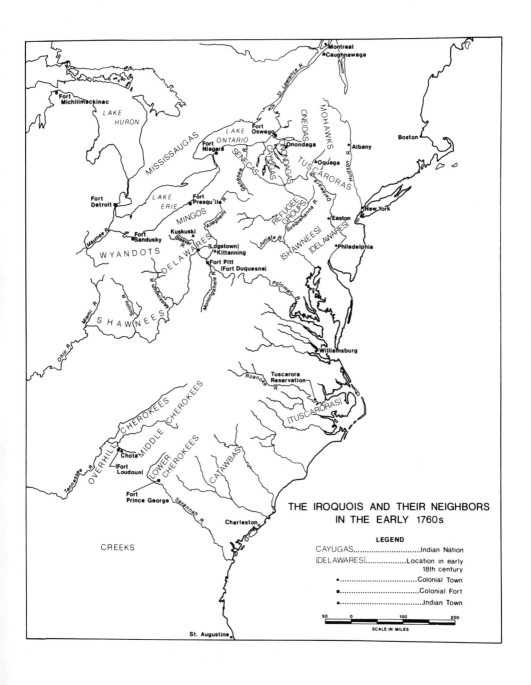

THE IROQUOIS AND THEIR NEIGHBORS
IN THE EARLY 1760s

LEGEND

CAYUGAS............................Indian Nation

|DELAWARES|.................Location in early
                                        18th century

•.....................................Colonial Town

■.....................................Colonial Fort

▲.....................................Indian Town

INTRODUCTION

DANIEL K. RICHTER AND JAMES H. MERRELL

T HE SUPREMACY of the Iroquois was never disturbed," wrote amateur historian and professional politician De Witt Clinton in 1811. "The conquests and military achievements" of those who called themselves People of the Longhouse "were commensurate with their martial ardor, their thirst for glory, their great courage, their invincible perseverance, and their political talents."[1] Clinton's celebration of Iroquois imperial power sails in the mainstream of an historiographical tradition that flows from Cadwallader Colden and William Smith in the eighteenth century through Lewis Henry Morgan and Francis Parkman in the nineteenth to Stephen Saunders Webb in the twentieth.[2] From villages strung across what is now upstate New York, the Five Nations of the Iroquois Confederacy—east to west, the Mohawks, Oneidas, Onondagas, Cayugas, and Senecas—seemed to wield influence vastly disproportionate to their numbers. For most of the European colonial period, they counted less than 10,000 people.[3] Yet, in Webb's words, the Iroquois "had as large an influence on the imperial marches of North America as did the French or English."[4]

Lately, however, scholars have more than disturbed the supremacy of the people Clinton dubbed "the Romans of this Western World." Recent studies argue that there was no forest empire ruled by Iroquois caesars, that the Confederacy's imperial pretensions were a fiction jointly promulgated by Anglo-American and native American politicians. The reality behind the pretensions was the "Covenant Chain," a complex set of alliances among Indians and English in which Iroquois and New Yorkers played dominant but seldom dictatorial roles. And the warriors of the Five Nations were not invincible; except for a brief period in the 1640s when they outgunned their opponents, they proved eminently beatable on the battlefield. Nor were Iroquois diplomatic skills especially great; most notably, the pivotal agreements of the "Grand Settlement of 1701" among the Five Nations and their European and Indian neighbors now seem more a French diktat than a bold stroke of native diplomacy. Finally, that venerable symbol of Indian political unity, the League of the Iroquois, has suffered in recent historiography; the seventeenth- and eighteenth-century League was riven by localistic tendencies, factional disputes, and ethnic rivalries.[5]

These new findings led, in March 1984, to the convening of a scholarly conference on "The 'Imperial' Iroquois." The weekend gathering in Williamsburg, Virginia, attracted approximately one hundred historians, anthropologists, and representatives of native American cultural organizations. At the first session, Francis Jennings — whose important book *The Ambiguous Iroquois Empire* appeared on the eve of the meeting — set the tone: "The theme of this conference is a myth," he declared; "the Iroquois never had an empire."[6] Eight more papers, the remarks of four commentators, and a number of lively debates involving the audience followed, but one thing quickly became clear: the existence of an empire of the sort described by Clinton, Morgan, and Parkman could no longer be supported. After a career of some 250 years, the whole Imperial Iroquois issue seemed dead.

The issues that were alive — and there were many — involved exactly what the Five Nations *did* have, if it was not an empire. "The idea of empire is really inconsequential," one Iroquois spokesman observed in comments from the floor. "The definition of Webster's or anyone else doesn't really matter to the Iroquois. They were a power to be reckoned with and they changed a great course of the history in North America."[7] Such remarks indicated that the time had come to reevaluate the Five Nations' role because, whatever the errors of the traditional view, the fact remained that the French, Dutch, English, and most Indians considered the Iroquois the dominant native power in the colonial east. The conference suggested a fruitful approach: perhaps future research should shift away from the familiar area of Indian relations with Europeans and towards contacts, conflicts, and connections among the Five Nations and their native neighbors.

For Indian life never revolved exclusively around the colonists. Transplanted Europeans, with their microbes and technology, their missionaries and settlers, obviously had an enormous impact on native history, and of course Europeans wrote the sources on which historians must primarily rely. Yet throughout the colonial period, the native peoples of eastern North America preserved their cultural autonomy and, to a degree only dimly perceived by colonists, pursued their own diplomatic and military agendas.[8] Analysis of the Iroquois contribution to seventeenth- and eighteenth-century North American history should, therefore, move beyond studies of the Covenant Chain system of European-Indian alliances to explore a heretofore shadowy realm of native American experience.

Moving beyond the Covenant Chain — both conceptually and geographically — is the purpose of this collection of essays on relations between the Iroquois and their neighbors in Indian North America. The story begins in Iroquoia itself. In Part I, essays by Daniel Richter, Mary Druke, and Richard Haan probe some secrets of Iroquois success in coping with internal change and external pressures. In Part II, Neal Salisbury, Francis Jennings, and Michael McConnell venture outside Iroquoia to examine contacts between the Six Nations and diverse neighboring peoples in New England, Pennsylvania, and the Ohio Country. Part III ranges farther afield, as James Merrell, Theda Perdue, and Douglas Boyce explore Iroquois dealings with southern Indian nations: Catawbas, Cherokees, and — to return the tale to its Iroquoia starting point — Tuscaroras, many of whom trekked northward from the Carolinas to become the Sixth Nation of the Confederacy in the early eighteenth century.[9]

The essays do not pretend to explore completely or conclusively the myriad relationships between the Iroquois and their neighbors. In particular, major peoples to the north and west of Iroquoia — Hurons, Ottawas, Algonquins, and others — deserve more attention than they receive here. So too do connections between the Six Nations and their kin who converted to Roman Catholicism and settled in such mission villages as Caughnawaga, near Montreal. Nonetheless, the following chapters present, we believe, an illustrative sampling of the variety and textures of relations among the peoples the Iroquois were once believed to rule. The sampling may not produce a definitive — or even always coherent — image. Indeed, the authors are sometimes in fundamental and often in minor disagreement; Haan and Jennings, for example, differ strongly on the early contours of the Covenant Chain. In scholarship such arguments are to be expected and even welcomed when an established paradigm ceases to function.

Ongoing scholarly debates and gaps in the picture, however, should not obscure the common themes that emerge. The Iroquois depicted in these essays are more divided among themselves and less domineering of others than they have generally appeared in previous scholarship. Defeat and disappointment visited them far more often than the conventional wisdom believes. Yet it cannot be denied that they cut imposing figures on the early American stage. Iroquois preeminence, these essays suggest, stemmed less from "martial ardor" or "thirst for glory" than from an extraordinary ability to adapt familiar customs and institutions in response to novel challenges, to convert weaknesses into strengths, and to forge alliances among themselves and with others that helped preserve native political and cultural autonomy. By making a virtue of necessity, the Iroquois may not have won themselves an empire, but they did win the respect, even fear, of native and European peoples near and far.

Whatever else these inquiries may tell us, we hope they will foster a clearer sense of the Iroquois place in colonial North America and inspire a new appreciation of the importance and complexity of interactions among native peoples. Traders, warriors, and ambassadors from Iroquoia ranged from New England and New France to Virginia and the Carolinas, from the Atlantic coast to the banks of the Mississippi. Their activities illuminate a host of different peoples and permit the study of a wide variety of contacts, friendly and unfriendly. Those contacts are crucial to historical understanding not only of the Iroquois but also of their native neighbors, not only of American Indians but also of the wider world in which Iroquois and Catawbas, Delawares and Narragansetts, French and English all lived.

I

PERSPECTIVES FROM IROQUOIA

ORDEALS of the LONGHOUSE

The Five Nations in Early American History

DANIEL K. RICHTER

F DIPLOMACY, like charity, begins at home, consideration of the Iroquois role in seventeenth- and eighteenth-century North America should commence with an examination of internal Iroquois political history.[1] This essay proposes a framework for analysis of political change in the Five Nations and finds an engine for that change in a series of social crises provoked by the European invasion. Amid each social ordeal, some Iroquois devised novel solutions within a framework of familiar cultural patterns. Their capacity to innovate without abandoning essentials of traditional culture — indeed to explain innovation in terms of cultural conservatism — provides one key to the Five Nations' survival and to the Iroquois' prominent role in the diplomacy of eastern North America. More than most native Americans of their region, the People of the Longhouse were able to adapt to the challenges of "the Indians' new world" while preserving their cultural identity.[2]

"I humbly conceive you have been kept in the dark, to say no worse of it, as to the nature of the Government of the five Indian nations," New York Governor Robert Hunter wrote to an unidentified correspondent in 1713.[3] The governor might have been addressing generations of subsequent commentators on seventeenth- and eighteenth-century Iroquois political history. Some of the darkness stems from the confounding of two related but distinct phenomena: the Iroquois Great League of Peace as a cultural and ritual institution, and the Iroquois Confederacy as a political and diplomatic entity. The first — the League — is undeniably old, relatively unchanging, and very much alive to the present day. The second — the Confederacy — developed gradually in the years following European con-

tact. It was in constant flux, and during the American War for Independence it virtually ceased to exist. The Grand Council of the League was
composed of the bearers of sacred sachem titles that descended in chiefly
lineages. The political and diplomatic leadership of the Confederacy was
much more fluid, and it consisted of men who had first gained influence
in the councils of their home villages. Only gradually during the seventeenth century did these local leaders form political networks spanning
the Five Nations, and those networks would never acquire the elaborate
and enduring structure of the Grand Council. The membership and ritual
of the two entities might at times overlap, but the functions of the councils
of the Great League of Peace and of the Five Nations Confederacy remained
distinct. The stability of the first and the evolution of the second delineate
a conceptual framework for analysis of political continuity and change
in Iroquoia.

The intellectual climate in which native American history has traditionally been written explains part of the confusion between the League
and the Confederacy. Only in the past few decades have scholars begun
to abandon the anthropological construct of a static, unchanging "ethnographic present" in favor of a more realistic emphasis upon process, change,
and adaptation; only recently, therefore, have Indians in the scholarly
literature begun to acquire a "history" of their own, in the sense that term
is usually understood.[4] For the Five Nations—despite an enormous and
sophisticated library of anthropological writing—the story has been little
different from that of other native peoples. Traditionally, most students
assumed that Iroquois political institutions persisted virtually unchanged
from the fifteenth or sixteenth century, when the League was founded, to
the nineteenth century, when ethnologists began systematically to record
native traditions.[5]

Foremost among those nineteenth-century ethnologists was Lewis
Henry Morgan. To the work of his generation can be traced the particular
variety of history-less history that confounded the League with the Confederacy. "At the institution of the League, fifty permanent sachemships
were created . . . ; and in the sachems who held these titles were vested
the supreme powers of the confederacy," Morgan declared. "The several
sachems, in whom, when united in general council, resided the supreme
powers of the League, formed, when apart in their own territories, the rul-
ing bodies of their respective nations."[6] Morgan's contemporary and sometime correspondent, missionary to the New York Senecas Asher Wright,
worked from the bottom up to paint a similar picture. "If any individual desired to bring any proposition before the general council," Wright explained,
"he must first gain the assent of his family, then his clan, next of the four

related clans in his end of the council house, then of his nation, and thus in due course of order the business would be brought up before the representatives of the confederacy" in the Grand Council. "It was a standing rule," the missionary continued, "that all action should be unanimous."[7]

Morgan's and Wright's portraits of Iroquois political organization were substantially influenced by the historical and personal circumstances in which they worked. Morgan's initial interest in the League stemmed from motives that twentieth-century anthropologists would find curious. At Cayuga Academy in Aurora, New York, the young author and several associates established a fraternal organization that gradually assumed a pseudo-Indian theme. The society soon expanded to include branches in several upstate New York communities and began to call itself "the New Confederacy of the Iroquois"; Morgan was its "Supreme Chieftain." In 1845, when a Rochester newspaper announced an impending League Council on the Tonawanda Seneca reservation, the Chieftain and a few other club members decided to attend, in order to learn more about the rituals and government of the people after whom their organization was named. The field trip was the beginning of the research that led to Morgan's monumental book, *League of the Iroquois.*[8]

All of this deserves mention not to belittle the earliest work of perhaps the greatest of nineteenth-century American anthropologists. Scholars should be grateful that Morgan studied the Iroquois at all, and in any event—whatever his motives—he conducted his later research with admirable rigor. The important point is that he attended his first League Council in search of information he could use to elaborate the institutional structure and ceremonies of his "New Confederacy." Moreover, he was inclined to assume that whatever he found had persisted relatively unchanged —in the minds of Indian informants if not in practice—since the earliest days of contact between Indians and Europeans.[9] And Morgan was ill-equipped to understand the intricacies of the nonstate, noncoercive politics characteristic of most eastern North American Indians in the European colonial period, though his later studies of kinship organization and the "kinship state" placed him far beyond most of his contemporaries in this regard.[10] In short, he went to Tonawanda looking for a "government" in what later theorists would call the "ethnographic present." And that is what he found.

Like Morgan, missionary Wright learned about Iroquois politics primarily from Seneca informants. Again, the particular historical context is important. Wright's long career (1831–75) spanned a period of intense social upheaval, bitter factional rivalries, and reprehensible land frauds involving the Seneca Nation. After the Buffalo Creek Treaty of 1838, in which a handful of drunken leaders sold off most of their homeland, Senecas deposed their hereditary sachems and installed a system of majority rule. This revolution sparked intense debates, which seem to have colored Wright's perceptions. The great virtue of the Senecas' old ways, he said, was the principle of government by unanimous consent, which had allowed Iroquois people to benefit from "the great and constantly increasing power of the confederacy, until their councils were divided by the bribery and Whiskey of the Whites." In Wright's account, the decay of unanimity and of the Grand Council's authority culminated in the debacle of Buffalo Creek and the troubles of the Seneca Nation under its new plan of majority rule.[11] This interpretation was fine political rhetoric for hereditary sachems trying to seize power from their nineteenth-century factional opponents, but it was poor history. Wright himself must have realized that the situation was more complex than his nice portrait of unitary unanimity indicated. He compiled a roster of the diverse participants in a "Six Nations Council of 1839," which shows clearly that, in the missionary's day, it was not just the League sachems who were in charge. But Wright, like Morgan, asked Indians to describe their traditional "government," and his informants obliged.[12]

A generation later the error was compounded, as Iroquois codifiers of *The Constitution of the Five Nations* and anthropologists such as Arthur C. Parker and J. N. B. Hewitt attempted to reconstruct "pristine" Iroquois political institutions in the ethnographic present. The anthropologists, and presumably some of the Indians, had read Morgan; his account of the League sachems' powers was a starting point for their own efforts. These men — whether Iroquois or Euro-American — had little more understanding of nonstate societies than did their predecessors. In addition, the compilers of the various versions of the *Constitution* were traditionalist leaders — many of them League sachems — who were engaged in political struggles with accommodationists and modernizers in their own communities on the New York reservations and at the Ontario Six Nations Reserve. They, like their Seneca predecessors, had every political reason to exaggerate the former powers of League sachems.[13]

Thus the doctrine of centralized government by the Grand Council became orthodoxy for both the People of the Longhouse and the scholars who studied them. From Morgan and Wright to Parker and Hewitt, the general scholarly literature, popular writings, and — to a more qualified and cautious extent — specialized studies of the Iroquois have portrayed an unchanging, highly structured Grand Council of League sachems who, from their capital at the main Onondaga village, both dominated the politics of their home villages and decided the collective fate of the Five Nations.[14] Yet the seventeenth- and eighteenth-century sources tell a different tale.

If, in the colonial period, the League Council actually exercised supreme power, one must conclude either that European writers were remarkably dense or that the Iroquois they met were remarkably secretive. There is ample evidence of each trait, but the lack of documentary support for anything like an all-powerful Council of League sachems is puzzling. Iroquois leaders, claimed Governor Hunter, could not "be confined to any certain number[,] there being no other election or nomination of such but the impression that the experience of their life and behaviour makes on the minds of the generality."[15] And indeed the hereditary names of League sachems rarely appear in the diplomatic records of the English and French colonies, while the Grand Council is hardly mentioned in the standard sources on which scholars rely for contemporary ethnographic information.[16] The richest of those sources — the *Jesuit Relations* — describe a few meetings of Confederacy leaders, but the evidence is ambiguous. Nowhere do French missionaries clearly link the personnel and ritual of the Grand Council with Confederacy-wide deliberations on matters of internal or external policy. The same is true of the writings of that other great colonial authority on the Iroquois, William Johnson — a man who, like the Jesuits before him, made it his business to identify and win over the real leaders in Iroquois communities.[17]

The leaders portrayed by Johnson and other chroniclers exercised anything but supreme power. The headmen presided — if that is the word — over a collection of intensely localistic village communities, each jealous of its own prerogatives, beset by internal factional quarrels, and host to scores of adoptive war captives and other newcomers whose loyalty to the League was suspect.[18] The Five Nations were, one English observer complained somewhat unfairly in 1681, "a stout, numerous, rapacious people, composed of many nations, receiving all sorts of outlying Indians, and therefore an ungoverned people, with whom no treaty can be depended on."[19] If ethnohistorians had never heard of Morgan's League of the Iroquois, they might well conclude that the Five Nations were, like many neighboring peoples, organized in a loosely knit confederacy of nonstate, noncoercive village polities, in which any form of sovereign power in the Western sense — located at Onondaga or anywhere else — was unknown. "Bretheren you know that we have no forcing rules or laws amongst us," a Mohawk headman proudly declared to leaders at Albany who wielded authority of quite a different sort from his.[20]

Of course none of this means that the League and its Grand Council of sachems did not exist in the colonial period; Europeans *were* dense, and Indians *were* secretive. That an institution so central to the Iroquois' identity can have been a nineteenth-century invention defies belief. Moreover, the case for the antiquity of the Great League of Peace and its councils is persuasive, as William Fenton and his fellow practitioners of ethnohistorical "upstreaming" have demonstrated. Iroquois "social organization and political institutions remained relatively unaffected" by interaction with Europeans during the colonial era, Fenton correctly observes. "Content changed but structure persisted."[21] There is the rub. How can the looseknit confederacy that emerges from the seventeenth- and eighteenth-century sources be reconciled with the perdurable League that must have existed?

One key lies in the nature of the Great League of Peace. The date of its founding is unknown; native traditions and scholarly interpretations point to various eras between A.D. 1400 and A.D. 1600, and not a single event but a series of alliances negotiated over a long period of time may have been involved. Nonetheless, the League's origins and purposes — if not its precise location on the Western calendar — are explained in a central Iroquois myth, the Deganawidah epic.[22] The epic is set in a distant period of incessant warfare among the peoples of the Five Nations. "Everywhere there was peril and everywhere mourning," observes one version. "Feuds with outer nations, feuds with brother nations, feuds of sister towns and feuds of families and of clans made every warrior a stealthy man who liked to kill."[23] The feuds, the peril, and the mourning all were part of a cultural pattern known as the "mourning war," which for the Iroquois, as for many other native Americans, was a principal means of coping with the death of loved ones. At the request of female kin of a deceased person, warriors raided a traditional enemy for captives, who would then face one of two fates. Either they would be adopted by a grieving family as an almost literal replacement for the departed, or they would be executed in rituals that were an integral part of the mourning process. Psychologically for the bereaved, socially for the community, and demographically for the population, the captives seized in mourning wars helped fill the void created by death and replenish the spiritual power of all concerned. But mutual mourning-war raids could all too easily become the endless feuds recalled in the Deganawidah story.[24]

According to the epic, the continual cycle of death, mourning, and warfare caused particular pain for a man called Hiawatha. The death of all his daughters in rapid succession robbed him of his reason; in his rage and depression, Hiawatha went off into the forest. During his wanderings, he encountered a being of supernatural origins named Deganawidah, who taught him rituals that removed grief and eased the mind. Offering strings of wampum, Deganawidah spoke several words of condolence: the first dried Hiawatha's weeping eyes, the second opened his ears, the third unstopped his throat, and so on until his sorrow was relieved and his reason restored. These condolence ceremonies were at the core of a new gospel, the Good News of Peace and Power, that would make mourning wars unnecessary. "When men accept it," Deganawidah said of his message, "they will stop killing, and bloodshed will cease from the land."[25]

Hiawatha and Deganawidah spread their Good News to the people of the Five Nations. After some initial resistance, the two men organized the Great League of Peace, with its Grand Council of approximately fifty headmen from the clans of the major villages of the Five Nations. These League sachems were divided into two "sides" or moieties — the Elder Brothers of the Mohawks, Onondagas, and Senecas and the Younger Brothers of the Oneidas and Cayugas — that exchanged the ceremonial gifts and the words of condolence that Deganawidah prescribed. "They hold every year a general assembly," explained Jesuit missionary François Le Mercier, who in 1668 produced one of the earliest European accounts of the Grand Council. "There all the Deputies from the different Nations are present, to make their complaints and receive the necessary satisfaction in mutual gifts,—by means of which they maintain a good understanding with one another."[26]

The most important League ritual occurred when one of the fifty sachems died. In rites that filled the better part of a day, members of the "clear-minded" moiety spoke the Words of Condolence to the mourning side and requickened the deceased sachem in the person of a kinsman chosen by the older women of the dead leader's lineage. Thus were kept alive the fifty sachems and, metaphorically, the League itself. Condolence rituals, ceremonial gifts, and requickening rites symbolically addressed the same demographic, social, and psychological needs served by the mourning war. In these ceremonies could be found the spiritual power that others gained from war. The Good News of Peace and Power, then, sought to replace the mourning war with what might be termed the mourning peace.[27]

The "peace" functions of the League Council must be distinguished from the "political" functions of decision-making and diplomacy characteristic of state-organized governments. The evidence suggests that, in the early seventeenth century, the Great League of Peace possessed few state-like characteristics: the Five Nations had little in the way of common foreign policy, no effective means of devising unified strategies, and no central government in the sense that term is usually understood.[28] Indeed, to look, as Morgan and so many others did, for state-like political attributes in the League and its Grand Council is to misinterpret some basic principles of seventeenth-century Iroquois political culture. The Grand Council was not designed to make policy decisions or to provide a central government for the villages of the Five Nations; it existed to preserve the Great Peace through ceremonial Words of Condolence and exchanges of ritual gifts. "Their Policy in this is very wise, and has nothing Barbarous in it," Le Mercier concluded, "since their preservation depends upon their union, and since it is hardly possible that among peoples where license reigns with all impunity . . . there should not happen some event capable of causing a rupture, and disuniting their minds."[29]

Beneath the missionary's ethnocentric language lie some penetrating insights about the Grand Council. The sachems' job was to prevent a "disuniting [of] their minds." In a nutshell that was what the Great Peace was all about, for to Indians of seventeenth- and eighteenth-century eastern North America, "peace" was primarily a matter of the mind. Headmen could not force anyone to forgo mourning-war raids; they could only advise, persuade, cajole, and invoke the obligations of kinship. As one scholar explains, "'peace' . . . did not imply a negotiated agreement backed by the sanctions of international law and mutual self-interest. It was a matter of 'good thoughts' between two nations, a feeling as much as a reality."[30] In a noncoercive society, "where license . . . [reigned] with all impunity," words and good thoughts were tremendously important, for only if everyone shared in the climate of good will could peace be preserved. Condolence rites eased grief and calmed troubled minds. The resulting emotional climate was "peace," not only for individuals but also for the clan, village, and nation to which they belonged and for the outsiders against whom their people might otherwise make war.[31]

A League sachem, a man entrusted with preserving the Great Peace, had to be of a special breed. The chiefly virtues most prized in Iroquois folklore are those associated with peace and harmony: imperturbability, patience, good will, selflessness. "The thickness of their skin shall be seven spans — which is to say that they shall be proof against anger, offensive actions and criticism," Deganawidah decreed of the League sachems. "Neither anger nor fury shall find lodgement in their minds and all their words and actions shall be marked by calm deliberation."[32] A character of such restraint — even passivity — is almost by definition incapable of the kind of strong and innovative leadership that the Five Nations needed to survive the ordeals of the European invasion. Moreover, had a League sachem exercised such leadership and thus necessarily provoked political opposition, he would have ceased to be a peacemaker. "And when it shall come to pass that the chiefs cannot agree," Deganawidah prophesied, "then the people's heads will roll."[33] So, the Grand Council appears to be an unlikely place to find political leadership of the kind Morgan sought. If the League sachems were to fulfill their traditional duties, they must remain aloof from everyday politics and diplomacy.

Where, then, might political leadership be found? The search for an arena of Confederacy politics that complemented the sphere of the peace rituals of the League leads back to the theme of innovation in response to a series of Iroquois social crises. The first crisis stemmed from the dual agents of change that Europeans brought to all native Americans: trade goods and infectious diseases. Although archaeological data show that some Iroquois obtained a few European goods during the sixteenth century, the Five Nations were relative latecomers to direct and secure trade with Europeans.[34] Not until the 1610s did Mohawks begin commerce with the Dutch, and not until much later did they and people of the other four Iroquois nations find a reliable market at Fort Orange (later Albany). These facts placed the Five Nations at a severe disadvantage in wars with foes to the north and east who could purchase French metal and make arrowheads superior to native flint weapons. The first great seventeenth-century Iroquois problem, then, involved a search for European trading partners. And once those partners were found, the trouble lay in finding suitable furs to barter, for the best pelts came from cold regions well to the north of Iroquois homelands. A further dilemma soon joined the list and quickly overshadowed the others. By the early 1630s, European microbes had begun their ghastly work in the villages of the Five Nations, and by the 1640s the Iroquois population had at least been halved. A demographic crisis combined with economic concerns to create the first great ordeal of the Longhouse.[35]

Individual Iroquois war chiefs, young men, and the mourning women in whose behalf they acted gradually found their way out of the crisis. The solution grew almost imperceptibly from one of the oldest of Iroquois traditions, the mourning war. Very early in the seventeenth century, first Mohawks and then other Iroquois warriors began targeting many of their mourning-war raids on the no-man's land surrounding the junction of the Richelieu and St. Lawrence Rivers. On that spot, easily reached from the Mohawk country by way of lakes George and Champlain, warriors would lie in wait for Algonquian traders bringing home goods purchased from the French. In a successful raid, men of the Five Nations could not only seize the captives their mourning kinswomen demanded, they could also pillage valuable trade goods.[36]

In the mid-1610s the St. Lawrence raids decreased in frequency, partly because of a show of French military force, but largely because the new Dutch outposts on the Hudson were providing Mohawks, if not yet people of other Iroquois nations, with a safer source of European goods. In the early 1620s, however, Mohawks nearly lost access to that source. A new leadership at Fort Orange tried to shift trade away from the Mohawks and toward their Mahican neighbors, whose ties with the Algonquian enemies of the Five Nations promised access to prime northern peltries. As they had already learned to do, Mohawks responded to an economic problem through the use of warfare. Between 1624 and 1628 they managed to push the Mahicans east of the Hudson, to open an unobstructed route to Fort Orange, and to teach the Europeans a valuable lesson: several Dutchmen who joined a Mahican expedition against the Mohawks lost their lives.[37] With the Fort Orange market secured, Mohawks, increasingly joined by others of the Five Nations, redoubled their raids on the St. Lawrence. Now, however, their targets were canoes moving downriver with furs, not those heading home with the fruits of bargaining with the French. A substantial portion of the pelts that Iroquois traders sold at Fort Orange after 1630 must have been stolen from the Indian enemies of the Five Nations.[38]

In coming years, as deaths from disease mounted, Iroquois warriors found a response to the demographic crisis in the same methods they were already using to deal with their economic dilemmas. The mourning war—formerly a matter of sporadic raids to seize a few captives and a practice that Deganawidah's disciples hoped would one day disappear—exploded into the orgy of blood known somewhat misleadingly as the "Beaver Wars." During the mid-seventeenth century, warriors from every village in the Five Nations lashed out at virtually all of their Indian neighbors—Hurons, Petuns, Susquehannocks, and others—in a desperate quest for sufficient peltries for the trade and sufficient captives to replenish Iroquois population losses.[39]

Plunder from these raids purchased great quantities of European goods. Necessarily, however, many of those goods were not tools and clothing that could improve life at home but guns and ammunition that fueled new campaigns abroad. Meantime the successful quest for captives produced major demographic shifts in the composition of Iroquois villages. "If any one should compute the number of pure-blooded Iroquois," one astonished French missionary observed in 1661, "he would have difficulty in finding more than twelve hundred of them in all the five Nations, since these are, for the most part, only aggregations of different tribes whom they have conquered."[40] The benefits of war, then, came at tremendous social cost: a seemingly endless cycle of death from disease, wars to find captives to replace the losses, pillaging furs to trade for guns, new wars, and more deaths in battle transformed the Great League of Peace into a Great League for War.[41]

Thus the resolution of the first Iroquois ordeal contained within it the seeds of a new social crisis. For, by the 1660s, the Five Nations could no longer ride the cycle of death and war; they faced defeat abroad and social chaos at home. Three developments came together in the mid-1660s to force the issue. First, the warriors of the Five Nations had lost the advantages that their plentiful supply of Dutch weapons had once given them. Their principal foes now were Mahicans, New England Algonquians, and Susquehannocks, all of whom had ample arsenals of their own.[42] The Iroquois simply could not continue to battle evenly matched foes on several nearby fronts while continuing raids on more far-flung opponents. Second, the French, who had occasionally been drawn into their Indian trading partners' conflicts with the Five Nations, were at last by the 1660s prepared to deal seriously with the Iroquois. In 1665 a new governor arrived in Quebec with a thousand elite troops and orders to use them. As if these developments were not enough, Iroquois trade ties crumbled as a result of the 1664 English conquest of New Netherland and of long-developing structural weaknesses in the Hudson River fur trade economy. The only way out was a comprehensive peace with New France and several of its Indian allies. In late 1665 Seneca, Cayuga, Onondaga, and Oneida headmen came to terms. A year and a half later, after a French and allied Indian army had burned the Mohawk towns, that nation joined the others in making peace.[43]

In the diplomacy that brought about a resolution to this second ordeal of the Longhouse, and in a chain of Iroquois-French negotiations stretching back to 1645, can be seen the beginnings of a Confederacy political structure distinct from the Grand Council. The key figures in mid-century Franco-Iroquois diplomacy were village headmen and influential local orators, most of whom evidently were not League sachems. The bases of influence for these leaders were individual villages, rather than a nation or the confederacy as a whole. Village councils consisted not only of hereditary sachems, but also of war chiefs, wise old men, and others who had achieved sufficient stature to have their opinions heeded and to speak effectively in the name of fellow villagers. "The number of these senators is not fixed," missionary-ethnologist Joseph-François Lafitau explained in 1724. "Each person has the right to enter the Council to vote when he has reached the age of maturity which has (attributed to it) as a prerogative, wisdom and understanding of affairs."[44] By far the most prominent of these mid-century village leaders was the Onondaga Garakontié, who gained great influence throughout the Confederacy on the basis of his considerable oratorical skills, his unequaled understanding of Europeans, and his genius for incorporating political and religious innovation within traditional cultural patterns.[45]

Like the warriors who fought the Beaver Wars, leaders of Garakontié's stripe walked in familiar ways as they struck out along new paths. In their dealings with the French, Iroquois diplomats adapted the language and rituals of the Great Peace to create the protocol of intercultural diplomacy that recent ethnohistorians have so richly described.[46] As with the adaptation of mourning-war patterns to new situations, the projection of Great Peace ceremonial practices to Iroquois-European diplomacy seems to have begun with Mohawks; the pattern was already established when Mohawk headmen treated at Trois-Rivières with Frenchmen, Hurons, and Algonquins in 1645. From that date forward, words of peace, rituals of condolence, and exchanges of gifts dominated the practice of European-Indian diplomacy in the Northeast.[47]

The implications of this brand of diplomacy for Confederacy politics are illustrated by two episodes of which the Jesuits left relatively full accounts. In 1656 a group of Frenchmen set out to establish a mission station at Gannentaha in the Onondaga country. Along the way to Iroquoia, their Onondaga escorts got into a tussle with some Mohawks—vivid evidence that there was little unity in the mid-century Confederacy. On reaching their destination, the French were welcomed several times by local headmen who used rituals similar to a portion of the Grand Council's condolence rites. Subsequently, French priests took the opportunity to preach to a gathering at Onondaga of leaders from all Five Nations. This seems not, however, to have been a Grand Council of League sachems. The meeting had been called, the Jesuits reported, to settle a dispute between Senecas and Mohawks and to discuss the French mission. Significantly, the French described the convocation as a "great council of war," and the proceedings show few of the classic features of the condolence ritual. Instead, a leader from each of the Five Nations "deposited his presents in the war-kettle."[48]

In 1661 another Jesuit embassy apparently did encounter "by a happy chance" a Grand Council about to begin at Onondaga. Father Simon

Le Moyne, who at Garakontié's invitation had come to treat with Onondagas, took the opportunity to present French peace terms to the assembled sachems. Le Moyne's description of the meeting, however, does not conform to the ethnological pattern of a League Council. Frenchmen rang a bell to call "all the Elders" together and opened the gathering with a Christian prayer. Le Moyne then made his speech, which was received in respectful silence except for polite acknowledgments that the priest interpreted as simple answers of "Yes" to everything he said. Then, observed the French envoy, "the Address concluded, the assembly adjourned, after the usual ceremonies and the exchange of compliments commonly made at these Councils." The sachems, it seems, went about their real business of ritual condolence after the Frenchman had finished. Only "some days later," when the leaders had reconvened — apparently outside their former ceremonial context and now without any Mohawks taking an active part — did Le Moyne receive a formal answer.[49]

Such episodes suggest that, by the 1660s, village leaders were meeting occasionally at Onondaga to discuss common concerns in a forum separate — though perhaps not entirely distinct — from that of the Grand Council. Mohawks seldom took part in the meetings, although Garakontié and other headmen from the four western nations sometimes traveled to their country for councils.[50] And by no means did the gatherings of Oneidas, Onondagas, Cayugas, and Senecas function as a collective government for the Five Nations. In 1661 Le Moyne addressed his remarks separately in turn to the headmen of each nation; similarly, in 1665 the western Iroquois leaders who made peace with New France spoke independently and only on behalf of their respective peoples. There was no anomaly, therefore (except in French eyes), in the fact that a year and a half passed before Mohawk leaders ratified the 1665 peace.[51]

However halting in terms of Confederacy unity, the diplomatic and political developments of the mid-seventeenth century nonetheless established important patterns. The new leaders' behavior conformed to ancient ceremonial practices, their supralocal roles grew smoothly from their status in traditional village councils, and their efforts created a Confederacy-wide network of headmen distinct from, but significantly not in place of, the Grand Council. There is no reason to doubt that some League sachems took an active part in the new Confederacy politics. They probably did so, however, not *as* League sachems but simply as influential men in their own communities. Some may even have used names other than their sacred council titles when acting in this novel sphere — hence the virtual absence of sachem names from the European records.[52] Still, it seems likely that most League sachems remained aloof from the new politics. Only in this way could they continue unchallenged to perform their vital roles as preservers of Iroquois culture and League spiritual unity. With the survival of the Great League thus ensured, other leaders were freed to struggle with the difficult and divisive secular problems of the Five Nations. In the ancient League and the emerging Confederacy, continuity and change coexisted.

The treaties that the incipient Confederacy leadership negotiated with French and Indian enemies in the 1660s allowed the Iroquois to weather another crisis. But again, the solution paved the way for a new ordeal. The Franco-Iroquois treaties of 1665-67 brought Jesuit priests to each of the Five Nations, inaugurating the most intense period of missionization that League Iroquois would ever experience. In Iroquoia, as elsewhere in North America, proselytizing inspired the growth of religious factions cutting across the lines of kinship that traditionally defined village politics. Over the course of two decades, divisions between Christians and traditionalists evolved into factional disputes between Francophiles and Anglophiles; the missionaries' converts and political allies forged close ties with Canada, while their factional opponents were driven more deeply into English arms. Many Francophiles migrated to mission villages in New France; thenceforth they were often collectively called "Caughnawagas," after the name of their most prominent settlement. Others stayed behind and watched as Anglophiles assumed dominance, forced the Jesuits to leave, and conspired with New York governors Edmund Andros and Thomas Dongan to create the Covenant Chain system of English-Indian alliances. The stage was then set for a renewal of the Beaver Wars and ultimately for the onset of the conflict Anglo-Americans called "King William's War." By the mid-1690s, military defeats abroad and bitter factional quarrels at home reduced the Iroquois to "a mean poor people" who, in the words of one Mohawk, had "lost all by the Enemy."[53]

Paradoxically, however, the military disasters and divisive factionalism of King William's War pushed the Confederacy council to its greatest unity and fullest elaboration. During the 1680s, the gatherings of village headmen that the French had witnessed in earlier years became regular meetings at Onondaga in which leaders of all Five Nations coordinated policies. There were several long-term roots of this development. First, for most of the seventeenth century, and certainly since the creation of the Covenant Chain in the 1670s, both New York and New France had, when it suited their purposes, treated the Five Nations as if they comprised a single political entity. The lesson was driven home at Fort Frontenac in 1687, when a French army marching against the Senecas kidnapped a number of Cayugas, Onondagas, and Oneidas and sent them to slave in the royal galleys. Second, Iroquois leaders were impelled to find new unity because Albany, where — if anywhere — common policies for Iroquois Anglophiles had been formulated since the 1670s, could no longer be relied upon for direction. It was not only a matter of English failure to fulfill promises of military support for the Five Nations; beginning in 1689, Jacob Leisler's Rebellion (New York's analogue to England's Glorious Revolution) inaugurated a long period of political turmoil within the province. Battlefield defeats and squabbling allies forced the Iroquois to rely on their own resources.[54] Finally, the death of several prominent headmen of individual villages — most notably Garakontié, his fellow Onondaga Otreouti ("Big Mouth"), and the Mohawk Tahiadoris — who had guided Iroquois peoples through earlier crises, opened the door to new forms of leadership. As a group of Mohawk warriors lamented in 1691, "all those . . . who had sense are dead."[55]

The immediate spark for regular meetings of headmen of the Five Nations was the need to formulate united Confederacy policies toward the French. The first such gathering to find its way into English records occurred in the summer of 1686. At Albany that July, a Mohawk orator announced — with what seems to be a recognition of the novelty of the event — that "the sachems of all nations have been assembled to discuss" military and diplomatic strategy and that "all the nations for seven days have been assembled in Onondage and have kept council." Beyond the fact that the meeting struggled with the contradiction between Governor Dongan's demand that they "keep quiet and not . . . take up the hatchet" and French missionary Jean de Lamberville's threat "that when the corn would be nearly ripe the French would come to kill" them, little is known about the proceedings. Still less is recorded about Confederacy councils that met in 1687, just after the French invasion of the Seneca country, and in August 1689.[56]

Rich accounts exist, however, of a council that convened in early 1690 to discuss Iroquois negotiations with Ottawas and peace proposals made by Louis de Buade de Frontenac when he began his second term as governor of New France.[57] In many respects, the proceedings on this occasion conform beautifully to Morgan's outline of Grand Council deliberations. The Words of Condolence, the exchanges of wampum, the role of Onondagas as "firekeepers" or chairmen, and the precedence of Mohawk and Seneca Elder Brothers are all present. But three jarring notes intrude: some eighty Iroquois headmen, not the theoretical fifty, participated; a delegation from Albany was seemingly treated equally with contingents from the Five Nations; and, with one prominent exception, the names mentioned in the sources do not belong to League sachems. Apparently this gathering was not a ceremony of the sachems of the Great League of Peace, but a working meeting of the political leaders of the villages of the Five Nations. This Confederacy council modeled its deliberations and ceremonial after those of the Grand Council, but its purposes and personnel were separate from those of that body. Again, innovation grew within a framework of traditional forms.[58]

Throughout the 1690s, Confederacy councils met several times a year and were the focus of intense struggles among Francophile, Anglophile, and neutralist factions. In keeping with Iroquois traditions, the real battles went on not at the council fire but back home in the villages of the Five Nations and "in the bushes" before and during the formal proceedings.[59] The shifting strengths of the three factions can be traced through the messages that the Confederacy council's wampum belts carried to Albany and New France and through the rises and falls of three Onondaga orators who emerged as factional spokesmen: Aradgi for the Francophiles, Sadekanaktie for the Anglophiles, and Teganissorens for the neutralists. Each of these men played key roles in bringing about an end to the Iroquois phase of King William's War in the comprehensive treaties with New France and its Indian allies that comprised the Grand Settlement of 1701.[60] In Iroquoia, Aradgi orchestrated capitulations to the western Indian and French foes of the Five Nations; at Albany, Sadekanaktie subtly redefined the English Covenant Chain; and at Montreal and elsewhere, Teganissorens labored valiantly to pull the diplomatic pieces together in a way that might preserve Iroquois independence. The Grand Settlement of 1701, therefore, should be seen not only as a diplomatic settlement abroad but also, and perhaps more importantly, as a delicate accommodation among Iroquois factions at home.[61]

Throughout the ordeals of the Longhouse, the capacity to innovate within a framework of tradition provides a key to Iroquois survival. The Great League of Peace endured, while within its forms and structures individual warriors and headmen adapted to the Indians' new world. When the advent of European trade and European diseases threatened to destroy Iroquois ways of life, people of the Five Nations drew upon their traditional patterns of warfare to shore up both their economy and their population. When warfare itself threatened Iroquois existence, headmen modified old rituals of peacemaking to evolve a system of intercultural diplomacy. When that diplomacy led to factionalism at home and a new war abroad, Teganissorens's generation used the diplomatic experiences of the seventeenth century to patch together the arrangements of 1701.[62] The pattern would continue long after Teganissorens was gone; a century after the Grand Settlement, when the American War for Independence had destroyed the Confederacy as a political entity, the prophet Handsome Lake reshaped Iroquois traditions to revitalize his shattered culture.[63] And, in the era of Lewis Henry Morgan and Asher Wright, when the future of Iroquois communities was again in doubt, League sachems drew upon a long heritage of innovation within tradition to insist that the Grand Council of the Great League of Peace had always been firmly in charge.

LINKING ARMS

The Structure of Iroquois Intertribal Diplomacy

MARY A. DRUKE

> He took hold of a Frenchman, placed his arm within his, and with his other arm he clasped that of an Algonquin. Having thus joined himself to them, "Here," he said, "is the knot that binds us inseparably; nothing can part us. . . . Even if the lightning were to fall upon us, it could not separate us; for, if it cuts off the arm that holds you to us, we will at once seize each other by the [other] arm." And thereupon he turned around, and caught the Frenchman and Algonquin by their two arms — holding them so closely that he seemed unwilling ever to leave them.[1]

IROQUOIS DIPLOMACY during the seventeenth and eighteenth centuries involved native peoples to the north, south, east, and west of Iroquoia, from the Penobscots to the Creeks, from the Narragansetts to the Sauks.[2] Subsequent chapters in this book deal with specific alliances; this one focuses on the structure of Iroquois diplomacy in general. Its thesis is that relationships of alliance and reciprocity were inextricably tied to leader/follower interactions within Iroquois villages, and that these relationships — which orators dramatized by the linking of arms — extended through Iroquois society and beyond to form the structural basis of diplomacy.

Alliance was a goal desired by Iroquois people in relationships with everyone in their universe. In addition to humans, there were numerous other beings who had access to power and could use it in either harmful or helpful ways. The man-being Hadu'i' (False Face), for example, was considered to be good when he helped to cure illness or to fight witches,

29

but evil when he brought disease. Animals, too, were conscious, active participants in the Iroquois world. Human health was under the control of some of them, who expected to be treated with respect.[3] Although the ideal was for all beings to provide assistance to one another, they did not always do so: offended animals sent disease; ill-tempered humans practiced witchcraft and brought misfortune to their enemies; beings in the Sky World created havoc if not given enough attention. The Iroquois account of creation, in which Tawiskaron and his grandmother attempt to harm Tawiskaron's twin brother Teharonghyawagon after the boys' mother dies in childbirth, is a reminder that even one's own kin can present serious threats.[4]

With the potential of all persons, including other-than-human ones, to use power in harmful ways, it was advantageous for Iroquois as individuals to make personal alliances in order to convince other persons to exert power for them.[5] The alliances of concern to us here rested upon personal relations between "leaders"—people whose talents and traits were valued and respected—and "followers"—those who were influenced by the qualities leaders were deemed to possess. The close personal relations between leaders and followers encompassed many facets of everyday life, including the direction of ritual, the holding of councils, the heading of war parties, the provision of advice and arbitration in personal disputes, the organization of agricultural activities, and the distribution of goods and supplies. Face-to-face interaction permitted continuous feedback between individuals. Leaders were in positions to suggest, guide, or cajole. When they were aware of followers' wishes, they used their contacts to help carry them out. If their own followers presented conflicting goals, leaders acted as central points around which conflicts were discussed. They served as pivots for organization of various matters and as spokespersons for presentation of followers' viewpoints to others.[6]

Kinship ties were fundamental in Iroquois society and were the basis of many leader/follower alliances. Members of a matrilineage—a set of people directly related through their mothers—commonly formed leader/ follower groups to accomplish necessary tasks. Females, for example, joined the oldest woman of their matrilineage (the matron) to plant, to cultivate, to harvest, or to gather firewood.[7] Matrilineages were grouped into clans, which had roots deep in the prehistoric past. Members of a clan were believed to be descended from a common ancestor. Actual genealogical links between people of different matrilineages within a clan had long been forgotten, however. Nonetheless, clan identity was a very important facet of Iroquois life, and within clans individuals frequently combined as leaders and followers. Military leaders, for instance, often raised war parties from among their own clansmen.[8] Although Iroquois kinship is most frequently classified as matrilineal, bilateral links—relations with one's father's clan—were also very important. Through bilateral ties women exercised leadership over their brothers' children. Such leadership was particularly important in time of mourning, as older women enforced their young kinsmen's responsibility to replace the dead of their father's clan through the acquisition of gifts, war captives, or scalps.[9]

Kinship relations figured prominently, therefore, in affiliation between leaders and followers. They were not, however, the only factors involved. Marriage ties also played a large role. In February 1764, for example, the women of the village of Oquaga spoke to their warriors, saying that they would give up their "Children, *Husbands*, and Brothers" to fight alongside English Superintendent of Indian Affairs William Johnson and hoped they would "observe his directions."[10] If a leader/follower group was not based on kinship or marriage, chances were high that the members came from the same or neighboring villages or from nations inhabiting contiguous areas. As a detailed list of Indians present for an expedition to Montreal in 1759 shows, even multinational parties were divided into village and clan groups.[11]

The personal relationships upon which Iroquois leadership rested extended throughout the society and served to weave individuals together. Kinship ties, expressed in terms of clan, defined a person moving to a new community not as an isolated individual but as a part of already established networks. These relationships tended to bind together individuals of different villages and nations as well. The number and names of clans varied from nation to nation, but three—Bear, Wolf, and Turtle—were common to each member of the Confederacy. A Cayuga of the Wolf clan, therefore, was accepted as kin by Mohawks of the same matrilineal clan.[12] Moreover, Iroquois kinship did not refer only to blood lines; indeed biological ties were not essential. In July 1755, for example, Hans, a Mohawk of Schoharie, declared that a number of the Turtle clan would join an expedition headed for Niagara under the direction of the English Major General William Shirley, because one of Shirley's recruiters had been adopted into that clan and was identified as a member of it. This affiliation was significant in allowing the agent to recruit the aid of Mohawk warriors.[13]

Any leader/follower coalition could extend its influence and its contacts by alliance with other similar units, not by being subsumed by them, but by joining them as allies. All alliances were thought to strengthen a person's or group's value to other potential partners. Members of an alliance maintained independence while also identifying with the extended relationship, for there was in Iroquois culture a sense of identity of self with the group. Instructions in 1783 to John Johnson, Superintendent and Inspector General for Indian Affairs in Canada, clearly stated that "the Chiefs are always to be distinguished [when presents are distributed] for by pleasing them, their Parties are pleased."[14] Thus, Iroquois leadership was not unitary but segmented into numerous leader/follower coalitions. The symbol of the League of the Iroquois as a circle of fifty wampum strings, each representing one of the fifty sachems, illustrates this very well: leaders join with others as distinct individuals to form the council of chiefs.[15]

Accordingly, the League of the Five (later Six) Nations was an alliance of distinct parts forming a united, and therefore stronger, front than any nation or coalition alone could provide. The League was of great value in Iroquois diplomacy, not only for the direct links between member nations that it afforded, but also as a tool to be used by individual nations to enhance their bargaining position in negotiations with others. In June 1768, for example, a Mohawk speaker succinctly stated in negotiations with the English that "altho' we be thought at present an inconsiderable People, we are the head of a confederacy that has Powerful Alliances."[16] Six years later, Mohawks of Canajoharie raised their grievances against the German settler George Klock in front of the whole League, "that they who know our Rank may Espouse our Cause as it is their Duty to do, and Convince the English that we have friends and Deserve attention."[17] Similarly, the Iroquois very specifically referred to attempts to extend alliances to tribes outside the League as a strengthening of themselves. In 1758, during the Seven Years' War, they said that they were seeking alliances so that neutrality would be feasible should they decide upon it, or so that they would not need to fear the other side if they decided to join either the English or the French.[18]

In alliances of leader/follower coalitions, leaders served as the points of articulation. As followers extended themselves by association with leaders who acted as spokespersons and advocates for them and organizers of their interaction with others, so the extension continued as leaders (with or for their followers) joined with other leaders. Alliance was sought first within the lineage, then within the clan, then the village, the nation, and the Iroquois Confederacy. Connections did not necessarily stop, however, at any of these levels. They could also extend to relations with people of other nations.[19]

Alliances between leader/follower coalitions served to strengthen persons, clans, and nations, as each stretched out to grasp hands with others. On a most basic level, humans who did not establish and maintain relationships — persons who had no friends, kin, or alliances — faced grim prospects. (Indeed, they were at times found destitute in or near Indian villages; William Johnson often remarked in his accounts that he had provided food and clothing, or a funeral, to a "poor" Indian bereft of friends.[20]) Iroquois made every effort, therefore, to create and strengthen personal and international connections. The Mohawk speaker quoted at the beginning of this chapter flamboyantly dramatized his hope that the alliance he was proposing should withstand great turmoil. He let go of the arms of the Frenchman and Algonquin and quickly seized their other arms to symbolize that the alliance should not be easily broken. Similarly, in 1775, referring to a chain of friendship between the Iroquois and English, an Oneida speaker stated that "when our ancestors first met, they agreed that they should take each other by the hand, and that no storms, not even thunder, should be able to break their union."[21]

To the Iroquois, alliances were dynamic, ongoing relationships, and if they were not kept alive — were not continually improved — friends might turn to enemies over minor differences, just as animal beings might send illness if not regularly solicited for good health. Connections, therefore, were constantly being reevaluated, refined, renewed, and kept alive in ritual form. Reciprocity — through gift-giving and exchange of wampum at councils as well as such things as aid supplied in time of need — expressed mutual commitment.[22] In 1751, for example, the Cayuga Ottrawana reported that Mississaugas confirmed their alliance with the Iroquois and promised "to keep it firm and strong." Such statements resound throughout the historic record.[23] The need for continued reassurance made personal interactions extremely important to the Iroquois in intertribal diplomacy. When Virginians insisted in 1719 that the Five Nations uphold peace with Indians in alliance with them, an Iroquois sachem expressly stated that "2 years ago the Governor of Virginia made complaints of some of their People doing Mischief in his Country and that they had desired he would come himself or Depute some Body to come to Albany with some of the Indians in Alliance that they might adjust matters Face to Face."[24] This was the manner of doing things. Despite rhetoric, hostilities might arise, and alliances were not infrequently broken, but documentary evidence of Iroquois diplomacy is full of efforts to establish, renew, or reestablish peaceful relationships.[25]

The kinship basis of many personal leader/follower relations was echoed in international arenas as groups used kinship terms for one another. Iroquois often addressed Delawares, for example, as "nephews" and were called "uncles" by the latter. Wyandots and Potawatomis were addressed as "brothers" and reciprocated with the same term for the Iroquois.[26] Moiety divisions — the separation of clans or other groupings into two roughly equal parts—were also features of interpersonal and intra- and intertribal affairs. Relationships among individual nations within the League of the Iroquois itself were expressed in these terms, with the Older Brothers being the Mohawks, Onondagas, and Senecas and the Younger Brothers the Oneidas, Cayugas, and Tuscaroras.[27] Reciprocity characterized such moiety relationships. This was especially evident in the opening of councils. In ceremony and rhetoric, a spokesman for one moiety would metaphorically "wash down" the body of the other to make it whole again. The other would then reciprocate, as in 1761 when Senecas, Ottawas, Potawatomis, Ojibwas, and Wyandots, meeting at Wyandot Town near Detroit, condoled with one another for losses suffered at the siege of Niagara the previous year.[28]

Other nations with whom the Iroquois interacted shared many of the same features of leadership. Through their Confederacy, however, it was the Six Nations who effectively provided a working model of the extension of leader/follower alliances from personal relations to more complex connections involving the interlocking of nations. On both intra- and international levels, councils were the means by which broader alliances of leader/follower coalitions were accomplished. As an Iroquois speaker said in 1693, holding councils "is our order and method on all occasions."[29]

Within the council framework, procedures incorporating reciprocity and emphasizing the renewal of alliances provided for constant and direct interchange between persons. The Jesuit missionary-ethnographer Joseph François Lafitau explained, in describing the councils of early eighteenth-century Iroquois villages, that women often met by themselves, as did warriors and peace chiefs, to discuss matters of interest or concern to their particular spheres. If the subject affected a large number of people, general clan councils were held after these meetings.[30] Thus, deliberations proceeded along certain lines, one being expertise; others were geographical and political. Clan councils usually preceded those of villages, and councils of nations preceded those of the Confederacy or meetings with other tribes. However, steps could be and often were skipped. Quite commonly, for example, village meetings were immediately followed by a general council of the Confederacy. At each step of the way, leaders served as links between groups of people.[31] When a Confederacy council was called at Onondaga, the central council fire of the League, local meetings took place first so that each unit would arrive with its ideal consensus articulated. Spokesmen went to Onondaga, or to any other incorporating council, as just that—spokesmen for their constituents, not independent individual decision makers. Thus Onondaga afforded the place for people of all of the Six Nations to meet and express the opinions of groups within each nation.[32]

Similarly segmented processes characterized negotiations between the Iroquois and other people. Meetings within Six Nations villages, if not within nations or the Confederacy as a whole, usually preceded councils with non-Iroquois. In the spring of 1768, for example, Oneidas, Tuscaroras, Cayugas, and Nanticokes from the village of Oquaga apologized for being late to a conference with Cherokees at Johnson Hall, the residence of William Johnson. Thomas King, their speaker, said that peace with the Cherokees was such a weighty issue that it had taken them a long time to decide upon it before coming to the general meeting.[33] Although such segmented procedures may not have been necessarily typical of nations with whom the Iroquois negotiated, it did characterize the Iroquois approach to international meetings. Moreover, segmentation was a factor directly involved in international diplomacy, because it was regularly incorporated into conferences in the form of private council meetings to which parties withdrew by themselves to consider an issue.[34]

Private meetings were not only an integral part of the larger diplomatic structure in which Iroquois were involved, they also served as means of focusing deliberations on the personnel or units specifically concerned with particular issues or interests. Yet this did not mean that closed doors provided a license for stealth and intrigue. There are numerous instances of Iroquois protests during the mid-eighteenth century when, for example, the private sphere was not considered appropriate for raising or settling issues. The Mohawk leader Canadagaye, for one, refused to answer questions put to him by Governor George Clinton in Albany in 1745, when Clinton was attempting to obtain the names of persons who had spread an alarm among the Mohawks. "It was like stealing to try to get this information in private, rather than in public," Canadagaye explained.[35] There is much evidence, too, of cases where Johnson discussed issues with sachems and war chiefs and was told that they could not answer him until they first consulted with their people.[36] It seems clear that one function of private councils was to allow matters to be deliberated by small groups directly concerned before issues and opinions were presented to a larger body of people. General councils appear, therefore, to have been forums for presenting the results of deliberations of smaller groups of people with perceived common interests.

Councils proceeded according to a highly regularized protocol. The first step was the invitation to meet. A runner would usually bring the message to the appropriate parties, "calling" them to council.[37] Apparently this determined who could present the agenda at the upcoming meeting, with the group extending the invitation being the one to open discussion on the matters at hand.[38] The site of the council also was usually suggested by the persons extending the invitation. Although some spots were favored, meeting locations — places where council fires could be lit — were many. Conferences between Iroquois and non-Iroquois occurred at various locales, sometimes at Onondaga, sometimes at Albany, sometimes elsewhere. In 1645, Mohawks met Algonquins, Hurons, and Frenchmen at Trois-Rivières. The Iroquois frequently negotiated with Indians to the west at or near Detroit. In 1756, Oneidas met with Shawnees, Chickasaws, and Mahicans at an Indian village called Otsiningo on the Susquehanna River. A meeting in 1776 of Iroquois, Shawnees, and Delawares with Cherokees took place at the Cherokee village of Chota.[39]

Once the location of negotiations had been established, the council (or more properly councils, since any negotiation consisted not of a single session but of a series of meetings) began with the arrival of the visiting party. The emissaries were greeted at the boundary of the village clearing with a ceremony commonly referred to as "At the Woods Edge," which consisted primarily of welcoming the visitors and, through speeches and exchanges of ceremonial gifts, metaphorically wiping the tears from the eyes, unplugging the ears, and cleansing the throat of those tired from a long journey.[40] The ritual included or led into ceremonies of condolence, in which each party mourned the other's dead. William Johnson noted in September 1761, in a footnote to a report of an Indian treaty at Detroit that brought together sachems and warriors from several nations including Iroquois, that condolence was always performed at the opening of meetings as a prerequisite to negotiations. Then delegates were usually given a couple of days to rest (or at least one night's sleep) before formal proceedings began.[41] Ethnologist Michael Foster has indicated that the initial ceremonies, with their stress on making bodies whole, opening eyes, and clearing throats, demonstrate a concern for "the channel," that is, for opening communications. Proceedings, focused as they were on making and (more importantly) maintaining connections through clear communication, were conducted to remind the parties of the advantages and general obligations of the alliance and the patterns of thought and behavior essential to its survival. The alliance itself, then, rather than practical details or specific contractual arrangements, tended to be the focus of council proceedings — much to the frustration of European observers, for whom the details mattered most.[42]

Once a conference started, leaders were not in themselves decision-makers but rather the foci on which discussions were centered and sentiments articulated. The give and take of consultation was, therefore, an important feature in interactions among leaders and between leaders and followers. Efforts were made at councils to discuss all perspectives on an issue. Lafitau, in describing "the manner of deliberation" at Iroquois councils, noted that

> each of the opposing sides first takes up the proposition in a few words and sets forth all the reasons which have been alleged pro and con by those who first expressed their opinion. He [the speaker] then states his own opinion and concludes with these words: "That is my thought on the subject of this, our Council." After their deliberation on whatever subject it may be, there is almost no reason, for or against, which they have not seen or weighed.[43]

Careful deliberations were very much a part of Iroquois council transactions with non-Iroquois as well. Rarely would answers be given to questions unless they had been carefully considered, at least overnight.[44] Wampum, or some other item of exchange, was presented by the speaker when a proposition was made. This would be kept by the other party or returned, depending upon whether the proposal was accepted or rejected. If the gift was kept, a comparable symbol would be given back.[45] Each proposition by one party was usually repeated by the other before an answer was given. This was done by specialist orators, often with prompting by other chiefs. It was undoubtedly an effective way to insure that messages had been properly understood before an answer was given. Great care was also taken to see that every item presented by one side was answered by the other.[46]

At councils, leaders provided advice, suggestions, and directives that were subject to review by followers. In many cases, great numbers of Indians who were not war chiefs or peace chiefs attended. Tradition held that these people were not to participate in council except through a chief acting as their speaker. It was often the case, however, that they were consulted by the chiefs informally, if not in private council, before final answers were given. The main reason for this was that the leaders did not "represent" their followers in the western sense, nor did they make binding decisions on their behalf. Leaders were dependent on their followers for their positions, and any decision that they made could be, and if repugnant enough would be, considered invalid. Often, council negotiations ceased until leaders could consult with other leaders and their followers, even if this necessitated their returning home to do so.[47]

Councils thus served as forums for discussing alternatives and, by process of elimination, arriving at agreement. Often, in those cases in which agreement did not emerge, new alignments arose between individuals with common interests or obligations, or those unwilling to compromise renewed their commitment to an alternative course of action. Thus, Adam, an Oneida sachem of Oquaga, commented to William Johnson in April 1757 that the Six Nations were divided among themselves and that "parties are like to arise at the Approaching Meeting at Onondaga."[48] Yet careful deliberations at council negotiations tended to mark decisions as firm and valued. People with different interests were familiarized with items of concern to others. Issues were discussed and weighed, as leaders tried to gauge opinions about the matter.

The presence or absence of support contributed to the reevaluation of the issues by parties already disposed toward a certain option. In 1761, for example, Seneca delegates urged Ojibwas, Ottawas, Potawatomis, and Wyandots to join them in war against the English. The western Indians rejected the offer and advised the Iroquois to give up the plan. The Senecas thanked the other Indians and added that they would "return home and acquaint the Chiefs of the Six Nations" and their allies "of the Desire and Intention of the Nations of Detroit."[49] Similarly, in 1774, repeated requests by Shawnees for aid against encroaching Virginians who had killed some of their people were rejected by the Iroquois, who sent the Shawnees a message advising them to "Leave the business of War, repent and mind peace alone." The message urged the Shawnees to "mind our words, They are strong, they are the words of the Six Nations. . . . [A]ll the Northern Nations have left their Belts in our hands and referred themselves intirely to our Government and determination, they have joined their words to us."[50]

As this joining of "words" suggests, the goal in interaction was unanimity. At councils, constant feedback, most of which took place in verbal discussions, allowed for alternatives to be evaluated. If, as was sometimes the case, more than one alternative was strongly advocated, this would become clear as interaction continued. When no arguments could convince parties supporting adverse positions that theirs were undesirable or impractical alternatives, attempts to extend alliances between parties with widely differing views would be suspended. Such was the case with the Six Nations and the Shawnees in 1774: "This is the third time, and the last that you shall hear from us if you do not hearken to us," the Iroquois informed them after reiterating that they should cease hostilities against the Virginians. The Shawnees did not listen.[51] In this, as in most instances where negotiations were halted, discussions were tabled, and those with contrary opinions acted independently of one another without overt antagonism. The Six Nations did not meet with the Shawnees again during the war, but they did continue efforts to convince Virginia Governor John Murray, Lord Dunmore, to halt actions against them.[52]

In some cases, hostilities flared and alliances were broken. In most, however, careful deliberations eliminated undesirable or less valued alternatives. After lengthy consultation, one course acceptable to all was left. Deliberation on matters of concern at council meetings allowed for spheres of influence and alliance to widen the solid base of direct leader/follower connections. Councils provided formal, open contexts of debate for people of different nations. The diplomacy that took place led to a familiarization with issues and concerns beyond local ones, as nations strove through individuals to link arms firmly with one another.

The imagery of interlinking parts that has been used here was not the only one the Iroquois employed to symbolize alliance. As the next chapter shows, metaphorical chains of friendship were also invoked.[53] The linking arms imagery, however, best captures the structure of Iroquois diplomacy, because it so graphically points to the pervasive personal leader/follower relationships upon which alliances were built.

COVENANT and CONSENSUS

Iroquois and English, 1676–1760

RICHARD L. HAAN

AMONG THE MOST SIGNIFICANT of the many recent advances in native American historical studies is a new appreciation of diplomacy's central importance in European-Indian relations. At the heart of what might be called the new diplomatic history of colonial North America lie the Anglo-Iroquois arrangements that appear in the records as the Covenant Chain, arrangements that Francis Jennings has termed "the Ambiguous Iroquois Empire."[1] The accepted wisdom now holds that the Covenant Chain dominated Anglo-Indian contacts in North America during the long interlude between the Beaver Wars of the 1640s and 1650s and the Seven Years' War a century later. Armed with such valuable insights, historians will no longer rely entirely upon Lewis Henry Morgan's "Iroquois League Council" to understand the Five Nations' institutional relationships with outside groups, nor will scholars focus exclusively upon military affairs. Both shifts in perspective are welcome, enriching as they do our understanding of the complexity of European-Indian relations.[2]

The purpose of this chapter is to bring our picture of the Covenant Chain into still sharper focus. For all the improvements recently made in that picture, there is still a tendency in recent studies to emphasize European understandings of cross-cultural relationships. Too often, Covenant Chain diplomacy is presented in the Eurocentric terms of centralized state systems, and portrayed either as an institution for sharing power with the Iroquois over other indigenous peoples of the eastern woodlands, or as a process by which the English eventually imposed sovereignty upon the Five Nations. Scholars generally note that the Iroquois insisted on their own independence and that English assertions of sovereignty fell upon deaf ears, but after that caveat, the tendency is to describe the English perception of the Covenant Chain — "a multiple alliance binding on tribes and

41

colonies," in Jennings's words — and then to assume that the Iroquois shared this perspective.[3]

An examination of the seminal period from 1675 to 1686, when the chain was forged, suggests that the Iroquois acted upon their own cultural and historical expectations, and that their perspective on the Covenant Chain was far more restrictive than the "constitutional basis" for Anglo-Indian relations the English intended. In fact, the origins of Covenant Chain diplomacy reveal that the relationship between Iroquois and English, each with their own view of the way things ought to work, was still *more* ambiguous than we thought. Furthermore, the misunderstandings inherent in the Covenant Chain — which, in Iroquois eyes, consisted of several distinct "chains" — raise serious questions about the adequacy of our understanding of Iroquois history during the eighteenth century.

The origins of the Covenant Chain are shrouded in obscurity. The paucity of records, and especially of native American accounts, is an obvious problem, but the difficulties are compounded because the observations of Euro-Americans are often clouded by motives of personal gain. Take, for example, Robert Livingston, for most of the period from 1686 to 1724 the New York secretary for Indian affairs. His records constitute the principal source for the era, and by 1700 his reputed expertise did much to gain him a seat on New York's provincial Council. From this vantage point, Livingston urged a series of governors to expand the fur trade into the west and better defend the colony's borders. While his position reflected a reasonable concern for New York's security, his arguments also served his own interests in undercutting the Albany monopoly on the fur trade and fostering his land speculations in the Mohawk River Valley. The quality of other English officials during the period does not make analysis any easier. New York governors exhibited — as did leaders in Whitehall or in Massachusetts, Virginia, Maryland, or South Carolina — a lack of concern for, or knowledge of, native cultures and their histories of contact with European colonists. As a result, much of the evidence reflects Euro-American perceptions and assumptions, brought into the record either by naiveté, intentional distortion, or confused translation.[4]

Even the most sensitive descriptions of the Covenant Chain tend to build upon the errors of colonial times and adopt a European posture, whether English, French, or Dutch. The new scholarly orthodoxy argues that the Covenant Chain was at first a pragmatic trading alliance between the Mohawks and the Dutch of Fort Orange (Albany). It was this alliance, a chain of "iron," that dominated Iroquois relations with New York for most of the seventeenth century. That pattern changed, the argument states, with the arrival of the English. Between 1677 and 1690, the chain with New York was made over into one of "silver." The change in metaphorical material not only reflected the English sense of a new arrangement of longer duration, but also an alliance that systematized Iroquois-English relations into a multicultural entity in which the two sides agreed to share power over the Northeast, and to do so with a decidedly anti-French bias. More specifically, the general consensus now seems to be that, beginning with New York Governor Edmund Andros in the 1670s and continuing with the joint actions of governors Thomas Dongan of New York and Lord Howard of Effingham of Virginia in the 1680s, the English, in concert with the Five Nations, divided up control over the Indians on Virginia's borders, encouraged the expansion of the Albany trade into the west, and assumed English sovereignty over northeastern North America.[5]

There is little doubt that this description accurately portrays the English Crown's desire to regulate its colonial empire at the end of the seventeenth century. The Restoration Stuarts relied upon quasi-military administrators called Governors-General to attempt to impose Crown prerogative government in the New World. For colonial officials like Dongan and Effingham, the goal of centralized administration, of course, fit well their expectations for making sense of Indian relations. What is in question is whether the Five Nations saw the Covenant Chain in quite the same way.

An understanding of the Silver Chain must begin with events between 1675 and 1677 — not that the Chain's origins are necessarily to be found at this time, but beginning there provides an important background for clarifying its subsequent ambiguities. In 1675 Governor Andros traveled to a Mohawk village to confer with leaders of that nation and, apparently, others of the Confederacy. In early 1676, he sought Iroquois assistance against Metacom ("King Philip"), whose allies were threatening the survival of the New England colonies. And in 1677 the Iroquois were invited to Albany by Maryland to discuss an end to the warfare then raging along the borders of the Chesapeake provinces. It is these events that recent scholars have pinpointed as the start of the Silver Covenant Chain. Jennings implies that the Chain stemmed from an English invitation in 1677, while Stephen Saunders Webb argues that the Onondaga leader Garakontié manipulated these meetings and eventually "defined" a chain of "silver" for the English.[6]

Upon closer inspection, however, these maneuvers, which did initiate new "chains" (the plural is intentional), were unrelated to the "Covenant Chain" that emerged a decade later. The developments between 1675 and 1677 were not joined in the thoughts of English officials at the time. The reason is simple: these early initiatives were intended to address immediate issues of border unrest that concerned two very separate colonies. Andros's dealings with the Iroquois in 1675 and 1676 are poorly documented and difficult to assess. But apparently, once he obtained the mercenaries he sought, the governor devoted little attention to Iroquois affairs. Maryland, too, seems to have had restricted goals. Its negotiator, Henry Coursey, had specific instructions: first, make a peace that would include Seneca assurances of the good behavior of the Susquehannocks, who, recently defeated in Maryland and Virginia, now lived with the Five Nations; second, obtain Seneca acknowledgment of a new Warriors' Path southward hugging the foothills of the Alleghenies.[7] In other words, neither Maryland nor New York was very interested in developing more intricate relationships.

The Iroquois response underscores the limitations of these developments. A Mohawk war party did attack Metacom's forces in 1676, yet no other Iroquois nation joined the expedition. The way in which the Five Nations agreed to Coursey's proposals the following year reflects the limited nature of Maryland's aims. The specific proposals Maryland sent to the Five Nations in the spring of 1677 set the agenda for the upcoming meeting at Albany and laid the basis for Iroquois responses. Significantly, the treaty minutes for 1677 held to these topics; neither side raised new issues, and the Iroquois reacted to Coursey's requests and to no others.[8] As shown in the previous chapter, traditional Iroquois leadership and decision-making patterns required the host of a council to offer clear proposals so that invited leaders could prepare by building consensus among their own followers. New proposals might be delivered at a council, but no answer was required from the participants on the other side of the fire unless the negotiators believed they already had agreement on the subject at home. If they were wrong, their people could reject the agreement.

Another hint of the Iroquois perspective on these meetings is the apparent lack of consensus among the nations of the Confederacy. A 1676 meeting with Andros is obvious on this point, for only Mohawks appeared in Albany. In 1677, delegations from each of the Five Nations did meet with Maryland officials, and those Iroquois who were present agreed to Coursey's conditions. But they did so, at best, as separate nations; the minutes contain no record of a general meeting in which the Iroquois as a united people appeared before the English of either New York or Maryland to bind themselves to the "covenant chain" being formed. Nor did any sachem or orator — not even the influential Onondaga Garakontié — emerge to speak for all Iroquois. Garakontié's conduct followed the general pattern: he rose and spoke in a council *attended by* the Oneidas, the Younger Brothers of the Onondagas, but he spoke only for his own people. The Oneidas met officially with Coursey later in their own session and presented their proposals to him by another speaker. This pattern of national councils was quite common during the colonial period. Indeed the records understate the lack of agreement among the Five Nations; not only was there no League Council authority binding the Iroquois, but the decisions made at Albany (or at any other council) applied only to those present at the council fire. As another Iroquois orator noted much later in the next century, the independence of each Iroquois village, clan, family, and individual was paramount: those who disagreed stayed away.[9]

The limits of the 1677 arrangements are also evident in the general tendency of both English and Iroquois to recognize that a "new chain" was being created that was independent of New York. It was a distinct relationship — of "clasped hands" in Indian metaphor — that saw the Iroquois, Maryland, and Virginia "grasp arms" in the fictive kin ties of "Brethren." Time and again, New York officials clearly distinguished this new relationship from their own. So did Henry Coursey: when he spoke to the issue, he encouraged the Iroquois to accept "this new chain" in addition to "yours with New York." Moreover, New York's lack of involvement was emphasized at each of the confirmation ceremonies when individual Iroquois nations exchanged gifts with Coursey. New York, for its part, acted as host to the southern colony, sponsoring its presence at the council fire at Albany and nothing more.[10]

The novelty of these arrangements is indicated, too, in the tendency of the colonial recorder to interchange the English metaphor of a "chain" with the Iroquois one of "clasped hands." The appearance of the Iroquois metaphor phrase in these treaty sessions suggests just how fluid relations actually were. For the Iroquois, the metaphor applied to *any* recognized alliance of friendship, whatever the particular conditions. And this is also how the English used it. Not until many years later would the phrase "Silver Covenant Chain" come to dominate New York treaty records and denote a *particular* relationship.

During these first councils of the 1670s, and those that followed into the early 1680s, neither side showed much interest in the complex relationships that scholars have attributed to these events. The meetings originated the Silver Covenant Chain only in the sense of introducing the English to the intricate Iroquois protocol required for public meetings. In retrospect, the ambiguity of Anglo-Iroquois relations was inherent from their very beginning. During the late 1670s, however, these problems were not obvious, because a limited agenda guided discussions. War parties from the Five Nations continued to cause unrest in the backcountry of Maryland and Virginia, leading both colonies to send a series of delegations to New York to insist that the Iroquois abide by the agreement of 1677. During the course of these meetings, Maryland officials seem to have become at least dimly aware that Iroquois assumptions about what had been agreed at Albany in 1677 did not jibe with English ones. The confusions would not be eliminated in the next decade, for English officials strove not to understand Iroquois society but to make the diplomatic map of the Northeast fit their own cultural assumptions.[11]

The process began in 1682, when Maryland officials, frustrated by their failure to achieve peace, "Considered of Some Expedient" to resolve the impasse. Their solution, presented in a memorandum of August 1682, called on the Duke of York's governor, "or some Person Commissionated by" him,

> . . . to Declare to those severall northern nations of Indians in leage and amytie with his Majestie in his Royalle Highnes The Dukes Government [of New York] that the Inhabitants of Maryland and virginia are alike Subjects To the King of England as your selves of new Yorke.
> [And] . . . That in having made a peace with the subjects of England att new yorke They must understand it includs all the Kings Subjects of Maryland and virginia.

These proposals, Maryland argued, should be delivered at "the Ratification of *your oune Peace* which wee understand is done yearly."[12]

In spite of Maryland's candid recognition of Iroquois expectations, when Effingham arrived in New York in 1684 to negotiate a final resolution to the Chesapeake colonies' continuing northern Indian problems, his actions suggest that little, if anything, had been done. But he clearly had adopted Maryland's proposals.[13] Howard informed the Five Nations that he had come to New York to assure the Iroquois of the peaceful intentions of Virginia's Indians and to create "a *new* chaine with you for Virginia and Maryland" (emphasis added). Effingham made it clear that this was a separate chain from New York's when he proposed "that the Covenant now made betwist us in this Prefixed house, in the Presence of your Governor [Dongan] may be firmly kept . . ., and that you doe not break any Link of the Covenant chain for the future, by your Poeples Comeing near our Plantacons."[14]

By the end of the year, groups from each of the Iroquois nations had expressed a willingness to join in Effingham's "Covenant chain," described as "silver" in a Seneca speech of July 1684. As the Seneca orator put it, "Here is Curler [*Corlaer,* the Iroquois council title for the governor of New York] present mening him that Represents his parson [and] there are foure arms which wee lock together in a Covenant Chaine. That is ower whole Cuntrey, my Lord howard Governor of Virginia, and my Lord Baltimore governor of Maryland[.] Let the Chaine be Kept Cleane and bright *as Silver* that the great tree that is can not break it a peeces if it should fall upon itt" (emphasis added).[15] There was still no general agreement. These councils brought the separate Iroquois nations together with New York, Virginia, and Maryland, yet no consensus on conditions had been reached *among* the Iroquois themselves on Effingham's propositions for peace. There was nothing to signify any agreement other than on an end to hostilities between the Iroquois and the English colonies to the south. The entire affair had simply generated yet another covenant chain, albeit one that included New York this time.

By November, conditions in the west led Dongan of New York to negotiate with the Five Nations to strengthen his province's separate connection to them. In so doing, Dongan obscured the significant differences between Albany's long-standing relationship with the Iroquois and the recent chain made between various Iroquois groups and Virginia, Maryland, and New York. Dongan's new conditions eventually became part of yet another silver covenant chain.[16]

A crucial factor in Dongan's decision was New France's intention to punish the Five Nations for their activities against Canada's western Indian allies. Beginning in the 1670s, certain Iroquois among the upper nations had sought to draw Ottawa trappers and traders into the fur trade complex centered at Albany. Because Canada's governor, Louis de Buade de Frontenac, wished to avoid open war with the Iroquois, he had disrupted these early negotiations through his influence among other Indian groups and, more directly, by building Fort Frontenac on the north shore of Lake Ontario. Added to these pressures were Robert Cavelier de La Salle's activities at Niagara and on Lake Erie, which were more direct assaults on Iroquois interests in the west. Apparently, La Salle's open support of the Illinois in 1679 angered enough Senecas to initiate a new round of hostilities.[17]

By 1683 Seneca and Mohawk war parties had attacked French traders in the west and La Salle's outpost on the Mississippi River. In response, Governor Joseph-Antoine Le Febvre de La Barre (who replaced Frontenac in 1678) decided to punish, if not conquer, the Iroquois. His plans began with a French assertion of sovereignty over the interior of North America, a claim based upon Jacques Cartier's early efforts and La Salle's more recent and more expansive explorations. From this premise, La Barre justified his protection of his Indian allies from Iroquois assaults. Thus, in the summer of 1684, he gathered some 1,500 French troops, Indians, and civilians at Fort Frontenac with the intent of attacking the Onondagas across the lake. An outbreak of Spanish influenza ruined La Barre's plans, however, and he soon sent word to the Five Nations to come to Quebec to receive favorable terms for peace.[18]

Many Iroquois probably welcomed the offer, but the threat to Iroquois interests remained, especially for those Senecas who met with New York during their negotiations with Lord Howard in the summer of 1684. While Virginia's diplomatic efforts proceeded along their own separate path, the discussions with Dongan exposed the fluidity of New York's new relationship with the Iroquois at this beginning of what would become New York's Silver Covenant Chain. During their negotiations with New York, the Five Nations requested the aid of their "Brother" against the French. Instead, the Iroquois found themselves listening to Dongan deliver a French request for reparations for the destruction of a canoe in the Illinois country. The Senecas — the principal participants in these discussions — made it clear that they had no effective remedy to the French threat. Dongan's only offer of assistance, which seems to have amused the French, was to give the Senecas plaques bearing the insignia of the Duke of York, to be put in Iroquois villages as a sign of his protection.[19]

The English response must have irritated the Senecas, and it probably reinforced any pro-French sympathies among them. Certainly the Onondagas, who were deeply divided, chose their own path. A large pro-French faction existed within this nation, given Garakontié's legacy and the continuing presence of Jesuit missionaries. The Onondagas had been the target of La Barre's ill-fated expedition, and they knew it. It is not surprising, then, that they ignored Dongan's demands. The Onondagas openly rejected English claims of sovereignty, asserting that as *brothers* — a specific reference to equals with reciprocal obligations — to the English of New York who offered little help, the Iroquois "must take care of ourselves." The Onondagas went further, explaining their willingness to forge still *another* covenant chain, this time with the French:

Brother Corlaer, We tell you, That we shall bind a Covenant Chain to our Arm, and to his [La Barre's], as thick as that Post (Pointing to a Post of the House). Be not dissatisf'd; should we not imbrace this Happiness offer'd to us, viz. Peace, in the place of War yea, we shall take the Evil doers, the Sennekas by the hand, and La Barre likewise, and their ax and sword shall be thrown into a deep Water. We wish our Brother Corlaer were present, but it seems the time will not permit of it.[20]

The words seem clear enough. The Onondagas were not joining the French and English into a single chain. They, and the colonial recorder, were using the phrase "Covenant Chain" in the same generic way as the Iroquois used the metaphor of grasped hands. What the Onondagas proposed was simply to make a treaty of peace with the French. And, given the recent French military threat, the large pro-French faction at Onondaga, and the failure of New York to provide adequate protection, the decision to negotiate made sense regardless of any long-range diplomacy. Furthermore, from an Iroquois perspective, such an agreement did not violate the covenant chains that still bound them to New York and the Chesapeake colonies.

By the summer of 1685, the Onondagas had failed to reach an agreement with the French, and the increased intransigence of the new French governor, Jacques-Réné de Brisay, Marquis de Denonville, eroded any consensus among the Iroquois about treating with New France. A hint of the altered circumstances came in September when an Iroquois delegation arrived in Albany with a proposal to stop negotiating with the French and a "promise that no more harm will be done there again." What makes the offer more than just the initiative of another faction acting on its own is that Garakontié's brother led the delegation.[21]

Dongan moved quickly to take advantage of the situation. Over the winter he offered a set of propositions to each of the Five Nations, propositions that were designed to alter significantly the context of the covenant chains made with the English since 1675 and to which, for the first time in his efforts, he applied the term "silver" as Virginia had done a year earlier. Dongan's intitial offering attempted to resurrect the fur trade and gain some control over its expansion into the west. The governor urged the Iroquois to end their wars in the region and asked the sachems to "incourage your young Indians to goe out a hunting and bring your Bever and Peltry no where but here wher you have always found Civil Entertainment." Dongan added that the Five Nations were not "to suffer any Christians that Shall come to your Country to trade with you without they Do have Corlaer[']s Passe." Both proposals were intended to weaken French influence: the first by avoiding open war, now that France and England had agreed to a European truce; the second by putting a halt to the purported activities of French traders on the Susquehanna River. By May 1686 Dongan, inundated with petitions from Albany to protect its trade from competitors who met Indian hunters before they arrived at the town gates, granted the outpost a monopoly on the fur trade with the Five Nations. But this was in no way antithetical to the major thrust of his general design. The governor linked these policy decisions to his revised version of the Covenant Chain, which he had reported to a Five Nations delegation the previous November. Now, for the first time, he called upon the Five Nations to include Virginia *in New York's Covenant Chain:* in other words, to create at Albany a single Silver Chain distinct from all other chain alliances.[22]

Clearly, Dongan viewed these conditions in terms of English sovereignty over the Five Nations; his insistence that the Iroquois were "neither to make warr nor Peace with any Christians without my approbacon" exposes his assumption that English law, not Iroquois cultural norms, would prevail. Furthermore, he insisted that for the future the Iroquois must rely solely upon New York to negotiate with the French. Dongan supported his case by insisting that the Iroquois would be safe from French attack once the Duke of York's coats of arms had been placed in their villages. To underscore his insistence upon Iroquois submission to English sovereignty, he ordered the Five Nations to forbid the French from settling at Niagara. As for the French Jesuits, restricted as he was by the Franco-English rapprochement under the Stuarts, Dongan urged the Iroquois not to disturb them.[23] It was a position he reinforced with respect to the fur trade. While Dongan promised not to permit "unlicensed traders in[to] the west," he expected that the Five Nations should "not Trade or Traffique, or Enter into any Covenant chain with any Christians french or English . . . without my Consent."[24]

The Iroquois who attended this council in May agreed to discuss Dongan's proposals, but this was to be expected, since the governor had delivered substantial amounts of wampum to "carry" his words. But Dongan had simply asked for too much. First, the Iroquois were too deeply involved in the western war to break it off so easily; many families still sought the satisfaction of revenge or captives for adoption. Second, the prospect of restricting the fur trade to Albany must have irritated those Iroquois families with ties to Canada and the trade there. Third, the demand to acquiesce in New York's authority reflected a kin relationship more like that of nephew to uncle than brother to brother. It should not be surprising that into the late summer of 1687, the Five Nations failed to generate sufficient consensus to respond to Dongan's revolutionary overtures. Indicative of difficulties were repeated reports that a major council at Caninda (near Onondaga) had been called but had never met. Given the competing pressures and the normal patterns of factional divisions in Iroquois society, there simply was no consensus between May of 1686 and the summer of 1687, and thus no decision. This may not have satisfied the English, but it was the norm for a divided Indian society.[25]

The French attack upon the Senecas in 1687 gave the Iroquois little additional time to ponder their answer carefully. In the fall of that year, Denonville struck the main Seneca villages and destroyed most of their stocks of corn. As if an open break with the Senecas was not enough of a problem for the French, Denonville compounded the damage by weakening an already small pro-French Onondaga faction. While gathering his forces at Fort Frontenac, he had taken into custody some Onondagas who had come to the post. Not wishing to lose the element of surprise, Denonville then rashly arrested a number of other Iroquois, held them incommunicado while his forces moved on the Senecas, and then treated them as prisoners of war, shipping them to France to row in the galleys that plied the Mediterranean.[26]

These maneuvers destroyed, at least for the moment, any French influence among the Iroquois, but they were insufficient to generate consensus on Dongan's Silver Chain. When King William's War erupted in 1689, many Iroquois were ready to join the English side — less from policy than to seek revenge for French provocations. And thus in 1687, when they renewed the Covenant Chain with New York, the Iroquois agreed formally to accept Virginia and Maryland as brothers of New York, to spy on the French for the English, and to trade only with the English in exchange for protection against French attacks. Upon close inspection, what the Iroquois did *not* agree to says much about the ambiguity of the Covenant Chain by this time. Including Virginia and Maryland into this set of agreements at the behest of New York (which hosted the council) did not eliminate the other "silver" chain that the Iroquois had forged with Effingham in 1684. Moreover, the Five Nations never acquiesced in Dongan's proposals on either the fur trade or on dealing with the French only through the English. In other words, the edifice Dongan had erected to support English sovereignty over the Iroquois was largely ignored.[27]

Even as Dongan celebrated what he perceived as a victory over the Five Nations, the inherent ambiguities of the Silver Covenant Chain were obvious. What the New York governor believed to be an alliance with multi-colony links — presumably superseding or incorporating Effingham's chain — was not. True, both the governors of Virginia and New York had referred to their covenants as being made of "silver," but that similarity could not cover up profound differences between the two agreements. Virginia was intent upon peace along its borders, while New York was concerned about the French and the threat of war. Besides, the Iroquois had agreed to both arrangements in quite separate meetings.

      That the Silver Covenant Chain developed against a background of profound cultural misperceptions has important implications for our understanding of later Iroquois history. This is not the place to retrace all the strands of that history; nevertheless, let me suggest how the shift in emphasis from Chain to chains can affect our understanding of Anglo-Iroquois relations after 1700. The patterns that emerge suggest that even the image of an "ambiguous empire" of diplomacy and guile is overly tidy, overstating as it does Iroquois unity and power in the great diplomatic events of the early eighteenth century.

      The logical place to begin is with the complex ambiguities that developed in the west. In 1687, Dongan had agreed to provide New York's protection against the French, but he had left the Five Nations, as they requested, free to deal as they saw fit with native groups west of Niagara. By the end of King William's War in 1697, the Iroquois were not only suffering defeats in the west, they were also threatened by war parties entering Iroquoia itself. To cope with these setbacks, they requested more help from New York. In 1698 Iroquois negotiators gained (after some opposition from New York's governor, Richard Coote, Earl of Bellomont) a promise to protect them from western Indian, as well as French, military aggression. The record of these negotiations, printed for public consumption to enhance Bellomont's claims to control of the Five Nations, repeatedly refers to the renewal of the Silver Covenant Chain, but the same minutes also underscore that this was a revision of New York's chain, not Virginia's.[28]

      These shifts in obligations emphasize the still-fluid nature of Anglo-Iroquois relations and the danger of considering the Covenant Chain to be a single entity. In 1701, during the councils that produced what scholars call the "Grand Settlement," arrangements with New York were further adapted to meet new conditions. New York, eager to confirm its alleged sovereignty over the Iroquois against similar French claims, promised England's protection of Iroquois hunting grounds in the west. The formal records list a "Trust Deed" that implies English sovereignty, but the

Iroquois probably read the agreement as brotherly assistance to defend their lands, not as a new relationship cementing English hegemony over the Five Nations. The misunderstanding persisted, however, as New York officials by the 1720s understood the deed of 1701 to convey ownership of the territory to the Crown. Meanwhile the Iroquois complained that New York failed to live up to its promises to defend them in the west, especially as the French establishment at Niagara grew from a small trading post into a substantial stone fort.[29]

Scholars have made much of the Iroquois decision in 1701 to remain strictly neutral between the French and the English, but what that decision did to rearrange the Covenant Chain with New York has sometimes been overlooked. While often viewed as directed by a common Iroquois purpose, in fact it reflected deep divisions within the Confederacy and its nations, divisions that had been exacerbated by a decade of war. Exhausted from a series of defeats, the Five Nations were so rent by factional disagreements over how to resolve their situation that they could not present a united front against the pressures of the French, the English, and the western nations. Thus the best that could be gained was to accede to a French demand for neutrality. This central facet of the Grand Settlement was essentially an abstention by the Five Nations: far from reflecting unity of purpose, it permitted a wide range of Iroquois preferences to coexist. Those who retained friendships with the French — most notably Senecas and Onondagas — continued to travel freely to Quebec and Montreal. Those with ties to Albany could do as they chose. Neutrality cemented peace in the west, thus permitting Iroquois hunters to move into the regions north of Lake Ontario and east of Detroit that they claimed as traditional hunting grounds. Neutrality also created a buffer to protect the Iroquois as long as all sides abided by the arrangement.[30]

It was this last point, however, that fundamentally revised New York's chain in 1701: the English definition of the Iroquois as dependent upon New York and thus obligated to help protect the colony had been effectively gutted. Thus, while the province thought that it had retained the allegiance of the Five Nations under English sovereignty, the Iroquois for their part had responded to reassert their own sense of their covenant with New York.

The Grand Settlement generated another ambiguity. For the next twenty-five years, the treaties of 1701 permitted a major faction led by the noted Onondaga leader Teganissorens aggressively to extend trade ties with the Indian nations of the Great Lakes. These activities were justified for a number of reasons, including access to hunting grounds, opportunities for trade, and the chance to undermine New France's power in the west by drawing its allies into the Albany trade market. It is important to note that Teganissorens's group of Iroquois worked actively to extend yet another covenant chain, sometimes also denoted "silver," into the west. From an Iroquois point of view, these arrangements were simply trading agreements, unrelated to the existing chains forged with either New York, New England, or Virginia. They linked western nations with New York, but almost exclusively for the purpose of trade; that is, they were in keeping with the concept of an "iron" chain, even though the records repeatedly use the term "silver." The aggressive actions of Teganissorens's group dominated French and English records for the next quarter-century, as the Onondaga-led faction consistently drew many groups into Albany's orbit. Such successes fed English hopes for expansion and French fears for holdings in the interior. That the English records should emphasize the unity of these alliances under English sovereignty is not surprising, given the origins of the Covenant Chain arrangements and, especially, the overriding English concern for legalistic forms to buttress claims of sovereignty.[31]

Where English officials wished to impose political unity, however, modern scholars should beware: the world of the eastern woodlands was too complex for simple explanations. The fluid nature of existing arrangements was a given among Iroquoian-speaking groups. As shown in chapter 2, alliances must be consistently renewed at face-to-face meetings. One simply could not know the mind of another without constant monitoring of directly delivered words. Without such procedures, it was nearly impossible for Iroquois peoples to keep track of who had agreed to what arrangements. When this native view of the diplomatic world came up against English legalisms, it is no wonder that misunderstandings resulted.

The tendency of recent studies to adopt the English perspective of the Covenant Chain as a unified entity shared between English and Iroquois is particularly problematic when Iroquois actions outside of New York are examined. For example, the multiple chains stressed in this paper force a rereading of Iroquois relations with Pennsylvania. The most important revision must be that Iroquois involvement with that province was not driven by matters of Confederacy or national policy, but rather by the limited vision of particular Iroquois groups and by very immediate and practical considerations. After the French fortified their post at Niagara in the early 1720s, New York, despite Iroquois objections, quickly established a military post at Oswego. The French and English presence in Iroquoia—and especially the penetration of fur traders into the interior of the continent—blocked Iroquois opportunities in the west and exacerbated trade tensions.

Thus, in 1727 a group of Iroquois, related to the recently deceased

Teganissorens and to Iroquois living on the lower Susquehanna River, appeared in Pennsylvania to open a new avenue of trade. These Iroquois knew little of the colony's concerns, but when they forged a new "chain of friendship" they were acting within the traditional, limited Iroquois understanding of such alliances. Contrary to the claims of some recent studies, these Iroquois did not represent the League Grand Council, though their arrival in Pennsylvania permitted provincial secretary James Logan to create the illusion of a relationship with the entire Six Nations. It was an image that he would use to oust the Delawares and thereby further his own ambitions in the Susquehanna Valley. Iroquois leaders who negotiated with Logan (in particular the Onondaga Canasetego) were probably unsuspecting accomplices in the dispossession of the Delawares. This probability, and the limited nature of Iroquois involvement (the major concerns of most Iroquois were New York and New France, not Pennsylvania), highlight the confusion that the Covenant Chain generated at the time.[32]

The confusion does not disappear when Iroquois activities farther south are examined. The so-called southern wars of the Six Nations probably do not reflect anything approaching a concerted policy. Rather, the scanty existing evidence points toward Iroquois involvement based upon kinship obligations between certain families (especially among the Cayugas and Senecas) and Iroquois and Susquehannock groups in Pennsylvania who continued a traditional form of warfare in the south. By the 1720s this was perhaps the only region where the practice of traditional warrior values was still possible. It is understandable that the south would appear as a trouble spot in English eyes, but those conditions do not translate into a concerted Iroquois diplomatic policy or influence over tribes to the south. Too much has been made of the apparent Iroquois intent of imposing tributary status on their southern neighbors. Iroquois perceptions were of a different order. Diplomatic protocol required that decisions be made through public face-to-face meetings, with the exchange of gifts — usually wampum — to carry the messages and to serve as symbols of reciprocity. With respect to the southern wars, when the English insisted upon peace, the Iroquois repeatedly demanded a public meeting at an established council fire, mediated by their fictive kinsmen of New York and Virginia. To do so was not to make the southern nations dependent; it was the only way within the native political system to know who was agreeing to what.[33]

Another area of misunderstanding surrounding the Silver Covenant Chain is Iroquois activity in the Ohio Country. Recent works have tended to recognize the independent actions of the groups that established themselves in the west after 1730 and negotiated with Pennsylvania after 1748. But these studies have also tended to assume that the native Ameri-

cans of the region acted in violation of the decrees of the Iroquois League
Council. Such an interpretation overlooks the decentralized nature of Six
Nations politics. For example, the Ohio leaders who appeared in Pennsylvania in the late 1740s to establish a covenant chain, or chain of friendship, with that province were doing nothing out of the ordinary. Iroquois
leaders in New York objected at times to the actions of these Ohio Country residents, but the tendency was to question who should be *included*
in these councils, not who had the authority to meet with English or French
delegations. Viewed from this perspective, Iroquois activities on the Ohio
in the 1740s and 1750s appear even more disorganized than most scholars
have discerned.[34]

The confusion in the Ohio Country raises yet another point that
is usually obscured by the prevailing notion of a monolithic Covenant
Chain. The increase in native activity in the area during the 1740s reflected
the seriously weakened position of the Iroquois after 1730. The western
chains forged by Teganissorens's faction during the first quarter of the century had neither kept Iroquois soil inviolate nor given Iroquois people clear
access to the trade or hunting grounds of the Great Lakes. After 1730, leaders of the Six Nations could not generate sufficient consensus to coordi-
nate efforts to attract western nations to Albany, even as they could not
prevent their own hunters from traveling with increasing frequency to the
Ohio. As a result, Iroquois diplomatic activity in the west declined. By
the 1740s the links of the chains extended into the west were so weak that
western nations were arriving in Albany to ask what had happened to their
brethren of the Six Nations. Unable to maintain either these relationships
or cordial ties with New York, Iroquois leaders were increasingly incapable of molding a unified response to English and French pressures.[35]

Into this vacuum of leadership stepped two remarkable men: the
Mohawk leader Hendrick and the New York magnate William Johnson.
Beginning in the mid-1740s and continuing through the 1750s, these two
joined forces to forge an entirely new chain that put Mohawks — rather
than Onondagas — at the head of Iroquois delegations. The new relationship gave Johnson more authority than previous English officials had been
able to muster, for the paradoxical reason that *his* "Silver Covenant Chain"
was more image than substance, restricted as it was largely to Mohawk
participation. But weak as this new chain was, it gave to English officials
the appearance of effective action. Johnson was well aware of his limitations: he spent much of the 1750s strengthening his position by trying to
create new chains with the independent Iroquois and other groups on the
Ohio and Susquehanna, then portraying the results as a single relationship in his reports to Whitehall. Perhaps the most ironic development of

the entire campaign came in 1760 at Detroit, where Johnson bypassed the leaders in Iroquoia, established a new council fire with the western nations, and pronounced the Silver Covenant Chain as strong as ever.[36]

The status of Iroquois involvement with European colonists, then, was even more ambiguous than Francis Jennings's seminal work has suggested. What successes the Iroquois achieved were due in no small measure to their image of unity and to the ignorance of English officials about the factional nature of decision-making among the Six Nations. In reality, by 1750 Iroquois influence in the Northeast was splintered. Iroquois society had always had divisions, but the failure of leaders to develop a clear response to English and French overtures in the eighteenth century made the Six Nations quite incapable of controlling their own diplomatic future. The disruptions to Iroquois society that would come in the wake of the American Revolution were merely epilogue.

II

NEAR NEIGHBORS

4

TOWARD the COVENANT CHAIN

Iroquois and Southern New England Algonquians, 1637–1684

NEAL SALISBURY

F ALL THE BOUNDARIES of Iroquoia, the least studied and least understood is the southeastern, where Mohawk relations with the Algonquian speakers of southern New England helped shape the history of Indians and Europeans alike in the northern colonies.[1] Several recent studies have noted the Mohawk role in defeating the New England native uprising known as King Philip's War (1675–76) and marked the treaty that followed as beginning the Covenant Chain system of alliances.[2] But most have paid insufficient attention to earlier relations between the two peoples.[3] For more than two decades after the Pequot War of 1637, wampum from New England supported Iroquois diplomacy and ritual, while the Mohawks contributed decisively to the balance of power in the Puritan colonies. Then this system collapsed under the weight of demographic and imperial pressures, and the Iroquois and New England colonies moved, uneasily and under the guidance of a new imperial leadership in New York, toward an alliance that subordinated or excluded the Algonquians. This paper seeks to reconstruct these developments, making clear that neither New England nor Iroquois history can be properly written without an understanding of the other.

Iroquois life during the Beaver Wars of the 1640s and '50s was marked by the intensification of rituals associated with warfare, diplomacy, death, and adoption. The critical component in all these ceremonies was wampum. The Iroquois used wampum "words" to cement social and political relations both among the Five Nations and with outside allies.

After a war, they employed it for the same purpose with erstwhile enemies. And wampum presents consoled the mourning relatives of the increased number of Iroquois dead, as exemplified in the myth of Deganawidah and Hiawatha.[4]

During the seventeenth century, the richest sources of the shells used to manufacture wampum lay in the coves and inlets of Long Island and the opposite mainland shore as far east as Narragansett Bay. The Mohawks had undoubtedly been obtaining shell beads from this region since before the arrival of Europeans. But their active interest began in response to the unsettling effects of Pequot and English expansion there. In 1631 the Pequots attempted to gain control of trade relations on the Connecticut and Thames rivers. As a result, they alienated virtually all the other Indians of the region as well as the Dutch in New Netherland and the English in Plymouth and Massachusetts Bay. After suffering a series of defeats at the hands of the Dutch in 1634, the Pequots confronted a military challenge mounted by the expansion-minded English and their Narragansett and Mohegan allies.[5]

The offensive launched by this coalition culminated in the well-known English massacre of several hundred Pequots in their Mystic River village in May 1637. Yet while the massacre broke the back of Pequot resistance to the English invasion of Connecticut, it did not exhaust the Indians' options or end the war. The end came only when the Pequot sachem, Sassacus, and about forty followers eluded colonial troops and crossed the Hudson River. There they requested the Mohawks' support by presenting them with wampum worth some £500. But the Mohawks had already accepted a similar gift from the Narragansetts in return for their support against the Pequots. Accurately perceiving that the future of New England's wampum coast now lay with the Narragansetts and English, the Mohawks captured and executed the Pequot petitioners, turning over the scalp and hands of Sassacus to his English pursuers. In so doing, they sealed the fate of the Pequots and their replacement by the new colony of Connecticut as a major power alongside the Narragansetts on Long Island Sound.[6]

The Pequot War had no sooner ended than tensions developed between the Narragansetts on the one hand and the English and their Mohegan allies on the other. At issue was control over the distribution of wampum. The colonists sought wampum in part as a substitute for scarce English currency; but for all parties, wampum served as a symbolic expression of allegiance. Since the English were attempting to colonize the region, they sought to subordinate the Narragansetts and other natives to themselves by extracting tribute in the form of wampum payments. To the Narragansetts, however, such payments were gifts freely presented to potential allies. During the 1640s, the Commissioners of the United Colonies (Massachusetts Bay, Plymouth, Connecticut, and New Haven) discovered time and again that the Narragansetts and their allies had given substantial amounts of wampum to the Mohawks while defaulting on payments to the English, and that the Mohawks had expressed support for the Narragansetts against the colonists.[7] The Commissioners assumed that these presentations represented gifts which the Narragansetts exchanged for Mohawk military support against the English colonies. That the Narragansetts were hostile to the United Colonies is indisputable. But this hostility stemmed primarily from the Commissioners' efforts to reduce, with the aggressive assistance of the Mohegans and their sachem, Uncas, the Narragansetts' land base and political autonomy.

Indeed, on those occasions in which a significant number of Mohawks seriously contemplated joining their southern New England allies in a concerted military action, their target was strictly the Mohegans, not the English. In 1647, for example, Uncas and a party of Mohegans attacked and robbed some Pocumtucks and threatened the Mohawks if they came to the aid of their Connecticut Valley allies. Though given wampum and urged to do just that by the Pocumtucks and Narragansetts, the Mohawks were divided, most "pleading their hunting season" and returning home. Shortly thereafter, the Narragansetts (who were similarly divided) downplayed the significance of the gift, claiming to the English that it merely confirmed an old friendship and that their only quarrel was with Uncas. In backing off from a military confrontation, both parties sought to avoid entanglement with the colonists, not out of fear but out of self-interest. For the Narragansetts, the decision was consistent with their strategy since the early 1630s: in order to avoid dependence on any single party, they cultivated as many alliances as possible, with Europeans as well as Indians. For the Mohawks, on the other hand, the plea of "their hunting season" suggests that collecting furs took precedence over avenging attacks on non-Iroquois allies.[8]

Three years later, it was the United Colonies Commissioners who recognized the wisdom of avoiding entanglement with the Mohawks. The occasion was their rejection of a proposal for an Anglo-French military alliance against the Five Nations. The proposal had been brought by Gabriel Druillettes, a Jesuit missionary who had recently succeeded in winning the Kennebec Abenakis of Maine to Catholicism and the French cause, and whose diplomatic skills New France now called on in the wake of the Iroquois' destruction of Huronia in 1649. In the following year, Druillettes succeeded — along with the Kennebec Abenakis and the Montagnais of the St. Lawrence Valley—in extending the French-sponsored anti-Iroquois alliance to four previously pro-Iroquois Algonquian-speaking groups: the Sokokis, the Pocumtucks, the Pennacooks, and the Mahicans. Since these groups were allied in turn with the other major Algonquian bands of southern New England and the lower Hudson, Druillettes confidently expected that all of the Iroquois' eastern supporters would now join his coalition. His task in 1651 was to extend his diplomatic offensive to the United Colonies.[9]

Druillettes argued that recent Iroquois attacks against the Abenakis and Sokokis represented an immediate danger to English trade on the Kennebec and a future threat to the colonies themselves. While Plymouth (which had the greatest interest in the Kennebec trade) was favorable, the Commissioners as a body rejected the proposal. Not only did they have no quarrel with the Mohawks and no desire to precipitate one, they recalled that during the Pequot War the Mohawks "shewed a small Respecte" toward them and had maintained amicable relations since. To make war on them now would only risk alienating the New England allies of the Five Nations and endanger both English settlements and Puritan missionary efforts among the Indians.[10]

Three years later, when the United Colonies again felt provoked by the Narragansetts, Roger Williams reminded the Massachusetts General Court of just how important the Mohawk-Narragansett connection was to the peace and stability of colonial society. These "are the two great bodies of Indians in this country, and they are confederates, and long have been, and they both yet are friendly and peaceabl[e] to the English," Williams argued. If the colonies went to war with one without making sure of the loyalty of the other, they would surely be defeated. Apparently the message struck home. In 1657, the Narragansetts, Pocumtucks, and Mohawks jointly petitioned the General Court for permission to attack their Mohegan rivals. Though predictably rejecting the plea, the Court went out of its way to praise the friendship of the three groups to the colony as one that was deeply rooted and beneficial.[11]

While fighting the Beaver Wars of the 1640s and 1650s, then, the Mohawks seem to have constituted a source of peace and stability in southern New England. Close Mohawk ties to the Narragansetts and to the Pocumtucks and other Connecticut Valley bands gave the United Colonies pause in their efforts to reduce Narragansett power and influence on Long Island Sound. As we have seen, the wampum that flowed from New England through the Mohawks to the other Iroquois tribes was a principal component of this connection. But what flowed the other way besides the Five Nations' reputation for ferocity? In repudiating Druillettes' proposed alliance against the Iroquois, the Commissioners maintained that "liveing att a distance from the Sea," the Mohawks "have littel entercourse in these parts."[12] Yet this claim is belied by other evidence that the Commissioners presumably did not wish to publicize, especially in New France.

Two of the most active fur-trading centers in mid-seventeenth-century New England were the Massachusetts portion of the Connecticut River Valley, dominated by the Pynchon family from its post at Springfield, and Narragansett Bay, where both Roger Williams and Richard Smith maintained operations. (In 1651 Williams sold his interests to Smith.) At both locales, English traders obtained furs from native allies in exchange for European goods. As local fur sources declined, these client bands relied increasingly on other Indian groups for pelts.[13] Given the amount of wampum that was passing from these groups to the Mohawks, the Iroquois were almost certainly reciprocating with skins obtained in the Beaver Wars, skins that kept the New England fur trade alive longer than the local beaver population alone could have done. The English merchants were by no means unaware of the Mohawks' commercial importance. From the time of Springfield's establishment in 1636, the Dutch traders at Albany decried the Pynchons' success in diverting Mohawk and Mahican trade to the Connecticut.[14] Moreover, as we shall see, John Pynchon was involved in a series of efforts to establish an English post on or near the Hudson. And for most of the 1640s, Richard Smith actually directed his Narragansett Bay operation from a home in New Amsterdam, where the Mohawks' commercial role was well understood.[15]

Historians of Indian-white relations in southern New England generally stress the very real tensions between the Narragansetts on the one hand and the English and Mohegans on the other. Yet, as these histories note, the two sides always managed to avoid open warfare.[16] How? Because the tensions were offset by the exchanges of furs, wampum, and European goods which linked English traders to the Mohawks via the Indians of Narragansett Bay and the Connecticut Valley. In the face of the recurrent war scares so often emphasized by historians, these exchange networks constituted a countervailing tendency toward peace and stability in southern New England.

This stabilizing tendency prevailed through the 1650s, but new pressures that arose thereafter finally shattered the fragile equilibrium of forces sustaining it, particularly the Mohawk link with the Indians of Narragansett Bay and the Connecticut Valley. The rise of overseas commerce

in New England during the preceding two decades relieved an earlier short-
age of English currency, ending settler demand for wampum as a substitute
medium of exchange. At the same time, a fast-rising population of family
farmers and the growth of land speculation made real estate a higher pri-
ority than the increasingly scarce furs or other goods and services that
local natives could provide.[17] The growth of the English colonies came at
the expense not only of the natives but of neighboring New Netherland.
Once wampum was no longer useful as legal tender, New England merchants dumped theirs in the Dutch colony — where it still prevailed — in exchange for furs and Dutch goods. With a scarcity of guilders and an abun-
dance of severely devalued wampum, New Netherland was beset with debt
and inflation, and its merchants were unable to procure sufficient supplies
of goods to trade with their Indian clients.[18] At the same time, John Pynchon and other New Englanders with access to wampum attempted to expand their fur-trading operations toward the Hudson and the Mohawks,
further undermining the Dutch.[19]

As the ties that bound them to the Iroquois and English weakened, the Mohawks' former allies in southern New England and on the
lower Hudson drew closer to their fellow Algonquian-speakers to the north
— the Sokokis of the upper Connecticut Valley, the Abenakis of Maine,
and the Montagnais — all of whom were allied with the French against the
Five Nations. As a result, the cycle of highly destructive raids and counter-
raids that characterized Iroquois relations with these Indians expanded
southward. A Sokoki attack on a Mohawk village in 1662 brought retaliation the following year in which, as in most such actions, the raiders suffered as many losses as their foes.[20] Nevertheless, the Mohawks frightened
the Sokokis into abandoning their recently besieged homes. While many
joined growing numbers of Abenakis in moving to New France, others took
up residence among allies and relatives at Pocumtuck and elsewhere.[21] As
refugees, the Sokokis and Abenakis were effective in galvanizing additional
anti-Iroquois sentiment, and those at Pocumtuck probably helped maneu-
ver that most influential of Connecticut Valley bands into active hostility
to the Iroquois. By July 1664 John Pynchon was unable to communicate
the friendly intentions of the English to the Mohawks, "for all the Indians
hereabouts" on whom he previously could have called for such a mission
were "at deadly feud with them."[22]

The break with the New England Algonquians compounded the
diplomatic and military isolation of the Five Nations in the early and
mid-1660s. Under attack by the Susquehannocks from the south and the
French from the north, the Mohawks sought additional diplomatic aid from
the English conquerors of New Netherland.[23] The New York government,

seeking to continue and strengthen the fur trade at Fort Orange (now Albany), signed a treaty with the Mohawks and other Iroquois in September 1664. The agreement assured the Five Nations a steady supply of trade goods, peace with the "River Indians" on the lower Hudson, and a free hand in avenging the death of a Mohawk sachem who had been murdered while on a peacemaking mission to Pocumtuck. In the following year, the Mohawks obtained their revenge in a massive attack that destroyed Pocumtuck, scattering its inhabitants among their better fortified Indian allies to the south and east.[24]

The New York alliance helped, but the Iroquois were by no means out of trouble. The war with the Susquehannocks continued, while the French troops recently arrived in Canada began building a series of forts from which to attack the Five Nations. The four western Iroquois nations quickly agreed to a peace treaty with New France in December 1665, but the Mohawks refused to go along. As the Connecticut Valley Indians and their allies counterattacked, the French invaded the Mohawk country in January 1666 and again the following July.[25] Under attack on three fronts, the Mohawks sought additional diplomatic aid from New York, pleading that "we do not want to be killed by the Mahikanders."[26] This desire was compatible with English goals — both at Albany and on the Connecticut — for an Iroquois-Algonquian peace that would restore stability to the fur trade and prevent the expansion of French influence among the Algonquians.[27] In September 1666, New York obtained an Iroquois-Mahican peace, but efforts to extend it to the New England bands failed as raiders from both sides continued to attack each other's villages.[28] Recognizing the limits of English protection, the Mohawks finally joined the other Iroquois nations in settling with the French, accepting three Jesuit missionaries "to cement the peace" and, they hoped, obtain protection from the Algonquians.[29]

While Iroquois diplomats were active at Albany and Quebec, the Pocumtucks and their allies extended their anti-Iroquois coalition to other New England bands. Though a proposed treaty between the Mohawks and the New England colonies collapsed in the summer of 1666, the Indians in those colonies must have discerned the potential danger of any agreement linking the Iroquois to Massachusetts and Connecticut (not to mention to New York and New France). In seeking to strengthen their anti-Iroquois alliance, the Algonquians were aided by the fact that, since the Pocumtuck-Mohawk break in 1664, the universally detested Mohegans of Connecticut had established ties with the Mohawks. Citing these ties, the Connecticut Valley bands approached such Mohegan enemies as the Narragansetts, the Pequots, the Massachusetts, and the Wampanoags of Plymouth.[30] The missionary John Eliot, playing on the record of Mohawk attacks in Massachusetts Bay, procured ammunition for his "praying Indians," some of whom had obtained their first guns from him twenty years earlier.[31]

It was probably the Massachusetts' firepower that entitled their sachem Josias Chickataubut to lead an attack by New England and New York Algonquians on the Mohawk village of Caughnawaga in August 1669. This was the last pan-Algonquian offensive to be mounted against the Iroquois from southern New England. According to their Puritan friend Daniel Gookin (who with Eliot advised against the expedition), the six to seven hundred Algonquians were ill-informed and ill-equipped for such an undertaking. By the time the slow-moving party of men, women, and children reached the village, the Mohawks (who had plenty of guns themselves) were well-prepared, and they easily withstood the Algonquians' siege. After a stand-off of several days, the invaders exhausted their provisions and ammunition, and many fell ill. As they attempted to retreat, they were ambushed by Mohawks, who killed more than fifty of their leading warriors, including Chickataubut. The Massachusetts, wrote Gookin, "returned home ashamed" and were "effectually convinced of their folly."[32]

The crushing defeat of the Chickataubut expedition led the governors of New York and Connecticut to seek a new Iroquois-Algonquian peace arrangement at Albany in November 1671. While the Mohawks and Mahicans were satisfied with the English proposals, many in the New England bands were highly suspicious. To begin with, the Connecticut Valley contingent that received the proposal was not an officially authorized diplomatic mission, but a large hunting party that happened to be nearby and was lured to Albany with promises of presents. At the ceremonies themselves, the English gave most of the presents — cloth, food, liquor, and wampum — and made sure that these gifts, as well as those that the Indians exchanged among themselves, were of precisely equal size and worth. But in the drinking that followed, an Algonquian was murdered, and the New Yorkers had to move the Mohawk delegates away quickly before the violence spread. Thereafter the Connecticut Valley bands remained reluctant not only because the meeting lacked their prior approval, but because New York was pressing them to return to Albany with more presents to confirm the peace. Besides distrusting the Mohawks' intentions, the Connecticut Valley Indians were alert to the symbolism that would be attached to their traveling to Albany. In John Pynchon's words, they "would fair stand upon equal terms with the Maquas and would not have them counted above them[selves]."[33]

In insisting upon "equal terms" — the application of the native prin-

ciple of reciprocity to the matter of status—the Connecticut Valley Algonquians were responding to a position already adopted by the Mohawks.
When the English had tried to organize a peace conference at Hartford five
years earlier, the Albany traders expressed their opposition to the Mohawks'
going to New England. As John Pynchon saw it, "unless our Indians go
thither there will be nothing done." This was the apparent sentiment of
a delegation of Mohawks sent to Hartford who sabotaged that conference
along the way by raiding the Connecticut Valley village of Norwottuck.[34]
It was a similar refusal to humiliate themselves before their foes that now
led the Pocumtucks and their allies to refuse to ratify the peace of 1671.

The problem of place was not critical in Iroquois-Mahican relations, for Albany had been established as their diplomatic common ground
since the conclusion of their war in the late 1620s.[35] Although the relationship remained tense, New York now exercised a fair measure of control,
reinforcing Albany's growing importance as the center of a new Indian-
European diplomatic order.[36] As a result, the anti-English Algonquians of
southern New England were now the ones who were isolated. By 1674, with
native-settler relations in southern New England approaching the break-
ing point, the inhabitants of two Connecticut Valley villages—Woronoco
and Pojassick—acknowledged the new reality by moving westward to the
more stable environs of Albany. John Pynchon was unable to understand
why the villagers "make so universal and general a removal," noting that
the few who remained behind wished the others had "not gone hard with
the Mohawks." According to Gordon Day, these emigrants founded the
"River Indian" community of Schaghticoke on the Hoosic River, some
twenty miles north of Albany. They were the vanguard of the much larger
refugee movement that soon followed.[37]

The Woronoco and Pojassick removals coincided with the return
of English rule to New York following the brief Dutch reconquest of 1673–
74. The colony's proprietor, the Duke of York (later King James II) and
his new governor, Edmund Andros, were more determined than ever to
use the colony as a base from which to impose imperial order on His Majesty's subjects—both Indian and colonist—in the northern provinces, especially in New England. A key element in this strategy was to be the
Iroquois Confederacy, as can be glimpsed from a renewal of New York's
accord with the Mahicans in February 1675. The balance of fear had shifted
from earlier New York treaties with Indians in which the Mohawks begged
for protection from the Mahicans. With France and England at peace and
their New England allies effectively cornered, the Mahicans suddenly found
themselves isolated and outnumbered in a colony where, as they put it,
"the English and Dutch are now one." In their admitted weakness, the

Mahicans and their Algonquian "River Indian" allies prayed that the Mohawks not attack them and "that they . . . not be exiled or destroyed by the English, something they have never done to the Christians."[38] Though the Five Nations did not participate directly in this agreement, their dominant position relative to other Indians in New York was made clear, and it signalled nothing less than a revolution in Indian politics in northeastern North America.

         While New York secured Mahican neutrality, New England moved to the brink of war. Though King Philip's War was essentially a conflict between natives and settlers, many Indians sided with the latter. The Mohegans and Pequots, many Massachusetts, and some Wampanoags participated in the colonists' cause and contributed decisively to their victory. These were Indians who had lived close to large numbers of settlers for more than a generation. The core of native resistance to the English lay in a broad swath of territory running northwest from both sides of Narragansett Bay through "Nipmuc country" in central Massachusetts to the Connecticut River. It encompassed Indians who had retained substantial autonomy until the early 1660s, thanks to their numbers and to their links with English traders, with each other, and with the Mohawks. In effect, they had continued to participate in a world of indigenous exchange even while growing increasingly tied to the colonial economy.[39] Following their break with the Mohawks, these groups continued to act together as an anti-Iroquois coalition, even though they lost the Mahicans and Massachusetts and in 1675 had to face the English and Iroquois simultaneously.
         At the outbreak of the war in June 1675, the role to be played by the Mohawks was clouded by English intercolonial tensions. The New England colonies desperately needed the second front to the west that New York and the Mohawks could provide, but they feared a resumption of Mohawk-Algonquian ties. Equally troubling were the stated aims of New York Governor Andros: to reclaim all territory west of the Connecticut River for the Duke of York and generally subordinate New England to imperial rule. In August 1675 Andros journeyed 100 miles beyond Albany into Mohawk country to secure support for the English war effort. But the Mohawks did not assume an active role until the Wampanoags entered New York in their quest for allies, threatening the newly established peace which had elevated the Five Nations to a dominant position among Indians in that colony.[40]
         That point was reached in January 1676, when the Wampanoag

sachem Metacom ("King Philip") and a body of his followers arrived at the new village of Schaghticoke. They hoped to overcome the neutrality of the Mahicans and other "River Indians" from the Hudson Valley, and to enlist the aid of several hundred northern Algonquian allies of the French who were present. But morale declined as epidemic diseases swept through the gathering. Then, with Andros's backing, a well-armed body of Mohawks attacked, driving the fragmented and dispirited New England Indians back to their own region, where winter, additional disease casualties, and a revitalized colonial military effort finally defeated them and ensured that New England would remain English.[41]

As the Mohawks pursued their enemies eastward into the Connecticut Valley, the New England colonists' misgivings about their new allies increased. In several well-executed attacks, the Mohawks scattered the Algonquians into small bands. Some of these bands surrendered to or were defeated by the English,[42] but others fled the region, mostly to Schaghticoke, which New York officially opened to them in May 1676.[43] A series of disputes over the status and disposition of the Schaghticoke refugees quickly developed among the Mohawks, the Mahicans, and the colonies of Massachusetts and Connecticut, for the English feared that the village would be used as a base from which to launch attacks on their towns.[44] At the same time, the Mohawks carried on their own war against the Indian allies of the colonies, particularly the Mohegans of Connecticut, who, like the Pocumtucks earlier, refused to carry presents to the Mohawks.[45]

In order to prevent the New England colonies from treating with the Mohawks and Mahicans on their own, as well as to advance Whitehall's broader imperial strategy, Andros decided to bring the New England colonies together with the New York Indians under his supervision at Albany. At a meeting in April 1677, the Mohawks and Mahicans each pledged to return any hostile New England natives to the colonies, and the Mohawks agreed not to raid any friendly Indians in New England. In return, the New England colonies renounced their power to treat with the New York tribes independently. While both Mohawks and Mahicans referred to the colonists as "friends" and "brethren," they insisted that all their meetings would henceforth be held in Albany with Andros in attendance.[46] With a carefully arranged symbolic hierarchy in which New York was supreme, in which the New England colonies and the Five Nations had secondary but equal status, and in which other Indians were deemed the "children" of one of the superior parties, the Albany conference of April 1677 constituted the seed of the Covenant Chain system of alliances.[47]

Yet in spite of this long-run significance, the New England–Mohawk treaty did not resolve the differences between its principals, for the Mohawks had not made peace with some of those colonies' "friend Indians," notably the Mohegans and the Massachusetts. For the remainder of 1677 and into the following year, Mohawk parties continued to attack these groups and to carry off captives, incidents that reveal the continued disparity between the goals of the Iroquois and those of the New England colonies.[48] They also illuminate the last-ditch efforts of two New England native groups to avoid submitting to the Mohawks. No final resolution of the Mohegan question appears in the documents. For the Massachusetts the issue was not settled until the Covenant Chain was renewed in July 1684. Only then did the Mohawks finally give up the idea of demanding direct gifts from the Bay colony's client bands and accept the colony as intermediary.[49]

By then few people, English or Iroquois, cared much about the southern New England bands. For thousands of these natives, King Philip's War had brought death, sale into West Indian slavery, or flight to New France and New York. Those who remained behind were isolated in segregated enclaves where they reconstituted their communal identities, but under conditions of extreme economic and political deprivation. Their defeat opened vast new tracts of land to New England's rapidly growing colonial population.

The Iroquois avoided such a fate. With the Covenant Chain, they joined New York in overseeing a system of alliances linking Indians and colonists from Virginia to Massachusetts. The Chain, along with their continuing ability to threaten the French, gave them a new lease on political life that would carry them well into the eighteenth century.

Andros forged the first links in the Covenant Chain out of the converging interests of the Five Nations and the New England colonies. These interests did not emerge suddenly at the time of King Philip's War; rather, they were rooted in nearly half a century of interaction between the Five Nations and various groups of southern New England Algonquians. During the middle decades of the century, Mohawk ties with the Narragansetts, Pocumtucks, and other bands bestowed commercial, political, and military benefits upon the Puritan colonies. Within these connections, autonomous Indian groups ventured freely into one another's territories as equals while the English, despite their fear of so powerful a native combination, did not dare challenge it. But when England and France escalated their imperial rivalry in North America and when economic and demographic developments in colonial New England strengthened the colonists' position, the supports for these Iroquois-Algonquian ties collapsed. In one sense, the treaty of April 1677 only legitimized the Mohawks' earlier interest in the Indian affairs of southern New England, with the colonies serving as somewhat reluctant beneficiaries. But it was the terms of this new interest — rather than the interest itself — that were unprecedented. Instead of the reciprocity among autonomous equals that had prevailed before 1660, the treaty and the subsequent evolution of the Covenant Chain established a hierarchy of power and status, reinforced by payments of tribute and by geographic centers of authority. To the Iroquois, this outcome embodied, among other things, a step toward the ideal of peace and cooperation among peoples. To the southern New England Algonquians, it marked the end of political autonomy and reciprocity. To us in the twentieth century, it denotes a new phase in Iroquois history and in the expansion of European power in North America.

5

"PENNSYLVANIA INDIANS" and the IROQUOIS

FRANCIS JENNINGS

THE COLONIAL HISTORY of Iroquois relations with the Indians of Pennsylvania is overshadowed by the myth of Iroquois empire. The myth, which originated with English colonial officials and in later years was perpetuated by historian Francis Parkman and anthropologist Lewis Henry Morgan,[1] drew extra support from a small selection of recorded treaty negotiations in Pennsylvania. In these, the Delawares paid deference to the Iroquois, and in one, dated 1742, an Iroquois chief asserted that his people had conquered the Delawares and "made women" of them. Good grist for the mills of male supremacists, this speech has been accepted at face value by historians and anthropologists until quite recently.

The whole corpus of this mythology is false. The Iroquois "empire" in the west has been analyzed elsewhere.[2] This chapter argues that the notion of "empire" in Pennsylvania distorts reality as much as that in Ohio. Like all enduring myths, the foundation of this one lay in tendentiously selected data, and its factual contradictions have been ignored or suppressed by various interested parties—among whom were keepers of Iroquois traditions of the Golden Age of Iroquois glory.

Pennsylvania is a construction made by lawyers. Within its artificial bounds, native peoples lived along three river systems: the Delaware, Susquehanna, and Allegheny/Monongahela/Ohio. Legend has it that the aboriginal inhabitants of the Ohio Valley left under pressure from other peoples sometime before the arrival in North America of Europeans.[3] When that European invasion began, it moved up the Delaware and Susquehanna rivers but was obstructed by the Appalachian mountain wall from flowing into the Ohio Valley. Thus, at the very beginning of the region's written history, the student must recognize distinct developments in what came to be called eastern and western Pennsylvania. In the east,

which is the Pennsylvania of this chapter, interlaced tributary streams made
one region out of the Susquehanna and Delaware valleys, and their springs
originated in the north close to the sources of other waterways that became the Hudson River and the Finger Lakes feeding into Lake Ontario.
For Indians, eastern Pennsylvania and all of New York were linked into
one great system of intercourse by canoe and by trails through the valleys.
Physical communication produced commercial and political relationships,
though it determined neither the character of those relationships nor the
varied statuses within them. When Europeans appeared at the rivers' ter-
minal bays early in the seventeenth century, they joined the preexisting
network and added their own influences to it.

A number of Indian peoples lived in this regional system. Some
of them disappeared before Europeans made direct contact, leaving three
dominant tribes or nations that dealt with each other and with the colo-
nizing Europeans in recorded relations of trade, politics, war, and peace.[4]
Within what was to become the province of Pennsylvania, the Delaware
(Lenni Lenape) people occupied the lower Delaware Valley and were allied
closely to the Minisinks of the valley's upper reaches. The Susquehanna
Valley, above its giant Chesapeake Bay, was home to the Susquehannocks.
Before the creation of Pennsylvania in 1681, Delawares and Susquehan-
nocks had had much intercourse with each other and with "New York's
Indians," the Iroquois Confederacy to the north.

When traders from the Netherlands, Sweden, and England pene-
trated the Delaware River, rivalry arose between Susquehannocks and
Delawares over access to the trading centers. Sparse documents suggest that
the Delawares tried to exert controls, but the Susquehannocks fought
through, after which the two tribes made peace and became allies on terms
of mutual advantage.[5] The Delawares thereafter enjoyed such remarkable
security that they did not build stockades around their towns.[6]

The Susquehannocks, however, were constantly embattled. They
conquered Indian peoples on Chesapeake Bay (exactly which ones and with
what effects are not clear), and they warred with the Iroquois to the north.
When Virginia was established, the Susquehannocks became trading partners with William Claiborne and were later drawn into his conflicts with
Maryland when that new colony claimed the Chesapeake islands where
Claiborne had set up trading posts.[7] Maryland's Calverts drove out Virginia's Claiborne in 1638, acquiring the Susquehannocks as enemies in the
process. Maryland declared war on those Indians in 1642, campaigned vic-
toriously against them a year later, but came to grief in 1644. Fortune
changed because still another new colony had sided with the Susquehannocks. New Sweden, founded on Delaware Bay in 1638, picked up the

trade that formerly had gone to Claiborne. Rather than let Maryland take it away by conquest, the Swedes armed and trained the Susquehannocks, and the Indians routed the Englishmen.

So many parties contended for dominance in the region that the situation could not possibly remain stable. To the north, the New Netherland Dutch provided firearms to the Iroquois, who inflicted great damage upon the Susquehannocks during the winter of 1651–52. The latter then protected their southern front by seeking peace with Maryland. They got peace and more arms at the price of a cession of all their claims to territory on the Chesapeake except for a small parcel at the bay's head. Shortly thereafter, in 1654, the Swedes forcibly took over Dutch posts in the Delaware Valley, whereupon the Dutch retaliated in 1655 by a quick conquest that terminated New Sweden. The Susquehannocks then found themselves in a very awkward situation: at war with the Iroquois who had been armed by the Hudson River Dutch, and allied with the Indians whose territory was occupied by the Delaware River Dutch.

Maryland's alliance became all the more important as the only feasible alternative to the Dutch, and Marylanders warmed to the relationship as their own interests became involved. Negatively, the Iroquois attacked Piscataway Indians of the Potomac River Valley "for being friends" to Susquehannocks and Maryland. Positively, Maryland's proprietor, Lord Baltimore, laid plans to use the Susquehannocks in a scheme to seize Delaware Bay. The Dutch presence and activities constituted the cement that bound Maryland with the Susquehannocks — but only up to a point. When Maryland demanded in 1661 that the Susquehannocks "destroy" the Delawares, the Indians declined to attack their own allies. As the Dutch at Delaware Bay clearly understood, Maryland's purpose was to claim the "rights of conquest" of "Maryland's" Susquehannocks. This storm blew over when Delawares and Dutch acted to conciliate Maryland, which was not yet ready to conquer with its own men.

For a while, Maryland's government trod cautiously in the midst of all the tensions. Though Baltimore enjoyed sanctuary in distant England, his officers' estates and persons in the colony's dispersed settlements were vulnerable to Indian attack. While the government temporized, the Iroquois struck. In 1663 a force of 800 Senecas, Cayugas, and Onondagas laid siege to the Susquehannocks' stockaded town, which was ready for the attackers with an equal force, 100 of whom were Delawares. The allies defeated the supposedly invincible Iroquois and sent the crestfallen raiders home within a week. In the same year, the Sokoki or Squakheag Indians of the upper Connecticut Valley inflicted calamitous defeat on a raiding party of Mohawks, Onondagas, and Oneidas. Notably, these Iroquois defeats occurred after the Iroquois triumphs of the Beaver Wars of 1649–55. Together with a smallpox epidemic, they wrought "sad havoc" in Iroquoia. Far from being the savage rulers of a wilderness empire, as old myth has portrayed them, the Iroquois were brought by the accumulated effects of famine, disease, and war "within two finger-breadths of total destruction."[8]

Between 1663 and 1676, the Iroquois defended their homeland against perpetual attacks by Susquehannocks from the south (backed by Maryland) and Mahicans from the east (backed by Massachusetts). In 1664 the Dutch backers of the Iroquois were conquered by the Duke of York's Englishmen, who made New Netherland into New York and incidentally upset the Iroquois system of diplomacy.[9] The French invasion of the Mohawk country in 1666 only increased Iroquois woes.[10] Far from presiding over a tributary empire, the Iroquois strove for more than twenty years simply to survive. They appealed to the merchants of Albany, the governor of New York, and, as late as 1673, the governor of New France to save them from their Indian foes.[11]

Because smallpox does not play favorites, the enemies of the Iroquois suffered equally from that plague. Neither were they immune to the casualties of battle. Already by 1664 the Susquehannocks had become willing to "imbrace a peace if Obteyned" but not "to sue for itt." Maryland's governor Charles Calvert was not willing, and neither were the Onondagas, for whom revenge had become an obsession. So the wasting war continued.[12]

Because Lord Baltimore wanted to prevent possible Iroquois interference with his campaign to seize Delaware Bay, he prevailed on Maryland's legislature to seek peace with the Iroquois Confederacy, and he smoothed the path by requiring the colony's Susquehannock allies to get out of the way. At his summons, they moved all of their people away from their river and into an abandoned Piscataway palisaded village on the Potomac just below where Washington, D.C., now stands.[13] The change proved disastrous, for it inadvertently involved the Susquehannocks in the tumults of Bacon's Rebellion in Virginia. After Virginians killed Susquehannocks in a hunting lodge, the Indians retaliated on Virginia's backwoods settlers. Virginia then mobilized militiamen against the Susquehannock stockaded village in Maryland, and Maryland joined its own militia to Virginia's in order to forestall possible claims of "rights of conquest" over Maryland's territory. Violating their own safe conduct, the besiegers killed five Susquehannock chiefs, after which the Indians escaped to the woods to take revenge in fragmented parties.[14]

Though the Susquehannocks could still punish, their tribal organization had been shattered. Scattered bands wandered about until New York Governor Edmund Andros, eager to prevent a general Indian uprising similar to King Philip's War, offered sanctuary within his jurisdiction among their old allies at Delaware Bay. When threats from Maryland made Delaware Bay too hazardous, Andros ordered the Susquehannocks to withdraw deeper into New York, and an Iroquois delegation offered hospitality.

The Susquehannocks split up. Some went off to Iroquoia. What appears to have been a minority stayed on with the Delawares. Maryland's bellicosity cooled, and in 1677 an embassy went to New York to make a general peace. Earlier in that year, as Neal Salisbury has shown, Andros had patched up peace for New England by creating the Covenant Chain confederation of Massachusetts, Connecticut, New York, the Iroquois Five Nations, and the Mahicans and Schaghticokes of the Hudson Valley. Not by chance, New York and the Iroquois leaders acted as a sort of steering committee in this multilateral alliance. When Maryland's ambassador arrived in Albany, empowered to treat on behalf of Virginia as well as Maryland, Andros swept the southern colonies into the same confederation and dictated similar terms of sanctuary for the Susquehannocks and Delawares within his jurisdiction.[15]

It is harder to see what went on in a separate, unrecorded meeting between the Iroquois and the Delawares. Its memory in Delaware tradition has been contradicted by later Iroquois assertions that the Five Nations "conquered" and "made women" of the Delawares.[16] Iroquois tradition is silent about the meeting, but I have not seen any Iroquois denial that it occurred. Apparently, however, the meeting did take place, and the importance of its sequels demands attention to what happened at it. The "conquest" propaganda may be dismissed out of hand: no sources, Indian or European, show conquest in battle. Iroquois and Delaware sources agree that the Delawares accepted the status of "women," but a deep cleavage appeared in the middle of the eighteenth century between the two sides' interpretation of the term, and the Delawares denied flatly that they had become metaphorical women by conquest. In 1677, however, all was amity. All the tribes within New York were to be protected, from each other as well as from external enemies, by the watchful Governor Andros, who had dealt personally with the Delawares for friendship and land cessions. It is especially notable, anticipating what was to come, that the Iroquois had nothing to do with Delaware sales of land to Andros or with Delaware treaties of friendship with the governor.[17] "Conquest" could not possibly have taken place prior to those arrangements because it would have required Andros to treat with the Iroquois *instead of* the Delawares.

According to their alternative tradition, in 1677 the Delawares accepted a status offered to them by the Mohawks — the "women's" status of mediating tribal peacemakers. There is a hint in the absence of stockades around Delaware villages that this status may have continued and confirmed a previously existing custom. It would have been natural enough for a tribe with the dignity of "grandfathers" to function as "women," and the mixture of metaphors would not bother Indians. In fact, a Cayuga tradition portrays the Delawares as peacemakers between Iroquois and Algonquian nations.[18]

Nobody seemed to think it strange that the disintegrated Susquehannocks should not be parties to the Covenant Chain treaty that so greatly concerned them; presumably their interest was represented by the Iroquois and by Andros. Delaware silence in the treaty minutes, however, requires some explanation, because Maryland's copy of the finished agreement names the Delawares as responsible parties to it.[19] It appears that when they agreed to be "women," they accepted the Iroquois as their spokesmen *in New York* but not necessarily elsewhere. According to a reminiscence by Delaware chief Sassoonan, the Iroquois sent their own representatives to live among the Delawares when Sassoonan had been "but small."[20] I infer that his maddeningly dateless reference applied to the period 1677–81, during which the Delawares as well as the Iroquois dwelt under Edmund Andros's protectorate and the Iroquois, especially the Mohawks, were his favored instrument among the tribes. Earlier and later than this period, the Delawares are on record as speaking for themselves.

What, then, was the role of that Iroquois delegate among the Delawares? Not much, apparently, as no other record mentions him. Nor are the Delawares mentioned in surviving records from the 1677–81 interval. At its end, when they come into view once more, they ceded land to newly created Pennsylvania, speaking and acting for themselves without any sign of the presence of an Iroquois.[21] It appears that the change of colonial jurisdiction abolished the Iroquois role as spokesmen. Indeed, the Iroquois found considerable difficulty speaking even for themselves in Pennsylvania because of intercolonial jealousies: New Yorkers wanted to keep the Iroquois from falling under Pennsylvania's sway, and Pennsylvania wanted to preserve "their" Indians from outside influence, such as New York's via the Iroquois. During William Penn's lifetime, Pennsylvania stayed out of the Covenant Chain confederation. In 1681, the Delawares and their guest Susquehannocks became "Indians of Pennsyl-

vania." But the other Susquehannocks, by their flight to sanctuary in Iroquoia, were to create great problems for William Penn.

Penn intended to clear the Indian "incumbrance" from his tremendous land grant by purchasing quitclaims, tract by tract, from legitimate
Indian landlords.[22] He initially had no trouble in the Delaware Valley. The
Susquehanna Valley presented greater difficulty, because its tribal owners
had disappeared into the Delaware and Iroquois polities. Penn was able
to purchase lands below the falls of the Susquehanna from a Delaware
who apparently represented the interest of the Susquehannocks at Delaware Bay, but the Iroquois claimed the valley above the falls.[23] They were
willing to sell to Penn's agents until the merchants of Albany intervened
to block the transaction, because of their fear that Penn's proposed trading
center at the Susquehanna would draw New York's Indians away from
Albany. Penn's charter complicated the matter by giving him a northern
boundary that would have included Iroquoia and effectively reduced New
York to little more than the Hudson Valley. The new governor of New York,
Thomas Dongan, frustrated Penn in 1683 by dealing for the Susquehanna
himself.[24] Though the Iroquois thought they were only putting the Susquehanna in trust to the office of the governor, Dongan wrote the deed
so as to make it an outright grant of the valley to himself personally.[25]
Not content, in 1686 he commanded the Iroquois to seize traders in the
valley, confiscate their goods, and deliver their persons to Albany. This
was too much for the Iroquois: "we dare not meddle therewith," they informed Dongan; "for a man whose goods is taken from him will defend
himself which may create trouble or warre." A year later, Dongan extended
his demand to include traders on the Schuylkill branch of the Delaware
River; this time the Iroquois responded more deviously — they agreed, and
did nothing.[26]

Iroquois restraint in the south seems to have been dictated by pre-
occupations to the west and north. Richard Aquila has well described the
"Twenty Years' War" against New France and its Indian allies, with the
war's disastrous outcome for the Iroquois.[27] Relevant here are the Iroquois
demands for support from their Pennsylvania tributaries during that war.
Unable to enforce such demands by their own power, they appealed to
Dongan in 1687. "We ask for help, much of it, and in a hurry," a Mohawk
spokesman declared. "Where can we run? There is a great crowd of Indians who would pursue us everywhere anyway."[28] Dongan rounded up
auxiliary warriors from within his jurisdiction, and as the war dragged
on, Onondagas and Senecas tried to summon recruits from the Delaware
Valley. Their demands were recited by Delaware chiefs to Pennsylvania's

governing council: "You delaware Indians doe nothing but stay att home and boil your potts, *and are like women,* while wee Onondages and Senekas goe abroad and fight against the enemie." Delaware chief Hithquoquean, supported by Mohocksey and Tammany, informed the council that his people, "having resolved among ourselves not to goe, doe intend to send back this their belt of Wampum," whereupon the Pennsylvanians offered protection, and that ended the matter. The event confirms the Delawares' status as women — they did not dispute it — but it also clarifies the nature of that status. They had rejected the Iroquois demands by their own decision *before* they notified the Pennsylvania council. Obviously they were not under Iroquois subjection, and no one at that time claimed that they were.[29]

The Twenty Years' War traumatized the Iroquois and reduced them to a shadow of their former importance. Disease and combat took such a toll of life that large numbers withdrew even from Iroquoia: a mixed band of Senecas and Susquehannocks retreated to safety in the latter's old homeland above Chesapeake Bay, where they became known as Conestogas; and a knowledgeable contemporary believed that two-thirds of the Mohawks had fled to Canadian missions.[30] Not again until the American Revolution did the Iroquois suffer such trauma, and the Indians of the Delaware Valley watched from a distance, unscathed, uncooperative, and protected by Pennsylvania. By 1701, when the Iroquois made peace with New France and its allies, the Five Nations had become just that — five nations. They maintained contact with, and demanded deference from, the Seneca-Susquehannock band that had fled from the war's carnage to settle in the Susquehannocks' old homeland, but they got little besides deference from the fugitives.

Until 1710 the Iroquois made little visible progress toward a position of importance in Pennsylvania. William Penn virtually ignored them. In Ireland, far from Indian observation, he bought Thomas Penn's "deed" to the Susquehanna Valley, and he confirmed the purchase by treating with the Conestogas.[31] Forbidding them to trade elsewhere than in Pennsylvania, he extended his protection over them and specified that they would be "responsible" for newcomers. A silent Onondaga chief observed the proceedings and signed the agreement, below the signatures of five local chiefs, "for and in Behalf of the Emperor" of the Iroquois.[32] The position is significant; when the Iroquois were in charge, they signed on top.

By this treaty and others, Penn created a "Chain of Friendship" between his colony and its resident tribes, distinct from and competing with the Covenant Chain presided over by New York and the Iroquois. Protected by Pennsylvania, the Conestoga region became a sanctuary for Indian refugees—Shawnees from the south and west and Piscataway-Conoys from the Potomac Valley. A shadowy Iroquois influence can be detected in the privilege allowed Iroquois war parties to march through the valley to campaign against their Catawba and Cherokee enemies in the Carolinas, but the tribal fragments at Conestoga looked to Pennsylvania for supervision.

Nevertheless, something was happening to make Pennsylvanians want a better understanding with the Iroquois. We catch a glimpse of that desire in some cryptic reports of events of 1710, and note that they were reported with discretion because New Yorkers regarded negotiations between Pennsylvania and the Iroquois as a "breach of the Covenant Chain."[33] Abuses by southern colonials caused Tuscarora Indians to send a delegation from Carolina to Conestoga to ask for sanctuary there. Informed of the request, the provincial government sent Colonel John French to negotiate. He demanded that the Tuscaroras first show "a Certificate from the Government they leave, to this, of their Good behaviour"—the only instance on record of a rebuff by a Pennsylvanian to Indians seeking hospitality.[34] Perhaps something else was said off the record. The Tuscaroras went home and did not return until three years later, after bitter war in the south and without a certificate.

In 1710 the Iroquois learned of that Tuscarora embassy and rushed their own delegation to meet it, but arrived too late to meet with the visitors from the south. So important was the Tuscarora matter that the Iroquois and the Pennsylvania government behaved uncharacteristically: the delegates sent a curt message to Philadelphia that they "expected" the governor, and Governor Gookin chose to go to them instead of requiring them to come to him. Was he expecting the message? It looks as though the meeting had been prearranged secretly in order to keep knowledge from New York. Certainly its minutes were excluded from Pennsylvania's official records; only one manuscript copy exists in what looks like rough notes rather than the usual treaty conference format.

The importance of the affair is plain. Colonel French, three Quaker members of the provincial council, and two other "gentlemen" accompanied Governor Gookin. Seventy Indians attended. Onondaga chief Teganissorens headed Iroquois chiefs from all of the Five Nations, and the peoples of Conestoga were represented by Seneca, Shawnee, Delaware, and Conoy chiefs. So far as the "minutes" show, Teganissorens did almost all the talking. He laid down thirty-one propositions that became a sort of charter for the Indians of the Susquehanna Valley. As the Pennsylvanians rejected only one substantive proposition (Teganissorens's claim to ownership of the valley), their agreement to the others may be assumed. The chief offered peace and hospitality to all Indian nations: "Indians might settle wherever Corn could be made"; "all strangers bound hither may have freedom without molestation to return or goe further as they please"; "the five Nations from the beginning have been like a wall to these places and if any danger appears will so again." Pennsylvania's tacit approval opened the door wide to the Tuscaroras.[35]

Thus was demonstrated one large component of Iroquois policy during what Aquila terms "the Iroquois Restoration" period, a period dominated by the admirable statesmanship of Teganissorens. Hospitality on the Susquehanna drew tributary "props" to the Iroquois. These were doubly valuable: when Iroquois war parties raided southern tribes, volunteers from the "props" joined the raiders, and when angry southerners marched north to retaliate, the Susquehanna Valley tributaries blocked passage to Iroquoia.

Teganissorens aimed also at reducing Iroquois dependence on New York, more specifically on the trade of the Albany merchants. This fitted well into the long-continued goals of Onondaga leaders, who were perpetually restless under Mohawk controls over access to Albany. Pursuing alternatives, Teganissorens solicited friendship with New France so eagerly that New York Governor William Burnet refused to treat with him. But that event came later. In 1710, at Conestoga, Teganissorens announced Iroquois alliance to Pennsylvania: "we are now one body, one heart and one head with them, and whoever draws the blood of one, it shall be taken as of the whole." Naturally there was a reason. "A free trade [should] be granted so the Buyer purchase where he best likes."[36]

There were reservations and odd quirks in this unpublicized alliance that made it not quite so wholehearted as it appeared in Teganissorens's proclamation. Pennsylvanians welcomed trade at Conestoga, from the Iroquois or any other Indians, and they turned a blind eye to the war parties passing through; but, as we have seen, they and the Conestoga Indians lacked zeal to join the Iroquois in wars against Canada. However, the pact enabled the Iroquois to expand their "beachhead" on the Susquehanna. As war heated up between southern Indians and the English in the Carolinas, the Iroquois acted as hosts on the Susquehanna to what Paul A. W. Wallace has called "displaced persons" fleeing from the slaughter.[37]

During the "teen" years of the eighteenth century, Conestoga-Iroquois League relations must be inferred from a few rather cryptic documents. The situation seems to have been similar to what is better known at mid-century, when "Mingo" Senecas in the Ohio Country assumed leadership over the mixed tribes there, treated independently with colonial governments, yet preserved ceremonial deference to the Confederacy centered at Onondaga. Categories defined by lawyers and European political scientists are irrelevant to the fluid arrangements made by agreement and preserved by custom (and more agreements) among the tribes. In these, the Shawnees at Conestoga were exceptional to the patterns observable among the others. Probably their special status was arranged at Albany in 1692, when they migrated east from La Salle's Fort St. Louis on the Illinois River. Previously, they had been at war with the Iroquois — had indeed been driven out of their Ohio homeland by Iroquois attacks. When they made peace and were accepted as tribal members of the Covenant Chain, they assumed a "guest" status on territory claimed by the Iroquois though within Pennsylvania's jurisdiction. In their case, the status implied a certain amount of subordination to their hosts.[38]

A clue to the differing statuses of Conestogas and Shawnees is provided by an incident in 1711. New York Governor Robert Hunter sent an "order" to the sachems "inhabiting in or near the Province of Pensilvania and on Sasquehannah River to march with their fighting Men to join the Five Nations" in a projected invasion of Canada. Twenty-five warriors marched from Conestoga to Philadelphia instead of to Albany. Being asked whether they were "under Covenants with the Five Nations to go to War, when they required them," the Indians said they had come because of New York's summons, and finally, after some unrecorded deliberations, they departed.[39] Twenty-six Shawnees, "under the Sinnekes," showed up at Albany three weeks later. The Senecas who joined the force were not distinguished by place of habitation, so some may have been from Conestoga, but no other "Pennsylvania" Indians appeared.[40]

Something happened in 1711 — perhaps related to this campaign — to cause Shawnee "King" Opessa to abdicate his post and abandon his people in disgust at their ungovernability. After an interval of apparent anarchy, they received a "new Elected King" in 1713, but not one chosen by themselves. He was Carondawana, an Oneida chief, and he had been chosen by the Iroquoians of Conestoga.[41] Conestogas and Shawnees continued to negotiate for themselves with Pennsylvania, but the Iroquois influence on the Susquehanna had become palpable.

Yet this influence was exerted within carefully observed limits, limits that appear in the proceedings of the great multilateral treaty at Albany in 1722. There, the governors of Virginia, Pennsylvania, and New York jointly demanded that Iroquois war parties stay out of Virginia and prescribed a boundary line that must not be transgressed. In any violation of the line, the Five Nations were made responsible for their tributaries as well as their own warriors. The Iroquois accepted the edict (though not without some lawyer-like stipulations) and specified the tributaries for whom they would be responsible. Of the Indians at Conestoga, the list included only the Shawnees.[42]

Limited though it was, Iroquois influence on the Susquehanna grew; on the Delaware, it remained practically nil. No Iroquois war parties paddled down that river, and no Iroquois chief laid claim to ownership of the valley, either by conquest or otherwise. After Pennsylvania's creation, the Delaware Indians governed themselves, but it is necessary to understand that they were not a unitary, integrated tribe. There were "Jersey" Delawares, "Brandywine" Delawares, and "Schuylkill" or "Tulpehocken" Delawares, each of which made treaties and ceded land independently of the others.[43]

The Tulpehocken community's head was given deference as a ceremonial paramount chief,[44] and as such he was entrusted by William Penn in 1701 with a wampum belt and message for delivery to the Iroquois. But it seems that the Delawares were cool toward rapprochement between the Iroquois and Pennsylvania, for that belt stayed in storage for eleven years, along with the wampum that symbolized the Delawares' tributary alliance to the Iroquois. No document explains why the Delawares decided to renew Iroquois relations after that long lapse; I can only guess that Pennsylvania's secret 1710 treaty at Conestoga had some relevance. It seems that the Delawares were being altogether too independent to suit the taste of some of William Penn's successors in the management of Indian affairs.

Chief of these successors was James Logan, who functioned simultaneously as secretary of Penn's private business and as secretary of the province's government. Logan had reason to diminish Delaware power. During Penn's absence he had helped to cheat the Brandywine community out of the lands that Penn had reserved for them and had kept Penn in ignorance of their protests. In time, Logan would tangle with all the Delawares, each community in turn. These facts cast a shadow on what he did to the records of the Delawares' renewal of Iroquois relations in 1712. Delaware chief Scollitchy had declared that his people were "friends" of the Five Nations bringing "presents"—a statement of alliance between peers. In the official record, Logan changed Scollitchy's words to "friends *and Subjects* of the 5 Nations" presenting "tribute" ("presents" being lined through).[45]

There was constant tension between Delawares and Iroquois, tension that was mediated by Logan, who acted for his own interests rather than those of any Indians.[46] In 1704 he opposed an Onondaga attempt to take the Shawnees off to Iroquoia;[47] a year later he kept some Conoy refugees from Maryland at Conestoga against the wishes of the Delawares, who wanted to take them to Tulpehocken.[48] At Conestoga the Conoys came under strong Iroquois influence, but Logan wanted them there for the same reason he wanted Shawnees there: they were assets to trade in that location, and he was a participant in that trade.

But the Indians had secrets of their own that not even Logan's highly developed intelligence network could learn. One of these secrets reveals the continuing limits to Iroquois authority. Though the Iroquois held themselves "responsible" for the Shawnees, in 1726 the latter joined the Delawares to defy the Iroquois on an issue of overwhelming importance. In that year, chiefs of the three peoples met secretly to consider an Iroquois proposal — the first of its kind — for interracial war. Iroquoia was being hacked off in pieces, and Albany merchants instead of defending their allies were among the hackers; the Confederacy concluded that it had to drive out all Europeans, English and French alike. This would require an uprising of all the tribes under Iroquois leadership, but Iroquois allies and friends would have none of it. Canadian Indians ignored Iroquois "orders," and in 1726 the Delawares and Shawnees bluntly refused participation.[49]

The event is noteworthy on several scores. By 1726 the Delawares had suffered even more than the Iroquois from territorial loss to encroachers. The Brandywine Delawares had lost all their land and migrated to the Susquehanna and Allegheny valleys.[50] The Tulpehockens under chief Sassoonan had been driven out of their valley by Palatine German immigrants in 1722. Thenceforth most of them went off to the Allegheny Valley ("the Ohio Country"), and Sassoonan was reduced to the status of guest in the Iroquois village of Shamokin at the juncture of the west and north branches of the Susquehanna.[51] Yet Sassoonan's forlorn chieftainship commanded such respect that he could successfully refuse to do Iroquois bidding.

The frustrated Iroquois had to cope with the reality of their inability to fight the Europeans without allies. They rebuked as "women" the Shawnees and Delawares, but they drastically revised their policy. Instead of war against colonials, they turned their hatchet westward, apparently with the hope of compensating in the Ohio Country for their losses at home. To facilitate war parties marching westward, they uprooted Pennsylvania's Shawnees and relocated them in villages along a line leading to the Allegheny Valley, where so many Delawares had already resettled on their own initiative.[52] No orders, for relocation or otherwise, were given to the Delawares remaining in the east, however.

The Iroquois had overestimated their control over the Shawnees. Those who went west exceeded orders by continuing until they were beyond Iroquois reach. Then they placed themselves under New France's protection, which the Iroquois did not dare defy.[53] To forestall loss of the Shawnees remaining on the Susquehanna's North Branch, the Iroquois Confederacy sent a new supervisor to take up residence in Shamokin, a location strategically interposed across the passage westward. Again, certain old myths require correction. This viceregent, the Oneida chief Shickellamy, repeatedly identified himself only as supervisor of the Shawnees;[54] though he accompanied Sassoonan to the latter's treaty with Pennsylvania in 1728, he merely observed. Sassoonan, who did all the talking, demanded compensation for his Tulpehocken lands, and Shickellamy approved by silence.[55]

But Shickellamy's public silence was not matched by private reticence. In unrecorded conversations, James Logan found him more congenial than that old complainer Sassoonan, and Logan turned to the Iroquois as a useful instrument for simplifying Pennsylvania's relations with all Indians. On their side, the Mohawks remained aloof, but the other Iroquois nations pursued closer ties to Pennsylvania as a welcome alternative to the frustrations imposed by the Mohawk-Albany combination. Sassoonan was isolated at Shamokin, bereft of influence, land, and people.[56]

In 1732, Proprietary Thomas Penn appeared in Philadelphia, just in time to propose warmer friendship to a delegation of Senecas, Cayugas, and Oneidas. Like Logan, Penn wanted tighter controls over Indians; also like Logan, he wanted to acquire the lands still in Delaware hands. (These were the Jersey Delawares and the related Minisinks of the region high up in the valley.) Iroquois aid seemed desirable — perhaps essential — for Penn's purposes. He proposed full alliance, "a new fire" at Philadelphia equal to the council fire at Albany. As an immediate project for the alliance, he asked the Five Nations to round up the emigrant Shawnees for return to Pennsylvania, and he offered his government's help. Intensely interested but skeptically realistic, the delegation's spokesman observed that the Shawnees could not be returned unless Pennsylvania prevented traders from going to their villages. It is clear that the Iroquois were not going to fling themselves against New France's protecting might, but they were very willing to consider alliance with Pennsylvania in more general terms.[57]

The Iroquois deliberated for four years. When they returned to Philadelphia in 1736, they did not explain the long lapse, but a reason is suggested by the absence once again (and for the succeeding twenty years) of the Mohawks. About this 1736 affair, the private papers of James Logan tell much more than the formal minutes. It was really two treaties: one held publicly at Philadelphia; the other out of sight at Shamokin, where interpreter Conrad Weiser represented the Penns. By the public treaty, Pennsylvania's government became a full member of the Iroquois Covenant Chain, which was now transformed to contain two special partnerships within it. As before, the Mohawks retained their tie with Albany, but now the "upper" Iroquois nations assumed a special relationship with Pennsylvania. The new council fire at Philadelphia burned as brightly as the old one. Yet, in this arrangement so strange to concepts of European law, *all* the Iroquois were linked in both special alliances; only some were "more equal" in the first, others in the second.[58]

In Philadelphia the Iroquois chiefs also dealt with the Penn family in the latter's capacity as chartered proprietors "of the soil" of Pennsylvania. The Iroquois sold their remaining interest in the Susquehanna Valley as far upstream as "the Tyoninhasachta Hills" (Blue Mountain) but refused to lay claim to Delaware lands. This did not satisfy Logan or Thomas Penn. Logan sent instructions to Conrad Weiser to get a "deed" at Shamokin. The Iroquois should "release" to the Penns "all their Claim and Pretensions whatsoever to all the Lands Between Delaware and Sasquehannah" up to Blue Mountain. Logan sent two letters: in one he wrote that "it was understood that they laid no manner of Claim to the Lands on Delaware River or on the Waters running into it"; the other explains that "they do not grant us any Land on Delaware, therefore observe to them that this is not at all intended by it but they only release and quit all their Claims there and as they make none it is in reality nothing." In return, Logan praised the "honest, wise, discreet, and understanding" Iroquois "for whom we keep our fire"; these Iroquois were so different from the other Indians in Pennsylvania — "weak and too often knavish" — that Logan proposed to treat with the Iroquois exclusively "in behalf of all or any of the others." Effectively this was a proposal for an alliance of Pennsylvania and the Iroquois *against* the Delawares and the Indians of the Susquehanna. The Iroquois accepted, and thus the eastern Delawares were "conquered."[59]

Thomas Penn felt secure enough after this agreement to swindle the remaining Delawares and the Minisinks out of their territory by the infamous "Walking Purchase" of 1737. He sold off large tracts for enough money to retire his family's debt and prepared to return to the greater amenities of a courtier's life in England.[60] Before Penn left, Sassoonan paid a ceremonial farewell visit and repeated his conception of the special status of the Delawares in Pennsylvania. Ignorant of Penn's new arrangements, Sassoonan explained "that he lives in the middle between the Five Nations and his brothers [of Pennsylvania]. He loves his [Iroquois] Unckles and he loves his Brothers and desires to have the paths that lead to both places [clear] and open." Someone, probably Logan, took care to suppress this too-informative document from the official records. It has survived only in a box of miscellaneous scraps in a private collection.[61]

Sassoonan found out quickly enough how obsolete his conception had become. Chief Nutamis of the Jersey (or "Forks of the Delaware") Delawares appealed to the Iroquois to require justice from Pennsylvania, and when the Iroquois came to treat in 1742, Sassoonan was a spectator. Governor George Thomas turned the tables upon Nutamis by calling on the Iroquois to suppress the complaining Delawares, and Onondaga chief Canasatego complied. Secure in Pennsylvania's backing, he ran to flights of oratorical fancy, asserting that the Iroquois had conquered the Delawares, without bothering to say when or where. He ordered them off their land and branded them "women" without the right to sell lands. In doing so, he conformed to the letter of the 1736 understanding with Logan. To expose that understanding would have been scandalous, so Canasatego covered it with his mythical exposition of the relationships between the peoples. Unfortunately, Canasatego's fiction has dominated histories to the present day, despite the clear and plentiful evidence to the contrary. But for the *eastern* Delawares in 1742, conquest was a reality.[62] Caught between the Iroquois hammer and the Pennsylvania anvil, they left the treaty council a beaten people and removed from their ancestral lands to places appointed by the Iroquois in the Wyoming Valley of the Susquehanna's North Branch.

There the eastern Delawares lived quietly until the turmoil of the Seven Years' War gave them opportunity to revenge themselves on the settlers who had taken over their lands (though they could not reach Thomas Penn, and James Logan had died). What happened then can be given only cursory notice here. The province's Quakers broke through the screen of secrecy shrouding the Penns' fraudulent land transactions and demanded restitution for those eastern Delawares. A "pine tree chief" named Teedyuscung emerged to prominence in the east and cooperated with the Quakers and with British general John Forbes, who was marching to the Ohio Country to conquer French Fort Duquesne. This rather odd combination forced a series of treaties at Easton, Pennsylvania, that resulted in four years of Indian peace, the reconstitution of the Covenant Chain, the fall of Fort Duquesne, and an agreement for western Indians to have a secure boundary free of encroachment by colonials.[63] This last became the Royal Proclamation of 1763 and was incorporated into the Quebec Act of 1774; it established the precedent for the "frontier" treaties of the United States.

All of these momentous sequels meant little or nothing to the remaining eastern Delawares. The pressures upon them increased, as settlers from Connecticut invaded their "Wyoming" section of the Susquehanna's North Branch and killed Teedyuscung. His people fled to join the Iroquois, and took revenge in the so-called Wyoming Massacre of 1778.[64] From that time onward, however, the history of all the Delawares is one of westward migration.[65]

6

PEOPLES "IN BETWEEN"

The Iroquois and the Ohio Indians,
1720–1768

MICHAEL N. MCCONNELL

IN NOVEMBER 1763, Superintendent of Indian Affairs Sir William Johnson declared that the Six Nations' claim to the "Ohio and thence to the [Great] Lakes is not [in] the least disputed by the Shawnees [and] Delawares," these people having been "subdued by the Six Nations and residing on land allotted to them for their use."[1] Johnson's comment was characteristic of a longstanding British view of Indian affairs. As early as 1727, New York's Cadwallader Colden had written of Iroquois conquests and asserted the Confederacy's own dependence upon the colony — creating, in the process, a convenient argument for British claims to vast territories in the Northwest.[2] These prevailing assumptions about the Iroquois and their role as part of an aggressive colonial empire, assumptions that have done so much to shape our understanding of colonial America, have also — thanks to Johnson and others — come to dominate later histories of the Six Nations' relations with Indians of the Ohio Valley.[3]

The reality was far more complex. Changing our vantage point — by looking eastward from the Ohio Valley rather than westward from Albany or Onondaga, and by considering deeds as well as words — develops a different picture of Iroquois influence over so-called dependent peoples. Instead of a secure corner of an Iroquois "empire," we see a volatile land, a prize in a high-stakes game that pitted various British and French interests against Indians trying to preserve their sovereignty in what they aptly called a "country in between." Instead of a land subdued and controlled by the Six Nations, there was an Ohio Indian world created by a variety of people — Shawnees, Delawares, and Iroquois. Into this world the councils of the Six Nations rarely intruded; and when they did, it was with little influence and less authority.

The first Indians to enter the upper Ohio Valley in the early eighteenth century did so not as invaders but as pioneers. The Eries and other cultures that had occupied the region for centuries past had, through a combination of migration, invasions of Old World diseases, and seventeenth-century trade wars, all but left the area by 1660.[4] As a result, the Delawares, Shawnees, and Iroquois venturing into the region encountered no opposition. These migrants arrived from several directions at roughly the same time, their routes largely dictated by the river systems that cut through the region. Senecas and other Iroquois gained access to the Ohio Country by way of the Allegheny River, and throughout the eighteenth century Iroquois settlements continued to dominate the river valley above Kittanning all the way to New York. The West Branch of the Susquehanna River provided Delawares and Shawnees access to the upper Ohio. From towns established in the 1720s and 1730s at Kittanning and along the Kiskiminetas River, the Delawares and Shawnees moved westward; eventually they pushed on to the Beaver River and down the Ohio to the Scioto River Valley.[5]

Meanwhile, other people had already laid claim to the western fringe of the Ohio Country. The Wyandots — remnant Hurons and Petuns — had relocated at the French trading post of Fort Pontchartrain (Detroit) after 1701 and began exploiting the lands immediately south of Lake Erie. Eventually they established a town at Sandusky in 1738.[6] Their occupation of the area, which went unchallenged by the new arrivals from the east, resulted in a rough division of the Ohio Country. West of the Allegheny drainage were the Wyandots; to the east were Delawares, Iroquois, and Shawnees.

Migration into the Ohio Country was the result of several factors: some pulled Indians into the region; others led them to consider the upper Ohio Valley a safe haven from problems at home. Iroquois movement southward appears to have been part of an ongoing Seneca expansion since the end of the previous century.[7] Delawares were lured by abundant herds of deer whose hides were the basic commodity of trade with nearby colonists. Both Delawares and Shawnees were driven west by conflicts arising from the rapid growth of colonial settlements between the Delaware and Susquehanna rivers.[8] Southern Delaware villages had already abandoned the Delaware Valley before 1720. From settlements along Tulpehocken and Brandywine creeks and in the Susquehanna Valley, increasing numbers turned their backs on familiar lands and on village "kings" too easily manipulated by the colonists. And these bands would move west once more, putting greater distance between themselves and European settlers.[9] Shawnees also participated in this westward movement, both in response to French offers of trade and as a result of conflicts with settlers and with the Six Nations.[10]

The eastern pioneers quickly reestablished themselves on the Allegheny Plateau. Their settlements were not refugee camps but village communities held together by bonds of kinship and custom. In addition, economic ties to British colonies continued. Pennsylvania traders, who followed their customers into the Ohio Country, built upon established relationships and helped create a trade nexus that spread westward to the Maumee River and eventually threatened the French trade and diplomatic network throughout the lower Great Lakes region.[11] Traders' records and archaeological evidence testify both to widespread exchange and to the Indians' intensive use of items from the peddlers' stock. Yet the presence of two maskettes from the Wyandotte Town Site, occupied in 1748, serves as a reminder that trade did not bring wholesale changes in native values or beliefs. Rather, such objects, which Indians used as amulets or as personifications of spirit beings, suggest persistence of basic values even as the dress, housewares, and settlement patterns of Ohio Indians continued to change.[12]

The creation of permanent towns and the ongoing trade with Pennsylvanians led to the steady growth in the number of Ohio Indians through the 1740s. In 1731, traders claimed that some 560 Indian men, representing perhaps as many as 2,000 people, were living in nine new Allegheny Valley towns. Nearly two decades later, Pennsylvania Indian agent Conrad Weiser learned from village headmen that some 800 warriors, or between 3,000 and 4,000 inhabitants, lived in the region bounded by the Allegheny and Scioto rivers.[13] While natural increase certainly accounted for some of the growth, of greater importance was the steady movement of people into the region, which continued until the eve of the American Revolution. The Ohio Country thus was a region in a state of flux, a land that witnessed far less order and stability than many of its residents (themselves often victims of similar circumstances in the east) might have wished. At the same time, however, such volatility made it difficult, if not impossible, for any one group to claim or maintain control, and it precluded the development of a single regional tradition that later arrivals might feel compelled to follow.

That some Iroquois, particularly Senecas, maintained claims in the Ohio Country is suggested by their assertions of special rights in the region. The foundation and extent of these claims are unclear, however.

A likely possibility lies in the destruction of the Eries in 1657. Claims to the northern reaches of the Ohio Valley perhaps originated with the incorporation of Erie captives, who may have passed their rights on to later generations of their adoptive Iroquois kin. The same process could have occurred with the Monongahelans to the south.[14] Monongahelan history has yet to be satisfactorily written, but none of their towns appear to have survived beyond the middle of the seventeenth century. Their seemingly abrupt disappearance may well have been a result of the wars that dispersed the Eries and other Iroquoian peoples in the lower Great Lakes region. Finally, the western Iroquois, especially the Senecas and Cayugas, may have established an indeterminate claim simply through the use and subsequent occupation of the upper Ohio region.

If the Iroquois did have a claim to these lands, they were slow to stake it. The resettlement of Indians from the east and north was at least a decade old by the time the Six Nations began to show any special interest in the lands west of the Susquehanna River. Generally, that interest tended to rise and fall with the concerns of the Iroquois' colonial allies, particularly Pennsylvania and Virginia. At the same time, conflict between members of the Confederacy and the Shawnees gave the Iroquois an opportunity to assert their control over western lands. In June 1732, Governor Patrick Gordon of Pennsylvania learned that the Six Nations, angered by the Shawnees' refusal to join in an alliance to thwart colonial expansion, had ordered them out of lands in the Susquehanna Valley and into the Ohio Country.[15] Such action implies Iroquois influence over the Shawnees in the east and suggests some Iroquois claim to the territory into which the Shawnees were to go. Though Six Nations authority in both cases was ill-defined, the governor and his proprietary superior, Thomas Penn, clearly assumed that the Iroquois could exercise such authority when, two months later, the Ohio Country became a topic of discussion at a meeting attended by Oneidas, Cayugas, and Senecas.

This Penn-Iroquois council, which was so important to the fate of the "Pennsylvania Indians," is no less significant for what it reveals about those nations who had already headed west. The proprietor observed that the Shawnees and Delawares then in the west were "under their [Six Nations'] protection." His logic rested upon the assumption that the westerners were merely splinter groups from the Susquehanna River towns, which were also considered to be under Iroquois control. Penn's interest in returning stray Indians to the fold grew out of concern about French influence in the west as well as his colony's inability to regulate trade or prevent violence between traders and Indians in the Ohio Country.[16] The assembled Iroquois confirmed Penn's worst fears by telling him that the

French had intended to send traders to the region. Furthermore, the Senecas had warned off one such man, named Cavelier. Yet the Iroquois speaker quickly added that they knew "nothing certainly of what passed between [Cavelier] and the Shawnees at Ohio." Finally, in response to Penn's insistence that they remove the Delawares and Shawnees from their new homes, the Iroquois suggested instead that the colony join them in recalling the westerners.[17]

The Iroquois ignorance of Cavelier's activities and their pointed reluctance to act alone in dealing with the Ohio Indians indicate that there were limits to their interest and influence there. The Covenant Chain had given the Six Nations (with colonial cooperation) some measure of control over Indians in the Susquehanna Valley. What the Iroquois may have understood — even if provincial leaders had yet to learn it — was that such cooperative control had limits.[18] By moving west, the Delawares and Shawnees effectively placed themselves beyond both the Covenant Chain and the reach of Iroquois-British authority. One measure of the distance migrating Delawares were able to place between themselves and the Anglo-Iroquois alliance was the ease and speed with which the migrants turned their backs on eastern village leaders, men whose authority had come to depend largely on colonial and Six Nations recognition. One of these Delaware "kings," Alumapees, failed completely in his efforts after 1732 to exercise influence over those Delawares living at Kittanning. Indeed, by his death in 1747, most of his people, including his own nephews, had put themselves beyond the mountains.[19]

If distance and time weakened ties to old homelands and loosened the grip of intercultural alliances, trade with Europeans in the Ohio Country helped build a new regional identity. Multi-ethnic trading towns such as Kittanning and Logstown stood at the center of a growing exchange system wherein Delawares, Shawnees, Iroquois, and British traders bartered merchandise, swapped information, and forged personal alliances that promoted both business and a sense of common interests.[20] Trade networks and regional cooperation continued to grow, promoted by Ohio Indians such as the Shawnees who told Governor Gordon that they were going "to the Ottawas to inform them of the good news we have from our brothers [the British] and to encourage them to come this way to trade."[21]

The expanding web of trade produced handsome profits for Pennsylvania and Virginia traders. Working through their Ohio Indian partners, they pushed their trading posts west until, by the mid-1740s, George Croghan and others were operating on the shores of Lake Erie — in the midst of what had previously been a French preserve.[22] The traders' aggressive expansion drew provincial attention westward. At the same time, it triggered French retaliation and turned the Ohio Country into a center of imperial conflict beginning in 1744. Ohio Indians quickly became active participants in the ensuing confrontation; they were enlisted by British traders with promises of plunder and assurances of aid from provincial governments. The Ohio Iroquois, or Mingos, for example, enjoyed a steady supply of weapons and other goods, which enabled them to settle old scores with French traders. The Mingos were also reinforced by members of the Detroit Wyandot settlement led by Nicolas Orontony, who took advantage of the conflict to move closer to British traders in the Beaver and Muskingum river valleys.[23]

Though the British and Mingos drove French traders from the field, King George's War (1744–48) had more far-reaching, disruptive results. In large measure, Indians had settled the Ohio Country in an effort to avoid conflicts arising from colonial expansion. Yet geography, conflicting colonial claims, and partisan activities by local natives themselves quickly turned the region into a cockpit of international and intercultural conflict, thrusting the Ohio Indians into the midst of the very turmoil they had sought to escape.

By the time warfare in the Ohio Country subsided in 1748, French traders had been swept from the area south of Lake Erie, prompting officials in Quebec to consider a more forceful means of regaining control of their inland empire. In the meantime, the Ohio Indians launched a dual campaign to forge alliances with Indians to the west and acquire military assistance from their parent towns in New York. The diplomatic efforts to the west produced a treaty with the Miamis that was endorsed by Pennsylvania.[24] The Mingos failed, however, to gain support from the Six Nations. In mid-November 1747, a Mingo delegation arrived in Philadelphia and complained about the "old men" at Onondaga and their repeated failure to consider requests for assistance from Ohio warriors who identified themselves as "of the Six Nations." Having been rebuffed by the Confederacy, the Mingos turned to their colonial trading partners for military aid. Moreover, they announced their plan to "kindle a [council] fire in their town," to which they had invited "all the Indians at a considerable distance round about them" the following spring, a bold step taken by men who identified themselves as warriors rather than council chiefs.[25]

The significance of the Mingos' actions did not pass unnoticed in Iroquoia. The independence displayed at Philadelphia and wholeheartedly endorsed by provincial leaders clearly upset some elements of the Confederacy, as Pennsylvania's agent Weiser learned. Weiser was at Onondaga to condole the recent death of Canasatego when he raised the subject of western lands and the prospect of Iroquois negotiations with the governor of Virginia. Explaining that the governor could not meet the Six Nations at Albany, Weiser suggested that presents intended for the Confederacy be given instead to the Mingos since, as he said, "the Ohio Indians were one and the same with the Six Nations and of their own blood." The Onondagas' reply was quick and to the point: the Mingos "were but hunters and no counsellors or chief mert, and they had no right to receive presents that was due to the Six Nations." Though the westerners might expect a share, they "must receive [it] from the Six Nations' chief under whom they belong," a statement the Onondagas repeated "over and over."[26]

The Onondagas' exchange with Weiser reflected the anxiety that developed within the Confederacy as shifting power relationships in the Ohio Country threatened their role in the eighteenth-century world. It is worth noting that the Onondagas directed their protests to the British; nothing suggests that similar messages were sent to the Mingos. Yet, as growing Mingo-colonial cooperation indicates, the Iroquois "mystique" of power and influence in the Indian Northeast was beginning to fade by mid-century.[27] Deaths of friends like Canasatego further reduced the prospects of Iroquois cooperation with the colonies at a time when many in the Confederacy were decidedly reluctant to abandon a studied neutrality and actively commit themselves to any colonial power. Debates over such a course of action exacerbated factionalism that expressed itself, at least on the surface, in the form of "pro-French" and "pro-British" groups within Iroquois towns. The British clearly feared that other opponents were gaining the upper hand inside divided Iroquois communities. Weiser, for example, made a point of reporting that Onondaga "was thick with French praying Indians."[28] What observers like Weiser perceived was a growing paralysis that prevented the Six Nations from taking decisive action in a region where, in theory, they and their colonial allies had mutual interests.

Internal dissension, loss of leaders, and a genuine reluctance to become embroiled in European conflicts only partly explain the widening gap between Six Nations' claims in the Ohio Country and the actions of supposedly dependent peoples living there. While colonial officials were seldom able to understand the complexities of Indian societies, Pennsylvania's Governor James Hamilton may have come closest to explaining what was in fact happening on the Ohio. Discussing his colony's decision to support the Mingos, Hamilton observed that "by suffering their young Indians to go and settle" in the Ohio Country, the Six Nations helped promote a "new interest" that challenged the Confederacy's claims to hegemony over the region.[29]

As Hamilton saw, the migrations that continued into the 1740s had put more and more Iroquois in the Ohio Country. Distance came to be measured in more than miles, however. By mid-century the Mingos, as well as their non-Iroquois neighbors, were looking upon the Ohio Country as home. Since Iroquois loyalties had always been rooted in the narrow confines of kinship networks and village communities, it was natural that the Mingos would gradually develop a strong attachment to their new homes.[30] It was especially predictable that their interest in affairs in Iroquoia would wane, especially when the Six Nations were being pulled in a variety of directions—toward Canada, the Susquehanna Valley, and Albany. Moreover, though many Mingos persisted in saying they were "of the Six Nations," the attachment of others within this group was weaker. To the British the term "Mingo" implied a mix of peoples—ostensibly Iroquois, but also including Fox Indians, Mahicans, and the descendants of captives taken in earlier trade wars, all of which may have served to dilute the Iroquois element in the Mingo population.[31]

Thus, though a cultural affinity remained between the Ohio Iroquois and their kinfolk in New York, regional interests and differences drove a wedge between them. Yet the Mingo community was not the only one hammering that wedge ever deeper. The "new interest" identified by Hamilton may well have been a reaction to Six Nations' inaction, a sense of being abandoned and set adrift by leaders in Iroquoia. As Mingos explained to colonists in 1747, the Six Nations had ignored their requests for help against the French, leaving the Ohio Indians to face the enemy armed with little more than "sticks and hickeries."[32] Six years later, the Confederacy again turned a deaf ear to pleas from Mingo warriors who were on the verge of losing their country to a French army.[33]

The issues went beyond armed assistance. Mingos were upset upon learning (apparently for the first time) the details of the 1744 Lancaster Treaty, whereby the Six Nations agreed to cede land between the Susquehanna River and the Allegheny Mountains. The Ohio Seneca headman Kanadacta (Black Kettle) protested by observing that, though the Six Nations continued to sell land, they "give us no account of the value." While he did not question an Iroquois claim to the land, Kanadacta insisted that *all* Iroquois be included in the deed. He went on to ask, on behalf of "the *Ohio Council*," that Pennsylvania's governor intercede for them and "recommend it to the Six Nations that when any lands shall be sold, we may have part of the value."[34] Kanadacta's request made sense to the Mingos: they used the territory in question, land that also served as an important buffer between Ohio Indians and colonial settlements. Finally, Kanadacta's reference to the Ohio council—as distinct from the Confederacy council at Onondaga—further suggests a widening gulf between the Mingos and the Six Nations of New York, a distance to which the Confederacy itself may have contributed.

British colonists with interests of their own to advance in the west were as vexed by Iroquois inaction as were the Mingos. Taking advantage of opportunities where they found them, Pennsylvanians and Virginians followed the Mingos in turning their backs on the Six Nations, at least as far as western affairs were concerned. The colonies' actions marked a turning point in Iroquois-British relations; the Anglo-Americans began to look beyond Onondaga and the Mohawk Valley to the Ohio Country and the Mingos' new council fire. No one captured the prevailing colonial mood better than Pennsylvania's provincial secretary, Richard Peters, when he concluded that "our only game to play now is with the Ohio Indians."[35] Worse still for the Six Nations, their most reliable link to British councils, William Johnson, agreed with Peters. Indeed, Johnson went further by observing how events had proven that Iroquois "fame and power may in some measure exceed the reality."[36]

British colonial ambitions in the Ohio Country and the Mingos' increasingly independent course of action converged at the Ohio Iroquois settlement at Logstown. Presented with an opportunity to strengthen their colony's influence among western Indians, Pennsylvanians responded quickly to the Mingos' call for help in November 1747. Within a year Conrad Weiser was on his way to the Ohio Country bearing the colony's presents and assurances of further aid. By meeting at Logstown and thereby lending legitimacy to their new council fire, Weiser added considerably to Mingo prestige and set a precedent for future councils.

Weiser's host at the Logstown meeting in 1748 was Tanaghrisson, known to the British as the "Half-king." A Seneca, though born of a Catawba mother, Tanaghrisson embodied the growing autonomy and influence of local Iroquois in regional affairs. His origins, like those of the people he came to represent, were somewhat obscure. His name was one of five attached to the 1747 message sent from Ohio Indians to Pennsylvania, and though his colonial associates deferred to him, it was left to later generations of scholars to elevate him to the lofty position of the Six Nations' "regent" or "viceroy" in the Ohio Country.[37] While these terms are anachronistic, it is possible that Tanaghrisson was the "Six Nations chief" referred to by the Onondagas, a man sent to mediate between the Iroquois and Ohio Indians. By whom he was sent or with what specific authority is uncertain. If he was indeed a Six Nations representative, he more than likely was serving those groups in the Confederacy whose own interests lay to the west, rather than representing the Confederacy as a whole. Whatever his real or assumed connection to Iroquoia, however, Tanaghrisson gained standing and influence among the Mingos by promoting himself and by becoming a broker between Mingos and colonists. One real source of his influence may have been reflected in French reports which referred to him as the leader of a band or village in the Ohio Country, not as the arbiter for the distant Six Nations.[38] Building upon a base of kin and personal allies, his authority enhanced by British generosity, Tanaghrisson eventually became the preeminent Iroquois in the Ohio Country.

Even before Weiser's arrival, Tanaghrisson seems to have created a rough consensus on the issues of trade and a British alliance which enabled him to cast himself as the individual best suited to promote Mingo interests. At a preliminary meeting held at Lancaster in July 1748, colonial officials agreed to send their agent to the Half-king.[39] Yet even as Weiser approached the Ohio Valley in September, Tanaghrisson's position appeared anything but secure. Indians from the Kuskuskies — perhaps including Wyandots as well as Mingos — explicitly challenged Half-king's authority, calling upon Weiser to meet at their town instead. Weiser refused, and the transfer of £1,000 worth of gifts to the Logstown Indians through Tanaghrisson could only have enhanced the latter's prestige while also silencing rivals. As a self-confessed "new beginner" at council business, Tanaghrisson needed and welcomed such signs of colonial support, which included personal gifts that could be redistributed among kinfolk and close followers.[40]

British assistance ultimately carried a heavy price for Tanaghrisson and the Ohio Indians, however. With each council meeting and exchange of gifts, Half-king moved closer to his Pennsylvania and Virginia allies — becoming, in effect, their Indian on the Ohio. At the same time, a rift appeared between Tanaghrisson and other Mingos. Different voices began to be heard, principal among them Kanadacta's, which hint at disagreement over the best course of action open to the Mingos. In the meantime, the Delawares and Shawnees appear to have remained in the background. They conducted their own business as opportunities arose, but for the moment apparently they were content to allow the Mingos, with their numbers and well-established channels to the colonies, to take the lead.

Taking the lead proved especially challenging for Tanaghrisson and his followers, especially after the French demonstrated that they were not only willing but able to match British words and gifts with men and guns. The expedition led by Captain Pierre-Joseph Céloron de Blainville, which entered the Ohio Country in 1749, angered and alarmed local Indians, many of whom responded by temporarily abandoning their towns as Céleron rowed past. All of the Ohio Indians were especially concerned that the captain buried lead plates declaring French ownership of the region.[41] Word of Céleron's visit undoubtedly intensified debate within the Mingo towns, while pushing Tanaghrisson and like-minded Ohio Indians closer to the British.

If Tanaghrisson and others anticipated decisive British counter-measures, they were to be disappointed. Pennsylvania's Assembly, dominated by Quakers, was reluctant to become embroiled in disputes beyond the mountains. Therefore it left the field to the more ambitious Virginians, who proceeded to use Indian uneasiness to extract further concessions for the recently formed Ohio Company. In 1752 agents for the colony and the company met Tanaghrisson at Logstown for what proved to be the Half-king's (and the Mingos') undoing. The purpose of the meeting was to secure Tanaghrisson's approval for the building of a "strong house" in the Ohio Country, which would provide the Ohio Company with irrefutable claim to lands west of the mountains. In previous meetings with colonial agents, Tanaghrisson had resisted all construction projects, doubtless understanding the implications of any European strongholds on native land. At Logstown, however, he caved in—though apparently not without a struggle. Unable to move the issue quickly in open council, the Virginians ordered interpreter Andrew Montour to privately "urge the necessity of such a settlement and the great advantage it would be to them as to their trade and security."[42] Under such pressure Tanaghrisson changed his mind and endorsed the stronghouse. What additional pressure Montour brought to bear is unclear, but by 1752 Tanaghrisson's position clearly depended upon the continued good will and largesse of his colonial allies.

Tanaghrisson's apparent willingness to overcome his own misgivings and cooperate with the Ohio Company may also have resulted from the realization that, had he proved uncooperative, the Virginians would have abandoned him in favor of direct negotiations with local Delawares and Shawnees. His fears in this regard were well founded. The previous year Croghan had asked the scattered and largely autonomous Delaware villages to select a "king" with whom the colonies could conduct business.[43] At the Logstown council Tanaghrisson managed to forestall direct contact between Delawares and colonists by staging a ceremony during which he "gave" the Delawares a king, Shingas, and continued the fiction that Mingo authority extended to other groups as well. Though Tanaghrisson appears to have taken in the Ohio Company's agents, the act was meaningless to the Delawares; Shingas had legitimate claims to leadership that were independent of the Mingos or the Half-king.[44]

Shingas's appearance on the historical stage marked the emergence of the western Delawares as an increasingly important force in regional affairs. Their efforts to distance themselves from the Mingos and chart their own course may have been prompted, like that of the Shawnees, by misgivings over the Logstown transactions. As a result, Shingas's emergence as a Delaware headman may not have been coincidental. He later attempted, unsuccessfully, to secure native rights in the Ohio Country and, having failed, took up arms against British frontier settlements and troops during the Seven Years' War.

While Tanaghrisson managed to maintain his credibility with the Virginians, the Logstown Treaty intensified, rather than lessened, Indian concerns about their security and sovereignty. Even as Half-king agreed in principle to a British trading post, his companion, Scarouady, warned the colonists that "we intend to keep our country clear of settlements." Tanaghrisson went further: "we live in a country in between" the English and French colonies, he told the French a year later; "therefore the land belongs to neither one nor t'other."[45] Yet by the time those words were spoken, the Ohio Indians found that being "in between" meant being caught in the jaws of an imperial vise. The Virginians, having come away from Logstown with the required Indian signatures, ignored Scarouady's warning and proceeded with plans to develop their claims in the west. The French, alarmed by the potentially dangerous Mingo-British alliance, sent another, larger, expedition into the Ohio Country and snatched control of the region from British and Indians alike.

Céloron's 1749 expedition had been merely a hint of possible responses to what the French considered a growing threat to interior trade routes and their own claims to the middle west. In the wake of the Logstown council, Governor-General Ange de Menneville, Marquis Duquesne, dispatched an army to rid the Ohio Country of British traders and speculators and to intimidate local Indians. By the end of 1753, at enormous human and financial cost, the army of Captain Paul Marin de la Malgue was in full possession of the upper Ohio Valley and had built forts south from Lake Erie virtually unopposed by the British and Mingos.[46]

Virtually, but not entirely. Tanaghrisson, in traditional fashion, issued three warnings to the French to leave the Ohio Country. His words had a hollow ring. Ever since the Logstown Treaty more and more Ohio Indians — including may Iroquois — had begun to separate themselves from Half-king and his British friends. By the time Marin's force moved south from Presqu'Ile, the Delawares and local Senecas had quietly accepted existing conditions. The Senecas went a bit further and supplied horses and labor for the newly built portage road from Fort Presqu'Ile to Fort le Boeuf.

They ignored the wampum Tanaghrisson sent calling for united resistance. Marin did the same with Half-king's warnings, refusing even to touch the message belts.[47] Tanaghrisson was powerless to do more. The response of his colonial allies, in the form of Colonel George Washington and his "army" of hastily-assembled Virginia farmers and tradesmen, was equally ineffective. And the Six Nations, to whom Tanaghrisson and Scarouady directed requests for help and mediation during the height of the French invasion, answered with little more than a suggestion that the Delawares (and, presumably, other Ohio Indians) "do nothing in that juncture" but "keep fast hold of the Chain of Friendship"—the Covenant Chain to which the Ohio Indians had not previously been bound.[48]

The Six Nations were not wholly unconcerned about events in the west involving lands they continued to claim as their own. Indeed, the Ohio Country several times became a topic of discussion between Iroquois sachems and colonists in 1753 and 1754.[49] What did concern the Six Nations was the all too familiar fact that they, too, lived "in between," and the latest round of imperial sparring might again involve the Confederacy. At the same time, while French armies mustered along the St. Lawrence River, the Six Nations were experiencing a particularly strained moment in their relations with neighboring New York, resulting in a Mohawk-colonial confrontation in 1753 that threatened to destroy the Covenant Chain.[50] How far this affected the western nations of the Confederacy is open to speculation, since the Mohawks, with much closer ties to the colony, dominated the exchange. Yet it appears that once again local concerns and self-preservation defined the parameters of the Six Nations' response to the Ohio Indians. The Senecas, closest to the region and with many of their own people living along the Allegheny River, chose a prudent course. According to Marin, their only response to the French invasion was to dispatch several matrons to the army to obtain assurances that their own towns would not be attacked, assurances Marin gladly gave.[51] It was not quite the response Tanaghrisson may have hoped for. And in the wake of Washington's defeat at the Great Meadows in July 1754, Half-king left the Ohio Country for good. The leader of Mingo refugees, he died later that year at Croghan's trading post at Aughwick.[52]

The arrival of French troops, the hasty departure of Tanaghrisson and the Virginians, and the war that engulfed the Ohio Country between 1754 and 1759 all helped transform the Ohio Indians' world. Though pro-British Mingos left the region, many other Iroquois (especially

Senecas) remained, along with Delawares and Shawnees. The war years were marked by the efforts of all these people to confront changes and challenges while still retaining as large a measure of sovereignty as possible. Most Shawnees cast their lot with the French, a decision reflecting long-standing alliances with French traders as well as growing antipathy toward land-hungry British colonists. As a result, Tanaghrisson's abandoned settlement at Logstown was rebuilt by the French at nearby Fort Duquesne for their Shawnee allies.[53]

Having closed ranks behind Shingas before 1754, the Delawares became more divided as the war dragged on. Many—including Shingas—were prepared to support the British if it meant that control over the Ohio Country would be restored to its native inhabitants. General Edward Braddock's tactless refusal to consider such a proposal, followed quickly by his defeat near Fort Duquesne, prompted Shingas and numerous other Delawares to begin their own war, with French assistance, against the now greater threat from colonists heading west.[54]

Not all of the Delawares followed Shingas to war against settlers, however. Some, most conspicuous of whom was Shingas's brother Tamaqua, sought to negotiate with the British through Pennsylvania. By early 1758 Tamaqua, representing an influential faction that embraced members of all three western Delaware clans, opened a dialogue with the colony and indicated the Delawares' willingness to end the war. The Pennsylvanians eagerly responded, twice sending Christian Frederick Post to the Delaware towns in order to arrange a truce.[55]

By the end of 1758, the abrupt departure of French troops and the inability of recently arrived British forces to occupy the Ohio Country effectively created a power vacuum that Tamaqua was able to fill to the Delawares' immediate advantage. Two measures of his success were the declining role played by Shingas and the increasing British tendency to refer to Tamaqua as the Delaware "king." During the next two years Tamaqua and the Delawares acted as peacemakers in the west, fulfilling an old and honored role in native politics which, generations earlier, had led other natives to refer to the Delawares as "women," the voice of wisdom and moderation in native societies.[56]

Although exchanges between Ohio Indians and British agents ran the gamut from trade to the repatriation of colonial captives, the Indians very quickly drew attention to the issue of who would control the Ohio Country. As early as July 1758, the Delawares expressed the hope that the British and French would take their war elsewhere. This, and the continued presence of British troops in the region after the capture of Fort Duquesne, raised Indian apprehensions. As one spokesman observed, his people were "jealous the English will take the land from us," a fear that overshadowed intercultural relations for years to come.[57]

In the give-and-take of Ohio Country diplomacy, the Six Nations were conspicuous largely by their absence. Prior to 1761, when several Mohawks accompanied Sir William Johnson to a regional council at Detroit, few members of the Confederacy had any compelling reason to involve themselves in western affairs, and most had strong reasons not to. The outbreak of yet another intercolonial war placed the Six Nations once again in the dangerous middle ground between contending European giants. Faced with falling population (much of it going west), torn by factionalism generated by distrust of French and British aims, and stung by the severe losses suffered by those Iroquois who did fight with the colonies, the Confederacy towns strove to maintain a safe distance from the conflict. Despite oft-repeated claims of sovereignty over the Ohio Country and hegemony over its people, the Six Nations refused Pennsylvania's request that they mediate a peace between the colony and belligerent Ohio Indians. Instead, the Iroquois disclaimed any influence in the region and argued that it was the colony's responsibility to end what it had helped start.[58] Not until the fall of 1758 would Confederacy leaders appear in the Ohio Country, and even then they came not as representatives of the Six Nations but as British messengers. Two Cayugas appeared at Tamaqua's town with news of the recently concluded Easton Treaty, along with a request from Pennsylvania that the Ohio Indians honor the agreements contained in the document and subscribe to the general peace it promised. The Cayugas made no effort to dominate the current discussions between Delawares and colonists, and Tamaqua clearly defined their role as secondary to his own, telling a French officer that the Iroquois would "assist" and "help" him in his role as peacemaker in the Ohio Country.[59] The Cayugas' request that the Delawares "be still and quiet" was largely irrelevant, since Tamaqua's followers had already decided to do just that.[60]

While the Six Nations played only a marginal role in Ohio Country diplomacy, the peace hammered out by Tamaqua and local garrison commanders presented the Confederacy and its British allies with new challenges and opportunities. The British conquest of New France in 1760 firmly fixed long-developing colonial interest in the lands and resources that beckoned beyond the Alleghenies. Yet the sheer expanse of territory now claimed by Great Britain taxed the crown's ability to regulate the west. This, the region's variety of native peoples, and the exhausted condition of royal forces, created problems of control and security that left British authority over the Ohio Country tenuous at best. Sir William Johnson, now superintendent of Indian affairs in the northern colonies, attempted to remedy this problem by creating or supporting a number of rival Indian confederacies, each dependent upon British trade and diplomatic influence.[61] In the Ohio Country this meant extending the Covenant Chain alliances across the mountains to keep the Ohio Indians subordinate to the Six Nations. The plan reflected Johnson's own definition of Indian relations more than realities beyond the colonial frontier.

Even though both Johnson and Six Nations leaders engaged once more in the rhetoric of Iroquois conquest and Ohio Indian subordination, this scheme had little immediate impact on Indians living along the Ohio River.[62] In large measure, the realities of British-Indian affairs in the west forced the superintendent and his agents to continue dealing with the Ohio Indians as sovereign groups; the few soldiers available for garrison duty, the need to regulate trade, and the growing importance of the Ohio Country in British strategic planning left Johnson little choice.[63] At the same time, Anglo-America's new westward orientation led to a significant decline in the Six Nations' role in British imperial affairs. While Johnson maintained close ties with the Mohawks and, through them, with other Iroquois, imperial interests led him elsewhere. Detroit, Michilimackinac, Fort Pitt — all of these were replacing Onondaga and Albany as centers of postwar Indian affairs. The implications of this westward shift were not completely lost on the Iroquois, who saw Johnson's trip to Detroit in 1761 to make peace with the Great Lakes Indians as a clear threat to their own standing as Britain's foremost native allies in the Northeast.[64]

While the Ohio Indians could conveniently ignore Johnson's rhetoric, they were forced to meet the more immediate challenges growing from a long, costly war and from British efforts to revolutionize Indian relations in order to reduce native independence. Losses suffered through fighting and periodic outbreaks of diseases introduced by foreign armies had placed great stress on kinship networks and village communities, resulting in the wholesale adoption of captive Anglo-American settlers. Added to this was the social and economic disruption resulting from the need to abandon vulnerable towns and to rely on increasingly unpredictable supplies of colonial food and hardware.[65] Yet the British met this distress with increased parsimony and a reluctance to negotiate in terms that native leaders considered acceptable. Trade prices soared even as Indian agents and army officers dispensed with such time-honored protocols as gift giving.[66] At the same time, British exchanges with natives that once were couched in deferential terms became more strident and demanding. To make things worse, royal agents tied a lasting peace to the repatriation of captives who, in many cases, were now full members of their adoptive communities; village leaders were powerless to meet this demand. But more threatening to native independence and regional peace were the continued presence of troops and the arrival of settlers. Garrisons originally defined as temporary wartime measures were greatly expanded, and new posts were built from Fort Pitt to Detroit. Meanwhile, squatters from Virginia turned up in the Monongahela Valley, while retired army officers attempted to establish settlements along the vital Niagara portage. Both developments violated the 1758 Easton Treaty.[67]

The Ohio Indians responded with growing hostility and greater unity. In 1761 Ohio Senecas circulated war belts and with them a scheme by which all Indians from the Ohio to the Great Lakes would rise against the British. The Senecas, through men such as Kiashuta, sent the belts as far west as Detroit before their plans came to the attention of British authorities and foundered on the rocks of tribal autonomy and mutual distrust. Significantly, it appears that the Seneca belts were not sent eastward to the Six Nations towns. When Johnson pressed them that year, Senecas living in the Genesee Valley professed ignorance of any belts or war plans. Johnson refused to believe them, arguing that it seemed unlikely that Seneca leaders would be ignorant of actions taken by their people on the Ohio; he pinned responsibility on the Senecas generally and their pro-French inclinations.[68] Yet the gulf that already existed between the Ohio Iroquois and the Six Nations of New York may have been sufficiently wide by 1761 to prompt Kiashuta and others to direct their efforts westward to Indians who shared their interests and problems.

While the Senecas advocated armed resistance to British expansion, the Delawares responded to colonial pressure in other ways. Following a now-familiar pattern, large numbers of Delawares moved out of the army's path, abandoning towns along the Beaver River and in the vicinity of Fort Pitt for new settlements in the Muskingum Valley of central Ohio. Once there, they welcomed a small but steady stream of migrants from the Susquehanna Valley. The concentration of Delawares in the Muskingum basin coincided with growing cooperation among the western Delawares, cooperation that first appeared during the Seven Years' War. This was reinforced in 1762 by a revitalization movement led by the prophet Neolin, whose message advocated a return to native ways and the rejection of European culture.[69]

Although Neolin's spiritual and political movement was not founded exclusively on a policy of hostility toward the British, the Delawares, too, began in the winter of 1762–63 to reconsider their stance in the face of continuing British expansion and aggression. The decisive factor appears to have been news of the Anglo-French peace negotiations. As one British agent put it, Delawares and other Ohio Indians were "struck dumb" upon learning that France had ceded Indian lands to Great Britain. This news led to a change in attitude all along the Ohio: as more natives came to fear that the "English would soon be too great a people in this country," Indians abandoned accommodation for armed resistance.[70] Tamaqua's voice of compromise was ignored in favor of others who advocated war. Notable among these was Netawatwees, whom many Delawares would soon recognize as their new "king." By the summer of 1763, Ohio warriors launched a preemptive strike on military posts and supply lines in an effort to stem the tide of colonial expansion. Their attack merged with similar actions taken earlier by Great Lakes Indians into a general struggle that nearly drove the British army from the west.[71]

The years following the Ohio Indians' war witnessed growing cooperation among the Indian societies in the region. Though unable to oust the British, Ohio warriors nevertheless refused to capitulate, and they took advantage of the army's limited striking power to negotiate an end to the fighting. Peace conferences were conducted by Ohio Senecas on behalf of the "Five Nations of Scioto," an alliance that also included Shawnees, Sandusky Wyandots, Delawares, and Munsees.[72]

The determination of the region's Indians to maintain control over the Ohio Country grew from a distinct regional history now several decades old and also a strong attachment to the land that had been translated into ownership by right of occupation. Thus in 1764 Ohio Indians negotiating with Colonel John Bradstreet offered to cede territory in return for peace, and they did so without acknowledging a superior Iroquois claim. Later, in 1767, Ohio Senecas urged their Shawnee and Delaware neighbors to defend "those lands [that] are yours as well as ours" against colonial squatters and speculators.[73]

Seen in this light, the Ohio Indians' rejection of the Six Nations-negotiated Fort Stanwix Treaty in 1768 stands not as a sudden assertion of independence but rather as the culmination of a process that divorced local native settlements from their parent communities. At issue in the 1768 boundary negotiations were the territory immediately east and south of the Ohio River and the Iroquois Confederacy's authority to sell those lands, which were claimed by the Six Nations but occupied by others who were not parties to the sale.[74]

From first to last, the Fort Stanwix Treaty was an Iroquois-Johnson affair. It proceeded from long-standing British assumptions that Indians living within or adjacent to territory affected by the cession were politically dependent upon the Six Nations, who would speak for all. By co-operating with Johnson, the Six Nations both assured their own security and confirmed their title to trans-Appalachian lands by deeding them to the crown. As it was finally drawn, the boundary line pushed British-controlled territory nearly to the Ohio River while leaving Confederacy lands in New York largely intact. In effect, the Six Nations maintained their own territorial integrity by selling land occupied by people on the fringes of the Iroquois world.[75]

The Ohio Indians, whose future was most directly affected by Six Nations decisions, were not opposed to a boundary line in principle; in fact, they appear to have welcomed an opportunity to define their lands clearly as a check on frontier settlers.[76] What ultimately angered many was the way in which the boundary was drawn. The process ignored the Ohio Indians, some of whom witnessed the treaty but were not included in the proceedings.[77] Indeed, it may be that the boundary described to them before 1768 was not the one outlined in the treaty, since Johnson took the liberty of moving the line farther west to accommodate land speculators in Pennsylvania and New York.[78] Johnson's altered treaty line — one accepted by the Six Nations but nearly rejected by his superiors in London — placed most of the land east of the Allegheny River within British jurisdiction and brought colonial boundaries much closer to the Ohio River. While the Ohio Indians did not occupy the lands in question, they used them for hunting, as a corridor for raids against native enemies in the southern piedmont, and as a buffer against colonial expansion. How far local Indians' claims extended is unclear, but their overwhelmingly negative response to the Fort Stanwix Treaty is unmistakable.

Ohio Indians' land claims fueled the anger that was evident to colonial observers as news of the treaty was carried west. According to Croghan, the Ohio Indians complained bitterly to their western neighbors, pointing out that the Six Nations had "shamefully taken all the money and goods to themselves and [had] not shared any part thereof with them," a singular lack of reciprocity that seemed to ignore the fact that "most of the country which was sold was their [the Ohio Indians'] hunting ground down the Ohio." Not only had the Six Nations run roughshod over local Indians' claims and rights, they also threatened the Ohio natives' economic future. The Ohio Indians, recalling what earlier land cessions had meant to their kin in the east, were well aware of the possible consequences.[79]

These feelings echoed those of Kanadacta nearly twenty years earlier, and the issues were much the same. The Six Nations, responding to the challenges posed by their relations with British colonies, abandoned reciprocal obligations to their own people in the west and to others whom the Iroquois periodically found it useful to call "dependent." That the Confederacy acted as it did suggests growing differences between what were becoming two distinct Indian worlds. Though Iroquois claims over the Ohio Country served them well enough at Fort Stanwix, in reality control over the region had long since passed to those living there.[80] Governor Hamilton's prediction, made in the 1740s, had come to pass: the Ohio Indians had indeed developed a "new interest" that increasingly led them into regional alliances and to challenge, in council and on the battlefield, Iroquois and colonial authority. They would continue to do so for another three decades after the Fort Stanwix Treaty, standing against Lord Dunmore's Virginians and the new United States until the Battle of Fallen Timbers in 1794 effectively transformed the Indians' Ohio Country into the Americans' Old Northwest.[81]

III

DISTANT FRIENDS AND FOES

"THEIR VERY BONES SHALL FIGHT"

The Catawba-Iroquois Wars

JAMES H. MERRELL

N MAY 23, 1751, "King" Hagler and five other Catawba Indians traveled from South Carolina to New York to make peace with the Iroquois. By the end of the summer the Catawba delegation was back home, its mission accomplished. During the course of a meeting with the Iroquois at Albany, "a Tree of Peace" had been "planted whose Boughs should spread quite to Carolina."[1] The encounter at Albany—the first time the two peoples had met in any arena other than combat—was a watershed in Catawba-Iroquois relations. Only a year earlier Catawbas had sworn to "fight them [the Iroquois] whilst there was one of them [Catawbas] alive, and that after their Death their very Bones shall fight the Six Nations." Little more than a year later the Catawba Nation would promise that "we have throwed them [their "Weapons of War"] into a great deep Water that has got no bottom where they are never to be found as long as there is one of us alive."[2] Thus the Catawbas' journey in 1751 marked the beginning of the end of a long and bitter conflict, a conflict that had enormous importance in the lives of both peoples.

At first glance the Catawba-Iroquois wars do nothing to dispel the image of ferocious Iroquois warriors roaming the East in search of victims. To the contemporary English colonists who saw them, and to scholars interested in the subject since, the Iroquois who visited the South were every bit as terrifying as the myth claims. According to John Lawson, an early Carolina explorer, the Six Nations "are the most Warlike *Indians* that we know of . . . , a Sort of People that range several thousands of Miles, making all Prey they lay their Hands on."[3] A century ago the anthropologist James Mooney, after studying the Catawbas and their neighbors, labeled the Iroquois "the great agents in the expulsion and extermination" of these peoples, and "their destruction by the Iroquois . . . [t]he great over-

115

mastering fact" in their history. "From the very first," Mooney continued, "we find these pitiless destroyers making war on everything outside the narrow limits of their confederacy, pursuing their victims on the one hand to the very gates of Boston and on the other to the banks of the Mississippi, and making their name a synonym for death and destruction from Hudson bay to the Gulf of Mexico."⁴ A closer look at Catawba-Iroquois relations reveals a more complex picture, however. The Iroquois were neither as ferocious nor as successful, and their Catawba foes neither as timid nor as battered, as Lawson and Mooney believed. This essay attempts a more balanced approach to the conflict: embracing both sides while taking the Catawba perspective, it explores the conflict's origins, probes its meaning to those involved, and weighs the consequences of its ultimate end.

Reconstructing the story is no easy task. Most of the action took place well away from colonial American settlements, and those colonists who did notice events in the interior often had difficulty sorting out who was killing whom. Many simply reported a "northern" war party on its way to attack "southern" Indians. More specific terms were often misleading: "Seneca" was common shorthand for the Iroquois Confederacy generally — including the allied peoples known as "props" of the Longhouse — while "Flatheads" might refer to Catawbas or any number of other southern peoples. Changes in the meaning of the word "Catawba" only added to the confusion. The entity Hagler spoke for at Albany in 1751 — seven towns and perhaps 2,000 people — was a collection of communities that had once been scattered across the southern piedmont. In the first half of the eighteenth century these groups — most of them, like Catawbas, Siouan speakers — had coalesced around a core of Catawba villages hugging the border between the Carolinas. In order to understand the Catawba-Iroquois wars, then, we must widen our scope to include the "props" of the Iroquois Longhouse and groups whose seventeenth-century homes stretched from central South Carolina to central Virginia.

Even with a broader focus, evidence for the opening act of the drama remains sparse. Colonists knew only that Catawbas had been fighting Iroquois "for a long time," "for many years past," or from "time immemorial."⁵ The Indians were equally vague. In 1715, for example, Iroquois spokesmen assured the English that Carolina Indians "are our antient enemys," indeed "they have allways been our Enemies."⁶ In fact, however, serious Iroquois incursions into the southern piedmont probably did not begin until the late seventeenth century. Enemies from the north had been harassing Virginia Indians in John Smith's day. But the very presence of the many native settlements Smith found along the rivers that drain into Chesapeake Bay, and the Five Nations' preoccupation with peoples elsewhere, probably limited deeper penetration until much later. Only after 1660 did word of northern intruders to frontier settlements begin to reach Jamestown officials.[7]

These visitors were only a nuisance at first. They did not become a genuine threat until the late 1670s, when Susquehannock Indians served as a catalyst for deepening hostilities. During the mid-1670s an attack by colonists in Maryland and several more by piedmont Indians in Virginia drove Susquehannocks out of the south and into the arms of the Five Nations.[8] Before the end of the decade Susquehannock warriors were returning south with their new Iroquois friends to even the score, and these war parties annually "in[f]ested" the Virginia piedmont, "plundering and destroying all . . . that lye in their way."[9] Virginia and its tributaries were not the only targets. Some warriors were merely passing through the colony on their way several hundred miles farther south to attack native settlements located "und[e]r the mountaines." In February 1682 one Virginia trader learned that the Iroquois had taken thirty-five prisoners from one village there and grabbed a handful of others from several smaller settlements. These marauders had "soe oppresst the Indyans," the trader concluded, "that they have made noe Corne [last?] yeare."[10] Unable as yet to match the Five Nations' easy access to European weapons, the piedmont peoples of Virginia and Carolina were easy marks.[11]

Over the next two decades the volume of Iroquois raids may have ebbed as the Five Nations were distracted by events closer to home. Piedmont villages never felt entirely safe, however, and by the time John Lawson made his famous trek through the Carolina interior in 1701 the Iroquois menaced the entire region.[12] Everywhere the English adventurer looked he saw evidence of their visits. Near the Catawbas stood seven piles of stones marking graves of the Five Nations' victims. Further along the path villages were banding together and building forts to withstand the blows of the Iroquois. Among the Keyauwees, a piedmont group several days north of the Catawbas, was a man who had fled Iroquois captivity, despite having half of each foot cut off by his captors to prevent escape. "This Fellow was got clear of them," Lawson remarked, "but had little Heart to go far from home, and carry'd always a Case of Pistols in his Girdle, besides a Cutlass, and a Fuzee." Others with their feet still intact felt much the same way: the Iroquois "are fear'd by all the savage Nations I ever was among," Lawson wrote, "the Westward *Indians* dreading their Approach."[13]

Apprehensive as the Keyauwee man was, he personified an important shift in the widening conflict. A decade or two earlier an upcountry Indian so well equipped for war was rare. By Lawson's day, however, traders from Virginia and Carolina had flooded the interior with European goods — a warrior *without* a musket was now considered remarkable[14] — and piedmont groups were able to fight firearms with firearms. Some Carolina nations went so far as to turn the tables on their Iroquois foes. In 1704 a party of forty warriors from the south arrived at an Indian village along the Potomac River. To the alarmed inhabitants there they declared "that they (of Carolina,) had been for many years attacked and Injured by some Indians from the Northw[ar]d, whom they had always hitherto taken to be those of Canada, but now found who they were, viz: the Senecars and those of Potomock and Conestogoe, and that they were Resolved to be revenged, and [to] that end three nations had Joyned and would shortly come up and either destroy or be destroyed by them."[15]

By the turn of the eighteenth century, then, the framework of relations was set. After the Grand Settlement of 1701 the Iroquois, freed from crippling conflicts with European colonists and native foes to the north and west, directed much of their attention southward.[16] The Catawba peoples, meanwhile, had acquired the wherewithal to hold their own and a clear sense of the enemy's identity. Over the next fifty years occasional talk of peace sank beneath wave after wave of warriors.[17] The Iroquois were generally the aggressors. Aided and abetted by displaced Shawnees (Savannahs) or Tuscaroras who, driven out of the south with Catawba help, knew the way back and had good reason to despise Catawbas, they carried the fight into the heart of the upcountry.[18] But like the angry band that showed up on the banks of the Potomac in 1704, a Catawba war party occasionally made its way north to return the favors dispensed by the Five Nations and their confederates.[19]

If the outlines of the conflict were becoming clear even to colonists, the reasons for that conflict were not. Some Virginia chauvinists were convinced that the Iroquois "come to the Southward to seek them selves better Habitations," traveling from their "cold, Barren, and Rockie Countrey and Soyle, into a Climate more happy and desireable."[20] But Anglo-Americans generally considered the bloodshed symptomatic of the Indians' "rapacious inclinations," their "over-boiling, revengeful temper," their "restless and martial Spirit."[21] Iroquois attacked Catawbas, concluded one observer, "meerly for the sake of Killing them."[22] Try as they might, most colonists failed to see the point of it all. "Surely you cannot propose to get either Riches or Possessions by going thus out to War," Pennsylvania Governor William Keith told the Five Nations in 1720; "For when you kill a Deer you have the Flesh to eat and the skin to sell, but when you return from War you bring nothing home but the Scalps of a dead man . . . and . . . got nothing by it."[23] "If they can steal anything and Kill

2 or 3 old women or men they soon return contented," a puzzled southern governor reported.[24] For once the French agreed with these English assessments, noting that "one or two scalps or the smallest prisoner satisfies them in an equal degree, and they return as victorious as if they had wholly destroyed the Nation they are about to attack. This is the mode of thinking among all Indians."[25]

In fact, the conflict's origins were probably more mundane than the discussions of climatic conditions or temperamental compulsions suggest. It may have begun with a handful of Iroquois looking for adventure. In 1662 a Jesuit missionary reported that some warriors from the Five Nations were "pushing their way farther down toward the South, without well knowing against whom they bear a grudge, seeking, they know not whom, and declaring war before they have any enemies."[26] It is also possible that the cycle of warfare was set in motion by a chance encounter somewhere in the piedmont. At least some of the earliest Iroquois visitors to the region were hunting not scalps or prisoners but pelts or deerskins.[27] Perhaps these parties quite unintentionally fell afoul of local natives.

Once blood was shed—whether accidentally or not—it was extremely difficult to limit further hostilities. James Adair, a trader among the Catawbas and other southern Indians during the mid-eighteenth century, described the explosive consequences of violence involving groups without some other means of settling disputes. Indians, "being destitute of public faith to secure the lives of embassadors in time of war, . . . have no sure method to reconcile their differences," Adair observed; "consequently, when any casual thing draws them into a war, it grows every year more spiteful till it advances to a bitter enmity, so as to excite them to an implacable hatred to one another's very national names."[28] This escalation from "casual thing" to "implacable hatred" may have occurred in the southern interior during the last decades of the seventeenth century, drawing the peoples into a war neither intended.

Whatever the cause of the Catawba-Iroquois wars, in a sense if a Catawba foe had not existed the Five Nations would have had to invent one. The Iroquois mourning-war complex, coupled with a desire to achieve individual status through martial exploits and a mission to expand the Great Tree of Peace to all nations, compelled men from the Five Nations to seek enemies, preferably remote ones.[29] Once found—or created—foes might eventually become friends by making the appropriate submission and entering the Iroquois Covenant Chain. That done, new enemies had to be found, for, as John Lawson discovered, the Iroquois "cannot live without War . . . ; if Peace be made with the *Indians* they now war withal, they must find out some others to wage War against; for, for them to live in Peace, is to live out of their Element."³⁰ Catawbas fit Iroquois needs admirably: small enough in size and far enough away to make massive retaliation upon Iroquoia unlikely, stubborn enough to resist peace overtures, they were the ideal antagonist.

Viewed from Iroquoia, war with the Catawbas made perfect sense. Less obvious is why the Catawba Nation accepted the role handed it by the Five Nations. It is tempting to portray the Nation as the plucky yet pathetic victim of the implacable Iroquois, to assume that its purpose in history was to be a target — its territory a mere training ground for young warriors, its people nothing more than a stock for replenishing Iroquois ranks and drying the women's tears. The temptation should be resisted. Catawbas were neither stupid nor masochistic; if truly devastated, they, like so many groups, would have visited Albany long before 1751. Why did Catawbas hold out against the current sweeping others to Iroquoia?

The simplest answer is that Catawbas, too, needed enemies, for they shared with the Iroquois a common culture of conflict. According to James Adair, southern Indians, like their northern counterparts, operated within a mourning-war tradition and fought "to satisfy the supposed craving ghosts of their deceased relations." "They firmly believe," Adair went on, "that the spirits of those who are killed by the enemy, without equal revenge of blood, find no rest, and at night haunt the houses of the tribe [kin group] to which they belonged. . . . Then they must go abroad to spill the enemy's blood, and to revenge crying blood."³¹ A desire to prove oneself as a warrior was also in the forefront of a Catawba's thoughts. "Our Warriors delight in War," Hagler told colonists, "and our young Men are equally pleased that they have an Opportunity of going to Battle."³² They "think its as good as A Ballplay," one Cherokee visitor observed, and "won't Leave off till [they] know who is the best."³³

Hostility toward the Iroquois shaped Catawba collective identity as powerfully as it shaped the identity of any individual. After 1700, enemy warriors unwittingly helped to create a more populous, more diverse Catawba Nation. Many Carolina Indian peoples already ravaged by disease found themselves unable to withstand raids from the north and came to the Catawba River Valley in search of shelter from the Iroquois storm. In the mid-1720s, for example, war parties from the Iroquois — recently become the Six Nations with the addition of Tuscaroras — fell upon Cheraw and Waccamaw settlements east of the Catawbas; within five years both groups had moved to the Nation.³⁴ Moreover, in a ploy reminiscent of the Iroquois themselves, Catawba headmen learned to use the threat of enemy raids to recruit new members, urging Indians still in the South Carolina lowlands to move upcountry and seek safety in numbers.³⁵ Catawba diplomacy and Iroquois visits were a persuasive combination: by 1743 the Nation had absorbed so many refugee groups that a visitor heard more than twenty different dialects spoken by its inhabitants.[36]

Once the Iroquois war had virtually emptied the region of native settlements and pushed survivors into the Catawba orbit, it was instrumental in sustaining the fragile entity it had helped create. Peoples in the Nation divided by language, culture, and history were united by their fear of raids from the north. Forays against the Iroquois joined men from different villages in a common enterprise that blurred old ties and created new ones, ties further strengthened after the battle when peoples celebrated victory or mourned defeat. The conflict also brought in its train heroes and stories that provided Cheraws, Waccamaws, and their Catawba hosts with a shared heritage. The headman Wickmannataughehee, who was captured by the Iroquois in 1717 but escaped and returned home; the woman who, taken prisoner in the same raid, slipped away and found her way south, only to be recaptured a year later and break free once more; the young Cheraw who took "a very lusty Seneca Man" near the Nation — these and many more, living and dead, gave a loose collection of formerly independent communities the stock of memories essential to any society.[37]

While certainly important, none of these factors singled Catawbas out. Every native group was determined to "avenge crying blood." Tutelos, Saponis, and Keyauwees were also driven together more by fear of another enemy attack than anything else. And hatred of the Iroquois helped forge a single identity among the geographically and linguistically divided Cherokees.[38] Yet all made peace with the Six Nations sooner than Catawbas, so again we must ask why that nation alone resisted, clinging to its independence and its hatred of the Iroquois when those around it were losing theirs.

The most likely explanation is that among Catawbas the benefits of warfare continued to outweigh its burdens, in large part because the Nation defended itself successfully. As late as 1750 a Virginia official could remark that they "are generally Victors over the parties of the Six Nations sent to War with them, being in their Phrase Great Warriors."[39] The Catawbas' fame as warriors was widespread. Governor James Glen of South Carolina was convinced that they were "the bravest Fellows on the Continent of America." Edmond Atkin, once a member of the South Carolina Council and after 1755 the crown superintendent of Indian affairs for the southern colonies, agreed that "In War, they are inferior [to] no Indians whatever." Even James Adair gave Catawbas equal rank with his beloved Chickasaws for a "warlike . . . disposition."[40] Indians in the Nation were quick to concur. "The Catawbaws are known to be a very Broud [sic] People," noted one colonist, "and have at several treaty's they had with the Cherokees used high Expressions, and thought them self stout warriors." "We are a small Nation but our Name is high," Hagler boasted to Glen.[41]

Many commented on the Nation's fierce reputation; few sought to explain it. Why were Catawbas feared and their Cherokee neighbors scorned?[42] If the Catawbas' renown predated the eighteenth century, it may have had something to do with their piedmont location. Cherokees could rely on their mountainous terrain for protection; coastal Indians enjoyed the advantage of swamps that impeded an enemy's progress or, in an emergency, served as a refuge. Ancestors of Hagler's Catawbas, lacking natural defenses, may have compensated by developing superior martial skills. In addition, aboriginal inhabitants of the uplands could have honed these talents further by defending themselves against powerful and aggressive societies that migrated to central South Carolina, drove out the indigenous inhabitants, and settled just downriver from historic Catawba territories. Piedmont peoples apparently did not get along with these intruders, and warfare was probably a fact of life in the area well before the first European explorer entered it.[43]

By the time Iroquois warriors began venturing south, then, the piedmont populations that made up the Catawba Nation were probably both thoroughly accustomed to and very good at killing people. Once established, the structure of Catawba-Iroquois conflict enhanced the Catawbas' reputation. War parties from the Six Nations tended to strike hunting camps, lone travelers, or villages when the men were absent; Catawba warriors would then pursue and strike back. The Nation's settlement pattern facilitated an effective response. As Glen observed, "the Situation of their Towns makes them stronger than any Indian Nation of double their Number for they are very compact all their Gun Men . . . can be called together in two hours time."[44]

Swift pursuit by skilled warriors determined to avenge dead kinfolk or rescue captured ones caught many a retreating Iroquois war party off guard. In May of 1745 the Pennsylvania Indian agent and interpreter Conrad Weiser crossed paths with an Iroquois acquaintance named Anontagketa as both were en route to Onondaga. The "footsore Indian" was "returning from an expedition against the Catawbas in which he had lost everything but his life. He had no shoes, no stockings, no shirt, no gun, no hatchet, no fire-flint, no knife — nothing but an old torn blanket and some rags."[45] Anontagketa was one of the lucky ones: upon many of his fellows, Catawbas were often able to inflict heavy losses, or, as the *South Carolina Gazette* phrased it, to "repay them in their own Coin, and with Interest."[46] The interest, and the Catawbas' fame, may have been compounded because attacking enemy warriors carried more prestige than killing or capturing women and children. Moreover, losses deep in enemy territory may have been especially hard for a people to bear. Those who perished far from home fell in what Adair called "unsanctified ground . . . distant from their own holy places and holy things," and therefore did not receive proper burial.[47] Some Indians went to great lengths even years later to recover the remains of their dead, but many corpses were left behind.[48]

The Catawbas' close relationship with the Anglo-American world considerably improved the odds in the Nation's favor. When authorities in Williamsburg or Charleston heard rumors about a northern war party heading in the Catawbas' direction, they sent word to the Nation to be on guard, along with arms and ammunition to strengthen its defenses. If neither the warning nor the weapons proved adequate, Catawbas found refuge in colonial settlements where Iroquois warriors were more reluctant to venture.[49] The Six Nations, frustrated and furious, complained that when a war party approached a village in the Nation colonists would "send them [Catawbas] Word by which Means they loose a great many People."[50]

Equally infuriating were the taunts Catawbas hurled at their enemies. If warriors from the Six Nations heaped verbal abuse on Catawbas, no one in the Nation ever complained to colonists about it. The Iroquois, shocked by such "spitefull and Offensive" foes, often did. One told South Carolina officials that "some Time ago we desired to have a Peace with the Catawbas Nation, who sent us Word that they had two Conveniencies, one for their Women, and one for us, and that they were Men and Warriours since which Time we are at War, and are of one Mind never to have Peace with them." According to the Iroquois, Catawbas rebuffed a similar message by sending "word that we were but Women; that they were men and double men for they had two P——s." Adair reported that northern Indians "were fully resolved to prosecute it [war with Catawbas], with the greatest eagerness, while there was one of that hateful name alive; because in the time of battle, they had given them the ugly name of short-tailed eunuchs." Such talk combined with Catawba success to add insult to injury and stiffen the resolve of the Iroquois. One disgusted sachem promised that the conflict "will last to the End of the World, for they molest Us and speak Contemptuously of Us, which our Warriours will not bear."[51]

The Catawba penchant for what their enemies considered treachery added sticks and stones to the arsenal of names and drove thoughts of peace still further from Iroquois minds. Cessation of hostilities was impossible, the Six Nations argued, for Catawbas could not be trusted. They were a "disorderly people," "an Irregular people," a "false People," "a deceitful People" who talked of peace and then made war, welcomed ambassadors and then butchered them.[52] In the most famous (or infamous) episode, Catawba warriors surrounded a retreating Oneida war party in 1729, proposed a parley, and then killed or captured the entire band when it came to treat for peace, including the renowned war captain Currundawawnah. For years neither side forgot this incident, Catawbas boasting of their great victory, Oneidas refusing to consider peace with the killers of Currundawawnah.[53]

Treachery, like beauty, is generally in the eye of the beholder. But even the Catawbas' friends privately admitted that they adopted "a Stratagem something too much like Treachery."[54] The Iroquois blamed it on the evil spirit "that dwells among the Catabaws and by which they are ruled."[55] A more likely cause may have been the chaotic process of forging a single society out of the many fragments that existed in the Carolina piedmont during these years. Perhaps lines of authority became tangled when so many different peoples came together in one place, making it difficult to maintain a consistent stance toward outsiders. Without some established means of making decisions, one group in the Nation might favor peace and welcome ambassadors; another, set upon war, might kill them the next day. This picture resembles nothing so much as the "ungoverned" Five Nations in the early 1680s.[56] Was the Iroquois Confederacy so thoroughly consolidated by the eighteenth century that such chaos was a thing of the past? If so, the Catawba peoples had not yet caught up. As one Shawnee headman contemplating negotiations with Catawbas put it in 1717, "there were many Nations under that name," and peace with one would not guarantee peace with all.[57]

The treachery, the insults, the Anglo-American assistance, the Catawbas' formidable skills — all of these ingredients combined to keep Catawba-Iroquois relations at the boiling point during the first half of the eighteenth century. Ironically, the Catawbas' very success contained within it the seeds of disaster. As victory followed victory and the Nation's reputation grew, so, too, did the number of native men elsewhere eager to make a name for themselves by returning home with a Catawba scalp or prisoner. "Such is the Honour in Indian Estimation to be accquired [sic] by Killing any of them," Edmond Atkin remarked, "that Indians as far remote as the [Great] Lakes go in quest of them."[58]

Other changes taking place in the second quarter of the eighteenth century also boded ill for Catawbas. The Shawnee populations that had left South Carolina for Pennsylvania early in the century moved again,

this time to the Ohio Country. Pennsylvania authorities had worked dili-
gently to stop war parties from these towns heading south, but once in
the Ohio the Shawnees were free to do as they pleased. To add to Catawba
woes, Cherokees made peace with the Six Nations in 1742, providing Iroquois war parties with an excellent base from which to launch raids on
the piedmont. And if this were not enough, the French stepped up their
efforts to win over Indians throughout the East and turn them against the
British. When Catawbas spurned French overtures, officials in Canada retaliated by encouraging attacks on the Nation.[59]

By mid-century Catawbas were fighting eleven different Indian
nations.[60] This unprecedented harassment converted the Nation from a
refuge into a target and threatened its very existence. Enemy raids, far from
binding diverse peoples together, now promised to drive them apart. Beginning in the late 1730s officials in Charleston began to hear occasional
rumors that some in the Nation "proposed now to withdraw themselves
from them [Catawbas], and to retire to some place of greater safety, where
they might have fewer Enemies."[61] Colonists managed to dissuade the mal-
contents each time, but life in the Nation grew steadily more precarious,
and occasionally it virtually ground to a halt. "[O]ur Enemies are so thick
about us," Hagler informed Governor Glen in the spring of 1750, "we cannot go from Home."[62] That summer Glen worried that "there seems to be
great danger of their being totally destroyed."[63]

Not surprisingly, in the late 1730s colonists thought that they detected in Catawbas a "turn . . . to a more pacifick disposition" toward the
Iroquois.[64] At the same time, at least some of the Iroquois appeared to
be similarly inclined.[65] But the road from "pacifick disposition" to actual
peace was long. For one thing, Anglo-American authorities could not agree
whether ending hostilities was a good idea. Some dreamed of a Covenant
Chain linking all Indians allied with the English.[66] Others differed, believ-
ing with South Carolina Governor Robert Johnson that "it is always the
maxim of our Governm[en]t upon the Continent to promote War between
Indians of different Nations with whom we Trade and are at peace with
ourselves[,] for in that consists our safety, being at War with one another
prevents their uniting against us."[67] A second obstacle was the Indians'
own attachment to warfare and their belief that such matters should be
of no concern to outsiders. Many agreed with Tuscaroras who, according
to one colonist, asked "why could we not let them that were Indians alone
to make war against Indians without our meddling with it." Another settler demanded to know what a party of "foreign" warriors was doing in
South Carolina, only to be told "that I had no Concern with what they
had to do there, their Business was with red and not white People."[68]

With time Indian "Business" very much affected white people, however. Settlers in every colony pushed deeper into the interior and cut across the paths warriors followed to enemy villages, with predictable results. As the skirmishes escalated it became clear that the war parties had to be stopped.[69] At the same time, growing fear of French power fostered a consensus on the wisdom of making peace. As one South Carolina official wrote in 1742, only a decade after Governor Johnson had stated his views, it was essential now "to prevent the Indians in the British Interest from weakening one another that they may be the better able to withstand the attempts of the French Indians."[70]

It was one thing for all to agree that warfare should end, quite another to bring Catawbas and Iroquois together. On both sides the headmen's lack of control over the warriors almost guaranteed that new attacks would disrupt delicate negotiations.[71] Colonial ignorance of or indifference to native protocol further cluttered the path. In 1738 New York's Indian agent Laurence Claessen asked Iroquois headmen to halt war parties about to head south. They "made answer that he was certainly jesting with them for if Corlaer [New York's governor] wanted them not to go he ought according to Custom to have sent a Belt of Wampum, but as Laur. Claasse[n] spoke without one they should not lay aside their Expedition."[72] According to a sadder but wiser South Carolina Council, Catawbas, too, were "very attentive to all Punctilios of Form." In 1741 the Nation ventured to send the Iroquois tokens indicating a willingness to discuss peace, but despite prompting from colonial officials Catawba headmen refused to go any further until the gesture was reciprocated.[73]

Once colonists caught on and the appropriate tokens had been exchanged, the antagonists had to be brought together, for the Iroquois insisted that "People do not make peace until they see those who ask it."[74] Debates over the location of the proposed council brought more delays. While the Six Nations maintained that Albany was the "Antient and fixt Place for all People to treat with them," Catawbas insisted upon "their own Towns or Country."[75] Colonists who proposed Philadelphia or Williamsburg as alternatives were told that the former was "too remote a Place" for Catawbas, the latter too far off to tempt the Iroquois.[76] These may seem like petty disputes; they were not. As Indian diplomats had made clear in the seventeenth century, the choice of meeting place reflected a people's prestige and was never selected at random. The Six Nations had formal ties to Pennsylvania, the Catawbas to Virginia. Thus traveling to Williamsburg would be the same as going all the way to the Catawba Nation and "would," Iroquois spokesmen argued, "be dishonourable to Us."[77] On the other hand Catawbas knew that, as Glen observed, "it was best to meet" their old foes in Virginia, "Otherwise it would look like following them to Beg for Peace."[78]

In the end, of course, Catawbas did just that. Hagler's readiness to travel all the way to Albany reflected the Nation's desperate straits at mid-century. Native enemies were only one of many troubles confronting his people. Disease steadily reduced the Nation's numbers, and the reservoirs of refugees Catawbas had drawn upon in the past were drying up. Settlers pouring into the interior drove out the deer, and with the animals went the traders and the trade goods, leaving the Nation dependent on the South Carolina government not only for supplies but also for protection from both enemy warriors and colonial planters. The Indians' plight gave Glen the leverage he needed to sweep aside any lingering doubts Catawbas may have had and put the Catawba delegation on board ship on May 23, 1751.[79]

Glen must have heaved a sigh of relief as he bundled six Catawbas, their interpreter Matthew Toole, and the colony's representative William Bull onto the aptly named schooner *Trial* for the voyage.[80] The long struggle had taken its toll in time, energy, and expense. At least Glen's job was done; for those aboard the *Trial* the "tedious" business was just beginning.[81] Ahead lay three long months of travel and delay, with little besides occasional low threats and moments of high drama to relieve the boredom. Shortly after the Catawbas' arrival in New York City, two drunk Mahicans accosted them and, "pretending to be Mowhaks[,] told them it was to no Purpose to expect Peace, with much more to the like Effect."[82] In Albany perfectly sober Caughnawagas who heard of the ambassadors from the south talked of plans to "rush in, bind them, and after making them dance the Death Dance, put them to Death."[83] To shield his guests from further verbal assaults (or worse), upon their arrival in Albany on June 25, Governor Clinton placed them in protective custody, with a mounted guard stationed nearby and a sentry posted at the door to screen visitors.[84]

The Catawbas were said to be "pritty uneasie," and they had good reason to be.[85] A "pensive" crowd of 130 Iroquois awaited Hagler and his men on July 8, when they finally emerged from their quarters to face their old foes. Over the next five hours the Catawba chief did what he could to ease the tension. His speech stressed the distance Catawbas had traveled, their sorrow that "Accidents" prevented their coming sooner, their eagerness for peace. To add weight to his words he couched them in an elaborate ritual that opened with solemn singing and the smoking of a pipe and ended with Hagler embracing Hendrick, the Mohawk sachem. From there the day's events quickly drew to a close amidst handshakes, presents, and the Six Nations' "Yo-Hah" of assent. Then an Oneida sachem announced that they would retire to consider Hagler's talk.[86]

Hagler had done all he could, but it was not enough. The Iroquois still harbored "a great many Objections," among them the memory of what these supposedly peaceful Catawbas had done to Currundawawnah and his party two decades before.[87] They had promised Hagler an answer to his talk that very evening or the following morning; but these deadlines came and went, and still the Iroquois council went on. At last, with the Mohawks urging peace, Governor Clinton "dawbing the Palms of their Sachims with Dollars," and William Bull slipping Hendrick money for "Secret Services," resistance finally melted.[88] On the morning of July 10, the Iroquois addressed the Catawbas, returning Hagler's kind words and expressing their own desire for peace, a desire now only one step from fulfillment. "Nothing now remained," they said, "but the mutual Exchange of Pris[oner]s, which was what they always observed in making Peace." The Catawbas must come back with these people within the year. Hagler, pronouncing it "a right and good Custom," pledged to return "in a short Time," and after further speeches and ceremonies the meeting broke up.[89]

The Catawbas had lived to tell about their trip into enemy country, and everyone was delighted with the outcome. When Hagler and his companions returned to South Carolina on August 16, Glen invited them into the Council Chamber to welcome them back and praise their efforts. He boasted to the Assembly of the peace "happily concluded," and the Assembly — which agreed with Glen on very little — assured him of its own "great pleasure."[90] In the Nation the "beloved old Men and Women" pronounced themselves "very thankfull" to Glen for helping to make peace, "which they were afraid it would not be."[91]

The celebrations were premature; that last step — the return trip with prisoners — proved a difficult one to take. Bull had fretted about it as early as July, warning Glen that "any Delay . . . would to all Intents and Purposes render fruitless all that had hitherto been done towards the Peace."[92] Glen took the hint: on August 26, only days after the Catawba delegation had left Charleston on the final leg of its long journey, the governor sent word to Matthew Toole that the Catawbas should return to Charleston with the captives in two weeks.[93] It was easier said than done. Toole replied that the Catawbas were going nowhere before spring. He and Hagler "strove all that lay in our Powers to get some of the Best of the Indians to go," Toole explained, "but could not get one."[94] The official explanation was that many of their people were ill and demanded care.[95] In the Nation's villages, however, other factors also played a role. Winter was coming, and everyone knew that "that is a cold Country."[96] Enemy raiders believed to be from the Six Nations had killed two Catawbas near the Nation shortly after Hagler and the delegation returned home, further dampening enthusiasm for the trip.[97] Finally, though no one admitted it, Catawbas may have had a hard time rounding up Iroquois to take north. In July Toole had informed Bull that the exchange of prisoners could pose a problem, because Catawbas had sold some of the people they had captured.[98] Others may have been adopted into Catawba families and were reluctant to leave. Thus when Hagler promised to come in the spring with "all the Slaves they have with them," he was sharply restricting the pool of candidates to those neither sold nor adopted.[99]

Events the following year demonstrated just how shallow that pool was, how low the level of enthusiasm, how fragile the peace. The Catawba delegation that arrived in Charleston brought with it only one Iroquois; there had been two more, but one had died recently and the other refused to travel by ship.[100] The delegation itself, which had taken a full two months to respond to Glen's summons,[101] was a poor relation to its predecessor the year before. Discouraged by Glen and recovering from a beating inflicted by colonial traders over the winter, Hagler did not go; Toole had been arrested for debt and was unavailable; South Carolina, to cut costs, chose not to send Bull or anyone else as its representative.[102] Whether the Iroquois missed these ambassadors or resented the fact that Catawbas had only one prisoner in tow is unclear, but their resistance to the peace remained strong. Plans to escort the Catawbas to each of the Six Nations were abandoned, as the Mohawks — again the Iroquois most disposed toward peace — "thought it most prudent" to bring the Upper Nations to them instead. At last "the usual Indian Ceremonies" were out of the way and the peace concluded.[103] The Catawbas remained among the Iroquois throughout the summer, and by fall were on their way home, by land this time, in the company of a dozen Mohawks.[104]

The Nation welcomed the visitors with open arms, receiving them with handshakes, pipes of peace, and feasts "as if they were our own Children."[105] The Catawbas hardly dared believe that "People that always came to us before with Bullets out of the Muzzells of their Guns . . . now come in Friends."[106] Captain Plans, the Mohawk leader, was equally pleased that "the Peace shall be continued, and the Path straight and open betwixt us, and shall be Brothers forever." Upon his departure after a month among his new friends he promised that "more of our People will come soon and keep the Path plain and open."[107]

It turned out that Captain Plans was only half right. More of his people did come, but many of them were bent on bloodying the path again. The Catawba-Iroquois peace would prove as difficult to sustain as it had been to conclude. Just how difficult is by no means easy to tell, for the identity of Indians attacking the Catawbas after 1751 is not always clear. Some were undoubtedly not Iroquois, but many were. Glen refused to believe it. Even during the summer of 1753, when Catawbas were so harassed that they could not venture out to hunt, the governor insisted that the Iroquois could not possibly be to blame.[108] Catawbas knew better: by August they were thanking Glen for his peace efforts but assuring him that "it was to no Purpose, for the Northern Indians have already broke it."[109] Only a month later William Johnson knew the truth too.[110]

It took Glen more than a year to admit that all of his hard work had been in vain. Only when word came from reliable sources in New York late in 1754 that a party of fifty Iroquois warriors was on its way did Glen finally relent. "I was in hopes that you might have been mistaken . . . ," he told the Catawba headmen. "But I cannot conceal from you that all your Apprehensions seems to have been well founded."[111] The following spring a Catawba woman who had escaped from the Iroquois staggered into the Nation to confirm the grim news. "They intend to cut off every Soul of the Catawbaws . . . ," she reported. "They knew where the Catawbaws fetched their Water and Wood and they would utterly destroy them."[112] An angry Glen sent word to the Six Nations that he could not believe the sachems there had sanctioned these actions: "I beseech you my good Friends [to] correct these irregularities of your young men and wipe away the blood of your Brothers the Catawbaws that has been unjustly spilt."[113]

Glen's consternation was understandable. Even as the peace fell apart, the reasons for making it were more compelling than ever. England, once again at war with the French, desperately needed to unite its Indian allies in His Majesty's cause. Disputes between northern and southern nations hampered British effectiveness, especially in the early years of the conflict. Some said that one reason no Iroquois joined General Edward Braddock's ill-fated expedition was their fear that they would have to march with southern Indians against the French.[114] Ironically, others joined the English at Fort Cumberland because they hoped Catawbas *would* be there and could more easily be attacked.[115] Still others went all the way to "the Catawba Country" for their prizes. In 1759 forty Onondagas passed through Pittsburgh with five Catawba captives, two of the prisoners known to a soldier there because they had served with him in the last campaign against the French.[116]

By 1763 northern war parties regularly "infested" the Nation, as they had for almost a century.[117] Now, however, they did so with the blessing of the English. With the French at last out of the way there was no longer any pressing need to make peace among His Majesty's Indian allies. Quite the contrary: the accepted wisdom once again argued that it was better for them to kill one another. "Whenever all the [Indian] Nations are at Peace," wrote General Thomas Gage in 1764, "I look upon it as a signal for us to take care of ourselves."[118] Sir William Johnson agreed. "I am humbly of opinion we had best not interest ourselves in it [the war between southern and northern nations] other than as Mediators between them," he wrote the Lords of Trade in 1765. If mediation failed, Johnson for one would shed no tears. "[L]et them carry it on as they please on both sides . . . for by this means we take off many dangerous Spirits who cannot be kept at peace."[119] The traditional cycle of conflict, again unchecked by pressure from colonial capitals, went on and on. George Washington considered it routine when he crossed paths with sixty Iroquois warriors heading south against the Catawbas in the fall of 1770 — and it was.[120]

The remarkable thing was that Washington could just as easily have come upon a delegation of six Iroquois then heading south to confirm the peace with the Catawbas.[121] Indeed, for two decades after the Albany congresses the unstable mixture of Iroquois warriors and ambassadors created such confusion in the Nation that when Catawbas heard of a party's approach they did not know whether to grab their peace pipes or their guns.[122] Some groups — like the lone Susquehannock in 1755 or the Mohawk man and woman two years later — were clearly not much of a threat; but others ranged from a half dozen to forty or more, just the right size for making war or peace.[123] Regardless of its numbers, if a delegation came in peace Catawbas were hospitable; no more charges of treachery issued from Iroquois councils after 1751. Instead, Hagler entertained the visitors at his own dwelling, while his people and his guests went off together to hunt deer, kill Cherokees, or (on occasion) plunder colonial plantations.[124] Ten years after returning from Albany Hagler still had the wampum and pipe given him there, and he was willing to display them to anyone interested.[125] Some Iroquois were.

If it was difficult to discern the intentions of each visitor, it must have been even harder to explain why some came to shake hands, others to take scalps. Perhaps young men were once again negating the peace initiatives of their elders. More likely is the possibility that the debate over war and peace divided the Six Nations, Mohawks preferring to end the conflict while the others insisted that it be carried on. Such a pattern of mind was evident at Albany in 1751 and 1752, and it may have held true thereafter. Iroquois war parties, when identified by nation, tended not to be Mohawks, while ambassadors generally were. It may also be significant that Catawbas sending a friendly letter to the Iroquois in 1758 directed it specifically to the Mohawks and received a reply only from "The Sachems and Chiefs of the Two Mohock Castles."[126] It would be dangerous to place too much weight on such distinctions, however, for as always, few colonists were capable of making them; colonial confusion about national identities among the Iroquois persisted.[127]

Whatever the precise chemistry that placed peace and war in such an explosive balance after Albany, before the end of the century the scale had tipped sharply toward the former. Washington was among the last to see the old plot being acted out. The eventual demise of the Catawba-Iroquois wars probably had little to do with Mohawk influence or a renewed Anglo-American peace offensive. For the Iroquois there were too many settlers in the way, too few Catawbas left — less than five hundred — to make the journey worthwhile, and, after 1775, too many problems closer to home to worry about. As late as 1791 Catawbas were still fretting about enemies "who, they had reason to believe, were at that time lurking in the neighbouring Woods in order to destroy them." The threat was identified only as "a distant nation, whose inveteracy against this little handful of people is not to be erased."[128] A decade or so later came the very last war party, and it followed the faded script to the letter: sudden attack on the Nation's settlement, pursuit, counterattack, Catawba victory.[129] The only new twist was that no other enemies followed the next spring, or the next.

The wars were over at last, with no grand peace treaty or bloody final battle to mark their passing. Was peace welcome? Catawbas had sung its praises from that autumn day in 1752 when a dozen Mohawks had arrived in the Nation to give the treaty tangible form. "I cannot but greatly express the Joy there is among our People . . . ," Hagler exclaimed to Glen. "It enables us to pay our Debts, and to cloth[e] ourselves and Families. We can sleep now without being afraid."[130] To their new friends the message was the same. "We so little knew the Benefitt of [peace] till Now for we can sleep in safety and hunt in peace, so that we have no reason to be affraid of any thing but Sickness."[131]

If the immediate benefits of peace with the Iroquois were obvious, its long-term implications were less clear and probably less welcome. Without the central thread provided by the Iroquois wars, without the Six Nations as a focus of enmity, the entire fabric of Catawba warfare came unraveled, and Catawbas stopped fighting the Iroquois or anyone else. For almost a century, war with the Six Nations had preoccupied Catawbas, and warfare itself could claim a more ancient lineage still. Its end, however gradual, must have had a profound effect on the Nation. How would "crying blood" be silenced, a young man's ambitions satisfied, ethnic diversity offset? The questions remained; the answers were no longer clear. For a time some warriors substituted runaway slaves or British troops for native enemies, tracing a complex pattern of camaraderie, skill, risk, and reward akin to that etched into Catawba experience by years of warfare. A few others put their increasingly obsolete talents on display in British theaters. But none of these alternatives survived the century.[132] After 1800 the wounds of warfare healed and the scars faded. Only the memories of old battles remained, handed from generation to generation long after the Iroquois stopped coming south and the last Catawba warrior passed away.[133]

8

CHEROKEE RELATIONS with the IROQUOIS in the EIGHTEENTH CENTURY

THEDA PERDUE

I N 1730 Sir Alexander Cuming, self-appointed emissary of the British Crown, declared the warrior Moytoy to be emperor of the Cherokees and instructed him to enforce British law in the nation.[1] Similar episodes occurred repeatedly among native peoples in North America: in the British mind, Indians became subjects of the crown, thereby losing the right to conduct their own affairs. A particular target of the British campaign for control was the Indians' foreign policy. Despite immense effort, however, the British rarely hit the mark. When it came to orchestrating native diplomacy, Anglo-Americans were not as effective as they thought they were, and Indian "allies" often surprised them by not being allies at all. The absence of central authority among native peoples like the Cherokees made it impossible for them to make an alliance that would be binding on the entire society; such an arrangement was as alien to Cherokees as an emperor was. Yet the British failed to realize that their political terms and structures had little relevance in native America, and they persisted in developing an Indian policy based on these fictions.

The British were no more effective in controlling relationships among native peoples in eastern North America than they were in dictating alliances. Indeed, British desires were only one factor governing these contacts; Indians had their own motives and agendas. A study of relations between the Cherokees and the Iroquois in the eighteenth century reveals the complexity of native diplomacy, the internal structures governing that diplomacy, and the ways in which those structures accommodated British pretensions and power. Cherokees and the Iroquois did not always march in step with the beat of the British drum. Instead, they tried to reach rapprochement with the intruders while also meeting the demands of their own societies and cultures.

135

In the eighteenth century, the Cherokees lived in towns built along rivers that drained the southern Appalachian highlands. Until the end of the century, each Cherokee town was politically independent: corporate decisions rested with town councils, and no centralized government existed. A common language and a kinship system of seven matrilineal clans whose members lived throughout the nation provided some unity. Cherokee, an Iroquoian language, is radically different from Muskogean, the language spoken by most native people in the South. The Cherokees spoke at least three and perhaps four different but mutually intelligible dialects that corresponded to geographic regions. The overhill Cherokees lived in what is today eastern Tennessee; the valley towns were along the upper Hiwassee and Little Tennessee Rivers in present-day northern Georgia and southwestern North Carolina; the middle towns were along the Oconaluftee and Tuckaseegee Rivers in western North Carolina; and the lower Cherokees lived in what became upcountry South Carolina. At times, these linguistic/geographic divisions took on political overtones. Immediately before the Seven Years' War, for example, overhill Cherokees tended to favor the French, while the lower Cherokees supported the British. Cherokee divisions were never as clear, however, as those of the Iroquois Confederacy.[2]

The Cherokees in the south occupied a geographical position somewhat analogous to that of the Iroquois in the north. Cherokee country lay between the seaboard inhabited by the British and the lands in the interior dominated by other Indians and by the French. Despite their location, Cherokees never became middlemen in intercultural trade as the Iroquois did; Cherokee hunting grounds provided so many deerskins that they had no reason to seek more from other nations. Moreover, the Cherokees did not live astride major routes into the interior, and southern traders could easily push past them to trade directly with western nations. However, the Cherokees were important trading partners of the English colonies (particularly of South Carolina), and colonial officials tried to appease them when they complained about high prices, unfair weights, tight credit, or watered rum.[3] The British had another compelling reason to promote good relations with this powerful nation: it served as a buffer against attacks by the French or their native allies. If Cherokees ever became enemies of the British, they had the ability to inflict considerable damage on the colonial frontier. Unlike the Iroquois, however, the Cherokees generally failed to use their strategic importance to maintain a position of neutrality. Except during the Cherokee War of 1760, most Cherokees allied with the British.[4]

The Cherokees depended heavily on the British for guns and ammunition as well as other trade goods. They lived too far from the French to be supplied adequately even when circumstances might have led them to favor the imperial rival of the English. Anglo-America did its best to supply Cherokee needs, and after the first decade of the eighteenth century British trade goods were readily available throughout the nation. Colonial governments often made gifts of supplies in recognition of the Cherokees' strategic significance. The South Carolina government, in particular, sent large quantities of powder and bullets to the Cherokees until most warriors turned against the British in the late 1750s. As late as 1759, when the Cherokees were on the verge of transferring their allegiance to Louisiana, the French complained that "the Cherokees have allowed themselves to be gained by the presents of the English."[5] The Cherokees used the guns and ammunition provided them by traders and colonial governments to hunt game or fight other Indian nations, including nations that also were friendly to the British.

Among the British allies most often involved in war with the Cherokees were the Iroquois. The origins of the conflict are unclear. William Johnson, the superintendent of Indian affairs for the northern department, described the Cherokees and Iroquois as "ancient" and "implacable" enemies. Major John Norton, a Mohawk who visited the Cherokees in the early nineteenth century, was equally baffled. "How these Contentions commenced," Norton wrote in his journal, "none of the ancients of either Nation can give any account."[6]

However or whenever they began, hostilities seem to have escalated — for Cherokees as for Catawbas — after the Grand Settlement of 1701. The increase in warfare may have come about at the instigation of the French or of British traders. On the other hand, war parties may have come south for war booty: typical accounts of attacks by Iroquois warriors often mention that the enemy seized skins or blankets and other trade goods.[7] Daniel K. Richter's argument that the southern wars of the Iroquois represented a return to the traditional mourning wars is particularly persuasive, and the desire for vengeance may have motivated Cherokees as well.[8] One Cherokee who narrowly escaped capture by an Iroquois war party he encountered while hunting claimed that "they wanted to take him alive." If he had been caught, his fate probably would have been adoption or torture. Norton wrote that the Iroquois had once taken an entire Cherokee village prisoner. A Cherokee war party rescued these captives, but many others were not so fortunate. There were, according to Norton, "numberless petty excursions" which "occasioned much effusion of Blood."[9]

Eventually the English began to object to this warfare between British allies, and the same arguments that changed people's minds about the Catawba-Iroquois battles were brought to bear on the Cherokee-Iroquois conflict. In the late 1730s the Lords of Trade headquartered at Whitehall in London described it as "extraordinary . . . that these five Nations who are protected by the British government should employ their force to destroy other nations under the same protection." Such warfare was "doing the work" of the French. The great fear, of course, was that the French would exploit these divisions in the ranks of Britain's native allies or that the nations involved would become so weakened by their own wars that they would not be able to help Britain in her conflicts. In the 1730s Spain posed an imminent threat, and Britain tried to mend relations with potential allies. For Cherokee warriors to be free to attack Spanish St. Augustine, attacks by other Indians had to be halted and retaliatory raids curtailed. The British also had another reason for promoting friendship among Indian nations. In the south, colonial settlement quickly approached the Cherokee country, and British settlers sometimes became casualties in native warfare. Virginians had particular cause to complain, because the Great Warriors' Path that brought Iroquois warriors south and took Cherokee war parties north ran along the frontier of the colony. A slight deviation from the path brought war parties into colonial settlements.[10]

Because of the dangers of native warfare, British colonial officials may have begun pressuring the Cherokees and Iroquois to negotiate in the late 1730s. But some evidence suggests that the impetus for peace came from the belligerents. The Cherokees may have wanted peace with the Iroquois in order to be free to join British expeditions against the Spanish, or they may have sought a truce because of severe depopulation by a smallpox epidemic in 1738. Norton related an oral tradition that some Cherokees had captured a party of Seneca warriors, and "through the Humanity of the Chief of the Village,— their lives were spared." As a result, "they began to negotiate, and Peace was concluded between them."[11] In July 1737, the governor of Virginia wrote his counterpart in Pennsylvania that a group of Cherokees "fortunately found means to fall into a friendly conversation with a party of the Five Nations [and] had sent with them deputies to conclude a peace for themselves."[12]

Although the Iroquois expected them, the Cherokee deputies did not appear. The next spring, the New York Commissioners of Indian Affairs sent word to the Iroquois that Cherokee and also Catawba delegations were on their way "to make a firm peace." The Commissioners' message encouraged Iroquois attendance at a conference in Albany and discouraged them from going to war against the southern nations. The Senecas, who first received the message, replied that the Commissioners must be "jesting with them." They had stayed home throughout the previous hunting season in anticipation of the Cherokee visit, but, they charged, the Cherokees had deceived them and murdered a Cayuga.[13]

When the deputies once again failed to arrive as scheduled, the Mohawks asked the Commissioners in 1738 to be sent by sea to Virginia in order to negotiate with the southern Indians. The Commissioners claimed that this peace mission was "all a Sham" and refused to sanction it, since Mohawk warriors had been carrying on the war all summer "with Additional Vigor." In December, Virginia complained to the Board of Trade that the Iroquois had scuttled negotiations by "a treacherous attack on the Catawba Indians." Despite the Board of Trade's recommendation that a "lasting friendship" be achieved between the Iroquois and the Cherokees and Catawbas, warfare continued throughout 1739 and well into 1740.[14]

In August 1740, New York Governor George Clarke met with the Six Nations at Albany and urged them to make peace with the southern nations. The Iroquois agreed to unite with their enemies "as one body, one heart, and one flesh but only if those nations were willing to send some of their headmen to the Six Nations within two years to confirm the peace." During this two-year period, the Iroquois promised to keep their warriors at home.[15]

In May 1741, a group of Cherokees and Catawbas met with colonial officials in Charleston. While the Catawbas demanded return of their prisoners, the Cherokees accepted a truce with the Six Nations and sent some beads, a pipe, and a flag seized from the French as a "token of the Cherokees acceptance and confirmation of the Peace." The Cherokees received a belt of wampum sent by the Six Nations and took it to their sacred town of Chota. One negotiator reported to Clarke that the Six Nations had been the Cherokees' most powerful enemy and that peace would be "a great advantage to the Cherokees as well as to his Majesty's service in these parts of his Dominions."[16]

In June 1742, representatives of the Six Nations met Clarke at Albany. They reported that a Cherokee had visited the Senecas earlier in the year to confirm the peace: "That Indian who we call Brother has cleared the way between us and them that there shall be no hindrance for the future from going and coming that way to transact Publick affairs. . . . We call him our Brother and have made him a Sachim of the Six Nations." They had sent him home with an escort, and he promised to return in the spring for further negotiations. The Catawbas, however, failed to send a delegation, and the Iroquois resolved that "the war must continue till one of us is destroyed."[17]

Under British auspices, the Cherokees and the Iroquois renewed diplomatic relations fifteen years later. In the spring of 1757, several groups of Cherokees—perhaps representing different regions or factions—converged on the Virginia frontier, met with a Mohawk delegation, and "promised to join them and prosecute the war against the French as long as they had a man able to fight." Four Cherokees continued to New York, where they met with Superintendent Johnson and representatives of each of the Six Nations in July 1757.[18]

The meeting opened with a ceremony of condolence for the benefit of the Cherokees. Although the Cherokees had no real parallel to this ritual, the delegates watched politely and then replied: "Perhaps you will expect a formal answer upon the ceremony of condolence to us. Brethren we are Warriors and do not understand these Matters and hope you will excuse us." The warriors next revealed their plan to attack the French on the Ohio. The representatives of the Six Nations responded favorably to the message of the Cherokee warriors and invited them to send a subsequent delegation to New York.[19]

In June 1758, the lieutenant governor of Pennsylvania granted permission for a Cherokee party of thirteen men, seven women, and three boys along with a few Mohawks to travel through Pennsylvania on their way to visit Johnson and the Six Nations. Stopping in Philadelphia, the Cherokees conducted a council with colonial officials. They expressed their enmity to the French, and said that the Iroquois, their "Eldest Brother," urged them to join with the British against the French. When their chief became ill the Cherokees were unable to proceed, but they sent the Iroquois wampum belts and the following message: "We have made a Road clear for you, and we will endeavor to keep that Road clear for our Brothers to walk in, in hopes that you will come and make use of that Road."[20]

These peace negotiations only begin to suggest the depth of Cherokee-Iroquois contacts during the mid-eighteenth century and the education that took place as a result. We know little about the lone Cherokee who had visited the Senecas or about his experiences among the Iroquois. Probably an Iroquois clan adopted him even as the Senecas made him a sachem. Adoption was common among both Cherokees and Iroquois. An oral tradition recorded by the nineteenth-century scholar Jeremiah Curtin (which probably referred to an event after the Seven Years' War) relates how a group of Seneca warriors gained admission to a Cherokee town and council by dancing, were adopted by Cherokee women, and became so much a part of Cherokee society that they played ball and went to war against the Cherokees' enemies.[21] For Cherokee and Iroquois, kinship terms were not merely quaint metaphors; they were essential for the conduct of human affairs. In negotiation, Cherokee and Iroquois used kinship terms whose meaning transcended cultural barriers.

On the other hand, wampum belts were not a common denominator for diplomacy. In 1741, the Cherokees sent the Iroquois trade goods and a war trophy as a token of friendship, while the Iroquois bestowed a wampum belt on the Cherokees. The wampum belt's significance as symbol and mnemonic device meant little to the Cherokees who carried it to Chota; it was merely a gift equivalent to the items they had sent north. By 1758, however, Cherokees had come to understand the significance of wampum belts, and they sent belts (of unknown manufacture) to the Six Nations to confirm the peace.

The Cherokees may have learned something about the ways of their northern "brothers" from Iroquois who lived among them. In the 1750s, in particular, some Iroquois made the Cherokee Nation their home for extended periods of time. In 1754, the trader Ludovic Grant reported that an Iroquois who had lived for many years in the Cherokee Nation interpreted for a captured warrior. Grant went on to note that nine of twelve warriors who agreed to escort a trader to Virginia were "Northward Indians" who had lived for some time in the overhill towns and were "almost naturalized."[22] These may well have been adopted war captives, or they may have been hostages kept by the Cherokees to guarantee the peace. On the other hand, a few Iroquois may simply have lived for a time in Cherokee towns. Brief visits became extended stays when, according to Norton, the Iroquois "were charmed with the kind hospitality with which they were treated by the Cherokees."[23]

Most of the Iroquois who lived among the Cherokees probably were using the Cherokee country as a staging ground for attacks on other Indians. In July 1751, the South Carolina Indian Commissioner conveyed information to the governor that warriors of the Six Nations were already returning to their villages with Catawba scalps. He reasoned that they could not have traveled south, made their raids, and returned home so soon: "Therefore, 'tis probable that they might have been amongst the Cherokees all winter, and taken the Catawbas on their Way Home."[24]

By permitting the Iroquois to live in and travel through their country, the Cherokees ran the risk of becoming embroiled in their wars. The Cherokees generally tried to remain neutral, particularly in their relations with other allies of the English, unless they had some personal interest in the hostilities because the enemy had killed Cherokees. In March 1752, Seneca warriors came through Cherokee territory with a Chickasaw woman, a Coweta captive, and an unidentified scalp. According to the trader Grant, they "made but a short stay." A few days later, six Chickasaws in pursuit of the war party arrived in the Cherokee town through which the Senecas had passed. In order to allay any suspicion that they had aided the Senecas, the Cherokees provided the Chickasaws with a guide. In 1754, Grant reported that twenty Iroquois warriors came to Chota on their way to raid the Creeks. In another attempt to maintain neutrality, the Cherokee headman and council gave "them scalps and stopped them from going."[25]

Thus far, the picture painted of Cherokee-Iroquois relations is a simple one. In fact, it resembles a paint-by-numbers kit. The British provided the outline of an Indian policy; the nations within the British sphere of influence put aside their own disagreements and united to counter the French threat. The Cherokees and Iroquois filled in the outline by agreeing to a truce in the early 1740s and then renegotiating an alliance fifteen years later during the Seven Years' War. This scenario, however, is to history as paint-by-numbers is to art. It is a simplistic and unrealistic portrait of relations between the Cherokees and the Iroquois.

The British believed that they had enlarged and strengthened the Covenant Chain that presumably bound their Indian allies to each other and to the Crown. They ignored the reality of native government and warfare. The fact was that Iroquois sachems and Cherokee headmen had made a peace they could not keep. Even during the two-year grace period from 1740 to 1742, Iroquois war parties raided the southern Indians. In 1743, Governor Clarke of New York wrote the Virginia governor that "the sachems [of the Six Nations] . . . endeavor all they can to restrain their youth from these excursions, but it is next to impossible." Norton attributed the resumption of hostilities after the truce to "the Evil Passions and consequent Machinations of some Individuals." According to Norton, the Cherokee son of a Seneca captive of the Cherokees organized an attack on a group of friendly Iroquois warriors who had been visiting in the Cherokee country.[26] In the fifteen years following the truce, Cherokee killed Iroquois and Iroquois killed Cherokee. In July 1751, for example, a Cherokee war party killed two young Iroquois warriors, and in 1752, Cherokees claimed at least eighteen Iroquois lives. The Iroquois, of course, retaliated. In July 1754, Ludovic Grant reported two attacks by the Iroquois and stated that the overhill towns had been particularly hard hit by these incursions.[27]

The presence of both friendly and hostile parties from the Six Nations in the Cherokee country caused problems for the Cherokees, who — like the Catawbas in the 1750s — could not easily determine the identity or intent of strangers. In 1755, for example, Grant reported that forty Iroquois had arrived at Chota. At first, the Cherokees were determined to kill the intruders, but they ultimately decided that they were friends. The Iroquois then objected to the presence of some Shawnees, whom they called "great Rogues and Liars." Grant agreed with this appraisal of the Shawnees, but he was inclined to apply it to the Iroquois as well: "Though they come into this Nation as Friends to these People, [they] seldom or never go Home without some of these Cherokee Scalps."[28]

The fact that Shawnees — French allies and traditional Cherokee enemies — were openly living in Cherokee towns in 1755 raises a new problem. At least some Cherokees seem to have been welcoming the overtures of the French. As early as 1754, one group of Cherokees returned French prisoners and requested a peace, and in 1756 a Frenchman who claimed to be a slave of Old Hop, the headman, was living at Chota and promoting French interests. In December of that year, it was reported that the French had made peace with the Cherokees "at a great expense in Presents," because they thought such an alliance was advantageous to Louisiana.

The Cherokees were not alone in their ambivalence. The following spring a few Cherokees accompanied a small group of Onondagas and Cayugas to Canada, an embassy which greatly encouraged the French.[29] Ironically, the British policy of promoting a Cherokee-Iroquois alliance may have been partly responsible for this Cherokee realignment: it introduced Cherokees not only to the pro-British Mohawks but also to other Iroquois nations less under the sway of the British.

Despite these reports from Cherokee country, the British did not believe that their old alliance was in jeopardy, in part because the Cherokees continued to pledge their loyalty to Britain. With Cherokee approval and even encouragement, in the 1750s the British built Fort Prince George among the lower towns and Fort Loudoun west of the mountains. These forts promoted the British interest and protected Cherokee towns when the warriors were off fighting French allies in the Ohio Valley. The friendship was not to last, however. A series of incidents along the frontier beginning with a 1756 attack by Virginians on an allied Cherokee war party and culminating four years later with the massacre of Cherokees held hostage by South Carolina led to war against the British. Although Cherokees captured Fort Loudoun and repulsed one invading army, the British defeated them, destroying fifteen towns and 1400 acres of crops.[30]

The Iroquois took advantage of the breach in British-Cherokee relations to revive openly their old enmity with the Cherokees. William

Johnson sent warriors against the Cherokees as early as 1760, and by the time Cherokees made peace with the British a year later, Iroquois war parties were common in Cherokee country. The Cherokees, weakened by invasion and by another epidemic, could hardly protect themselves, much less retaliate.[31] When raids increased in 1763, the Iroquois blamed Cherokees for the escalation. Seneca warriors supposedly had visited the Cherokees in 1763 "with an Intention to renew and brighten the Chain of friendship." According to the Iroquois, after the delegation concluded its negotiations and headed home, Cherokees attacked the delegates, and "we returned the Blow — Since which we cant enter their settlement, they meeting us abroad as Enemies."[32]

The Iroquois may well have blamed the Cherokees for what was actually an assault by Virginians. But whoever began the war, Cherokees clearly suffered most. General Thomas Gage reported that they "were much harassed by the Northern Indians, and desire our Mediation to Negotiate a Peace." John Stuart, the southern superintendent of Indian affairs, believed that peace was advantageous not only to Cherokees but also to British colonists. He wrote William Johnson in 1766: "The Cherokees by their Sufferings in their War with us, and perpetual Incursions of the Northern Tribes are much reduced, and at this time do not exceed two thirds the Number they consisted of about ten Years ago." Because this depopulation threatened to tip the balance of power among southern Indians in the direction of the "insolent" Creeks, Stuart urged that the Cherokees be spared further suffering.[33]

Virginians were particularly concerned about continuing warfare, and they complained that Iroquois heading toward Cherokee country frequently attacked frontiersmen. The Iroquois, arguing that colonists had settled near the Warriors' Path in western Virginia, urged the governor to clear the way. The problem was not resolved, and colonists and warriors became involved in a series of skirmishes. In 1763, Indians complained to Johnson that not only had the English attacked a Cayuga war party but returning Seneca warriors had lost two Cherokee prisoners and four scalps to Virginians. Johnson explained the problem to the Board of Trade: "The Inhabitants will be imprudent, the Indians impertinent, the latter think they have a just right to carry on a War against their Antient Enemy's, . . . the former having a confirmed hatred for all Indians are glad of every opportunity that offers for insulting their small war parties, . . . and when any insult is offered there are always indiscreet Indians who will readily retaliate fourfold." Unhappy with the disruption along the frontier and flooded by Cherokee requests for peace, Whitehall recommended mediation.[34]

Johnson, however, opposed peace, and other colonial officials agreed with him. Since the British had eliminated the French threat, they no longer feared a Franco-Indian alliance. Indian wars now could be regarded as nothing more sinister than disputes between "ancient enemies." In fact, Johnson believed that the Cherokee-Iroquois war, like the conflict once again raging between Catawbas and Iroquois, would prove beneficial to the British colonies. For one thing, any attempt to dissuade the Iroquois from raiding the Cherokees jeopardized British relations with them, because the two peoples, Johnson wrote, "have been a long time such implacable Enemys that any words we might make use of on that head might tend to inflame their Jealousy, and create suspicions which they are already to[o] apt to entertain concerning us." For another, Johnson believed that the war kept "many Turbulent Spirits particularly to the Nor[th]ward employed," and that an increase in native casualties was in Britain's interest. In other words, Johnson considered this warfare so debilitating to both nations that they could not effectively challenge British power. Now that the French had been defeated, the British could permit the Indians to destroy each other.[35]

Johnson finally gave in to pressure from colonial governments and to orders from the Board of Trade. In 1766 he approached the Six Nations about a peace. The Iroquois agreed to negotiate, but only if the Cherokees would "Submit themselves and their Country to their mercy, wh[ich]," Johnson concluded, "I don't apprehend they will yet readily do." The Cherokees, however, wanted peace desperately, and they made plans to send a delegation north. Fearing attack if they took an overland route, a delegation of eight Cherokees, including the Anglophile Attakullakulla and Oconostota, the Great Warrior who had led the struggle against the British in 1760, sailed for New York in November 1767. After their arrival, the delegation stayed in the city long enough to attend a performance of *Richard III* before reaching Johnson Hall in late December. The representatives of the Six Nations did not assemble until March.[36]

When the conference finally began, Oconostota addressed the delegates. He reminded the Iroquois of the wampum belt that had been kept safely at Chota, and then presented belts from the Cherokees to each of the Six Nations. He also conveyed a belt to them from Cherokee boys, who wished only "to venture out to hunt Birds and Rabbits without risk of being carried away or killed." Next came a belt from the Cherokee women to Iroquois women, because "it is they who undergo the pains of Childbirth and produce Men, Surely they must feel Mothers pains for those killed in War, and be desirous to prevent it." After the Iroquois spokesman reprimanded the Cherokees for their failure to live up to earlier agreements, the Six Nations accepted a treaty of peace, friendship, and alliance with the Cherokees, "having buryed the Axe and opened the Road."[37]

The new alliance was soon put to the test. In the fall of 1768, the Cherokees and the Six Nations agreed to land cessions intended to revise the Proclamation Line of 1763, which had divided Indian territory from lands open to British settlement and prohibited colonists from moving west of the line. Sir William Johnson, however, violated his instructions and negotiated a cession with the Six Nations at Fort Stanwix that included land also claimed by the Cherokees. In the end, the crisis was resolved in 1770 when Stuart and the Cherokees agreed to a compromise line.[38]

The land controversy probably did not disrupt the alliance, because neither Cherokees nor Iroquois had much use for the land in question, which lay between the Kanawha and the Holston rivers. It was the Shawnees and Delawares south of the Ohio River, not the Cherokees or the Iroquois, who suffered most from the Treaty of Fort Stanwix. Delegations from these unhappy nations visited Cherokee towns to try to stir up opposition to the treaty, but the Cherokees, according to Johnson, were "temporizing with the Shawanese till the sense of the 6 Nations was obtained." The invasions of the Cherokee War, the long conflict with the Iroquois, famine, disease — all had severely weakened the Cherokees, and they did not want to risk another war with the Six Nations. What the Cherokees really wanted was an alliance with the Iroquois and joint war parties against western nations, including the Choctaws and the Indians living along the Wabash River.[39]

A Cherokee delegation traveled north in the spring of 1770 to affirm the alliance with the Six Nations and to request a congress with all northern Indian nations. In July, Johnson met at German Flats with well over two thousand Indians representing Cherokees, the Six Nations, Canadian Indians, and "Dependent Tribes." The purpose of the conference, at least as far as the Cherokees were concerned, was to organize raids on western Indians. An Oneida headman acknowledged the purpose of the Cherokee visit and commented that his people also had "received several insults" from western nations. Nevertheless, the sachems of the Six Nations concluded that war with the Cherokees' western enemies was inadvisable. The sachems may have been taking their cue from William Johnson, who opposed this particular native war. He had been in a position to profit from the Cherokee-Iroquois war, since their land was coveted by his speculator associates, but the lands of western Indians were of little value at the moment. At the conference, Johnson and the Iroquois sachems prevailed. The Six Nations decided to live in peace not only with the Cherokees but also with nations to the west. The Cherokees, whose western ventures were probably contingent on Iroquois support, publicly accepted the sachems' decision and reaffirmed their alliance with the Iroquois.

Dissent existed, however, and its source boded ill for the peace to which all parties present officially had agreed. When their turn came to speak at the great conference of 1770, Iroquois warriors expressed their unhappiness with the sachems' call for peace: "We are not well pleased with our Sachems for neglecting to acquaint us with what they purposed to say this morning, and for not giving you our particular thanks for calling, and meeting us this day, as the occasion of this assembly is principally on *our* accounts, upon a matter in which *we* as Warriors are particularly interested. And, they well know it, for, *there* are the men (pointing to the Cherokee chiefs) whose business they all know is Chiefly to us warriors, to invite us to engage their troublesome neighbours with whose conduct we are likewise much dissatisfied."[40]

The result of this dissent provides an interesting parallel to what had happened to earlier Cherokee-Iroquois alliances. Under British auspices, the Iroquois officially had been at peace with the Cherokees, but beyond British control the two peoples had carried on the war. Now they officially were at peace with each other and with Cherokee enemies in a truce encouraged by the British and proclaimed by the Iroquois sachems. But within months of the conference, Johnson reported that he had met a war party of Senecas and Cayugas that had gone south to attack the Choctaws and returned with four scalps given them by Cherokees. The Choctaws do not seem to have been merely isolated victims of Cherokee-Iroquois ire. General Gage observed that the Iroquois now attacked not the Cherokees "but any Nation they [the Cherokees] should desire them to strike." Gage pointed out the problems created by the presence of Iroquois warriors in Cherokee villages: "I believe the Alliance the Cherokees have made with the Northern Nations, has rendered them more insolent towards their Neighbours, than they used to be, for I have heard of their killing Some Creeks, and also falling on a Party of Chickasaws, which was likely to draw them into Quarrells."[41]

The Cherokee chiefs and Iroquois sachems apparently had made a British-sanctioned peace that had about as much validity or effect as Cuming's coronation of Moytoy in 1730. In part, this was because "Cherokee" and "Iroquois" implied a unity that did not exist: the terms had more meaning for British Indian policymakers than they did for native peoples. The Iroquoian nations that formed the Confederacy sometimes pursued a common course, but at other times (as the American Revolution would demonstrate) they went their separate ways. The Cherokees had an even less centralized government and no concept of delegated or coercive political power until very late in the eighteenth century. The Iroquois certainly understood this, even if the British did not. In 1756, an Iroquois spokesman told the southern superintendent, Edmond Atkin, that "the Seven Towns living on the North[west] side of the Mountains are also our friends — the lowest three [overhill] towns are in the French Interest."[42]

The Cherokee-Iroquois councils reveal another division within native societies, this one between chiefs or sachems and warriors. Iroquois warriors, for example, dissented from the decision the sachems made in 1770: the sachems proclaimed peace, the warriors went to war. Reflecting a similar division, the Cherokee warriors who visited the Iroquois in 1757 had respect for but no interest in ritual. Peace was the primary business of chiefs and sachems; when the British wanted peace, they sought alliances from these people. War, on the other hand, was the business of warriors, who sometimes pursued their occupation in violation of truces negotiated by headmen.

This division may have provided native people with a pragmatic solution to a vexing problem. British economic and military might, particularly after the Seven Years' War, could not be ignored. Both Cherokees and Iroquois, however, had a religious and social obligation to retaliate against those responsible for the deaths of kinsmen. In fact, as James H. Merrell has already pointed out, the desire to avenge "crying blood" was a primary motivation for war in the eighteenth century. When the chiefs and sachems negotiated a truce, they appeased the British; when warriors killed the enemy, they satisfied the need for vengeance.[43]

Divergent courses of action were also inevitable because no leader could effectively control the activities of his people. There was no centralized government, no police force, and no judicial system. Governed primarily by a communitarian ethic that placed the good of the group foremost, individuals sometimes differed over exactly how to promote the general welfare. Thus a delegation of Cayugas, Onondagas, and Cherokees could visit French Canada in 1757, while most Cherokees and Iroquois favored the English. Thus some Cherokees considered the Six Nations their "Eldest Brothers," others regarded the Iroquois as the enemy, and no one could force adherence to either position. Unanimity among Indians existed primarily in the objectives, the desires, and the minds of Europeans.

For that reason, European policymakers were often astounded and perturbed when chiefs made agreements that individual Indians ignored.

Colonial ignorance was not bliss, it was dangerous: if, for example, the British had heeded the lesson taught by persistent warfare between Cherokees and Iroquois in violation of the truce of 1741, they might not have been so surprised when Cherokee war parties raided the colonial frontier in the late 1750s even as Cherokee chiefs tried to negotiate a peace with colonists. But the lesson was lost on colonial pupils. In this, as in many other cases, the British had far less power over their Indian allies than they liked to believe. At the same time, native peoples probably had more control over their foreign relations than the British realized. Headmen could make treaties; implementation, however, rested with the people. Both peace and war could characterize relations between the Cherokees and the Iroquois in the eighteenth century because of the nature of native politics. Rather than reflecting a weakness in political organization, the coexistence of peace and war may well indicate strength and flexibility. It enabled Cherokees and Iroquois to adopt a formal posture that appeased the British while simultaneously pursuing a different course that satisfied the internal needs of their societies.

9

"AS the WIND SCATTERS the SMOKE"

The Tuscaroras in the Eighteenth Century

DOUGLAS W. BOYCE

IN THE FALL of 1752 Bishop August Spangenberg and other Moravians visited the Tuscarora Indian reservation in Bertie County, North Carolina, hoping to procure land rights should the few hundred Indians still there decide to leave. The Moravians were encouraged by the fact that so many Tuscaroras had grown dissatisfied with reservation life and had gone north to join the Iroquois, while "others are scattered as the wind scatters the smoke." Those remaining live "in great poverty," Spangenberg wrote, "and are oppressed by the whites."[1]

The winds of change battered the Tuscaroras repeatedly during the colonial era. As smoke settles in valleys somewhat sheltered from the wind, so groups of eighteenth-century Tuscaroras sought security and a better life in a number of locations from the Carolinas and Virginia to Pennsylvania, New York, and Canada. Throughout the colonial period the loyalties of the Tuscaroras shifted dramatically as they encountered different peoples and places. The Five Nations of the Iroquois played major but often unpredictable roles in Tuscarora efforts to deal with the winds of change. Sometimes they were foes, at other times friends. This essay attempts to make sense of the complex character of Tuscarora-Iroquois relations. After following the Iroquois south to examine their early contacts with Tuscaroras, it goes on to suggest how Iroquois sponsorship and ultimate adoption provided new opportunities—and new challenges—for those Tuscaroras who became the sixth nation of the Iroquois Confederacy.

When first encountered by English settlers, Tuscaroras occupied the northern half of the inner coastal plain of what is now North Carolina. While the Tuscaroras and the Five Nations are both Iroquoian-speaking peoples, the two had lived apart for over 2,000 years,[2] and archaeologists working in eastern North Carolina have verified a long period of *in situ* development for the Tuscaroras.[3] As many as 25,000 Tuscaroras may have lived there before the arrival of the first European explorers during the sixteenth century. By 1700, more than a century of new diseases, disrupted communities, slave raiding, fertility decline, and other factors had reduced Tuscaroras to some 5,000 people living in fifteen villages.[4]

European observers commonly lumped all of these towns together, but Tuscarora life was highly localized. Their scattered horticultural farmsteads and small village centers were linked more by a shared ethnic affiliation than by any cohesive political structures. Village autonomy with transient alliances for mutual assistance was the rule. Within each community the social organization was egalitarian. A few European accounts and some variation in grave goods found in late prehistoric burials suggest status differentiation beyond age and sex. But there is no clear evidence for anything resembling a stratified chiefdom akin to nearby societies to the north and south.[5]

Although the Tuscaroras must have heard about the sixteenth-century explorations of the Spanish and English to their north, east, west, and south, regular contacts with Europeans did not begin until fifty years after the English settled Jamestown. Excursions of explorers and traders from Virginia were followed in the late 1650s by permanent colonial settlements on the northeastern edge of Tuscarora territories. The two peoples were soon so heavily engaged in trade that in 1670 a Virginia explorer described Katearas, a Tuscarora village, as "a place of great Indian trade and commerce."[6] A decade later Tuscaroras were journeying as far north as a fort on the Rappahannock River near modern Fredericksburg to trade.[7] These ventures were so successful that in 1691 a Virginia colonist reported that European goods were abundant in many Tuscarora settlements.[8] At the same time, however, relations between Virginia and Tuscarora communities were characterized by mutual distrust. Colonists complained that Tuscaroras were hunting on patented lands, native leaders countered by charging that colonists were selling Tuscaroras into slavery, and there were occasional kidnappings or killings by both sides.[9]

The character of relations between the Tuscaroras and the Five Nations during these years is much harder to uncover. Any assumption about ethnic or linguistic kinship providing an inevitable cooperative bond must be laid aside,[10] for in the later seventeenth century Iroquois raiding parties to the south included some of the Tuscaroras as targets. The origins of this conflict, like the opening salvos of all of the southern wars of the Iroquois, are shrouded in obscurity. The northernmost or Upper Tuscaroras, who dominated the trade with Virginia, were not bound by any treaties with the colony, but they did befriend some of Virginia's tributary Indians. It was this association that probably brought them into conflict with the Iroquois. The catalyst was the Susquehannocks, whose turbulent relationship with colonists and with the Five Nations has been chronicled elsewhere in this volume.[11] Beaten by Virginians, Marylanders, and various piedmont Indians during the mid-1670s, most of the surviving Susquehannocks returned north, where they settled their differences with the Five Nations.[12] Meanwhile Virginia officials granted these piedmont groups tributary status.[13]

It seems likely that Tuscaroras entered this confusing picture because angry Susquehannocks considered them guilty by association. These Susquehannocks, probably with French assistance, convinced some Iroquois warriors to help them gain revenge against Virginia and its tributary Indians. In the last quarter of the seventeenth century attacks and rumors of raids by northern Indians in the backcountry were common, and at some point Tuscaroras also became targets. In July 1703 an Iroquois raiding party killed five Nottoways, captured their headman, and informed colonial officials that they were "in search of the Tuscarora Indians."[14] A year later the Nottoways, along with representatives from five other tributary peoples, asked Virginia authorities for permission to "go north to conclude a Peace with the Senecas" and to allow two Tuscarora men to go "for the same Purpose."[15] If Tuscarora ambassadors went along, they failed to end the fighting; Susquehannock and Seneca attacks did not cease.[16] North Carolina's Surveyor General John Lawson, the expert on native societies in the colony, noted in 1709 that the Iroquois were "mortal Enemies to all our Indians, and very often take them captives, or kill them."[17] "If you go to persuade them to live peaceably with the *Tuskeruros*," Lawson continued, "they will answer you, that they cannot live without War."[18]

Apparently desperate, Tuscarora representatives traveled to Conestoga in June 1710 to ask for peace with the Susquehannocks and the Five Nations and friendship with the people of Pennsylvania.[19] At a conference with colonial officials and representatives from the Five Nations, Delawares, Shawnees, and Susquehannocks a month later, an Onondaga spokesman stated that since a "peace between the Tuscarores and them being now in agitation, None of the Young people here Should Warr against that Nation."[20] The resolution of these hostilities was at best partial; a year later the Susquehannocks remained at war with the Tuscaroras.[21]

Disruptive as hostilities with the Susquehannocks and Iroquois might be, the challenge posed by colonial expansion in North Carolina was an even greater threat to Tuscarora existence. In contrast to the Upper Tuscaroras, the southern or lower villages had the worst of both worlds: they benefited only indirectly from trade with Virginia, and they suffered directly from the growth of colonial settlements. North Carolina did virtually nothing to regulate relations with Indians, and the exploitation of these Tuscaroras and their Indian neighbors became intolerable.[22]

At last these abuses were too much to bear, and in September 1711 the Lower Tuscaroras joined with several smaller groups in the region to launch a coordinated attack on North Carolina's English settlements. Almost immediately, Upper Tuscarora villages insisted that they were not involved, and to back up their words they agreed to help the colonial governments subdue the hostile Indians. Unfortunately, colonists failed to distinguish friendly from unfriendly Tuscaroras. In January 1712, John Barnwell led an army of Indians and colonists from South Carolina on a rampage through the region, plundering and burning both Lower and Upper Tuscarora villages. A year later James Moore followed in his path. Together the two expeditions killed or enslaved over one thousand Tuscaroras, and the rest fled to isolated piedmont areas of North Carolina and Virginia.[23]

The Five Nations may have had a hand in both the outbreak of war and the return of peace. Contemporary observers were convinced that the Five Nations, or at least some elements of them, encouraged the Lower Tuscaroras to attack the colony and promised help. Barnwell captured several Lower Tuscaroras who admitted that "12 Senecas came and made peace with them, and told them that the Whites had imposed upon them. . . . [T]hat they [the Tuscaroras] did not fear the want of ammunition for that, they would come twice a year and furnish them with it."[24] Virginia's Lieutenant Governor Alexander Spotswood also claimed that the Five Nations were involved, in part because one of their men had been killed while hunting in his colony; according to New York's Governor Robert Hunter, the French had incited the Five Nations to help the Tuscaroras.[25] If the Iroquois were indeed helping to stir up trouble for the English, they soon turned around. By July 1712, they agreed to do what they could to restore peace in North Carolina. Late in December, colonial militia captured seven Tuscaroras—and a peace envoy from the Five Nations. When he discovered the envoy's identity and mission, North Carolina's Governor Thomas Pollock freed the captives.[26]

The Iroquois role in making both war and peace is by no means easy to explain. Perhaps there was a shift in strategy from before to after the war. Perhaps the peace emissary represented the official Five Nations response and the warriors were unsanctioned. Perhaps the Iroquois, or some segment of them, collaborated with the Lower Tuscaroras while tensions with the Upper Tuscaroras continued. Whatever transpired, the Five Nations seem to have realized, in the final analysis, the importance of attracting additional friendly peoples to help maintain their own position in the Northeast. As a French official wrote in September 1715, the Five Nations "have never appeared so haughty as they are at present for they have been strengthened by the accession of a nation . . . who were settled near Carolina and took refuge among them."[27]

Some 1,500 or 2,000 of the Lower Tuscaroras who fought the English managed to avoid death or captivity and fled north to accept an invitation to enter the Longhouse of the Five Nations.[28] As early as June 1713, the New York Commissioners of Indian Affairs either guessed the Five Nations' plans or received intelligence that the Tuscaroras had been invited north. They told the Iroquois that "not upon any pretence whatsoever" should they "receive any of the Tuscaroras amongst them nor permitt them to settle with them."[29] The Iroquois paid no heed: on September 10, 1713, Governor Hunter wrote that the Five Nations could not be dissuaded from receiving the Tuscaroras.[30] Ten days later a Longhouse orator began to break down colonial opposition to the Tuscaroras with an emotional plea on their behalf.

> These Indians went out heretofore from us, and have settled themselves there; now they have got into war, and are dispersed and have abandoned their Castles. But have compassion on them. The English have got the upper hand of them; they have abandoned their Castles and are scattered hither and thither. . . . [W]e request our Brother Corlear to act as mediator between the English of Carrelyna and the tuskaroras, that they may be no longer hunted down, and we assure that we will oblige them not to do the English anymore harm; for they are no longer a Nation with a name, being once dispersed.[31]

The Five Nations played heavily on their linguistic affinity with the Tuscaroras in convincing colonists to allow their "kinsmen" to "return home." The Five Nations' speaker also touched on a sore spot in their relations with New York on the matter of the Tuscaroras. In July 1712, the Iroquois had asked that New York officials be sent to mediate between the Tuscaroras and the North Carolina government.[32] The New York Commissioners refused even to entertain the request, thereby angering the Five Nations' delegation. The allusion to this in the speech above seems to hint that the Iroquois believed New York must bear some of the blame for the continuation of hostilities. Whatever the case, on September 25, 1714, when the Five Nations informed colonists "that the Tuscarore Indians are come to shelter themselves among" us, New York officials made no objections.[33]

The pace of Tuscarora emigration northward through Virginia must have been slow, so that children and old people could rest and find food. Once in Iroquoia, the Tuscaroras' steps slowed still more and even stopped altogether for a season or a year. Some emigrants may have settled briefly in what came to be called the Tuscarora Valley on the Juniata River in Pennsylvania. In 1713 these or others halted two miles west of what is now Tamaqua, Pennsylvania, where (according to tradition) they erected a village and set out apple trees, only to move on again after two years.[34] Eventually the refugees established themselves closer to the heart of the Five Nations. Oquaga, an important Five Nations village on the Susquehanna River, received many Tuscarora remnants. Gideon Hawley, a missionary to the diverse Indian peoples living there during the 1750s, found two Tuscarora villages in the vicinity, including some of the "first settlers" who had arrived years before from Carolina.[35] Other emigrants went still farther into the center of the Longhouse. A September 1714 remark by the Five Nations that the Tuscaroras were "among" them may indicate that some emigrants had already reached one of their later-known villages near or with the Oneidas.[36]

The only information about those Tuscaroras who joined the Five Nations from 1713 to 1722 comes from the chronicles of the Society for the Propagation of the Gospel in Foreign Parts. Early in 1716 the Society's missionary to the Mohawks, William Andrews, was warned by his interpreter not to go to Onondaga because he would have to pass through the country of the Tuscaroras, who were said to be cannibals harboring a deep hatred of colonists.[37] The Tuscaroras were also blamed for stirring up the Oneidas and Mohawks against Andrews's endeavors. Certainly the new arrivals had little use for the missionary's message. When they passed his mission at Queen Anne's Fort on their way to trade at Albany, they mocked "at Mr. Andrews when he would offer to talk to them about Religion; and when he proffered to go to their Abode, they absolutely forbad him."[38] The Tuscarora hostility is understandable, but it also helps explain why there is so little in the colonial records about them.

The Tuscarora emigrants had cast their lot with a Confederacy that attempted to play the French and English against one another during the first half of the eighteenth century. The occasional successes of this policy resulted in the Five Nations receiving economic and political concessions from each of the European powers courting them. The balance of power could be maintained by the Iroquois only if they could seriously threaten military action or convincingly promise military assistance. It was perhaps the need for more warriors that led the Five Nations to welcome the Tuscaroras and other peoples. Despite their added strength, and despite all of their threats and promises, the Iroquois were often incapable of concerted action, for localism remained a powerful force working against Confederacy unity. Thus the traditional Tuscarora pattern of village autonomy tempered by multi-ethnic alliances had its parallel in the affairs of the Longhouse, and before long the scattered Tuscarora towns in Iroquoia had fitted themselves readily into a political culture somewhat akin to what they had known in North Carolina.[39]

The environmental setting of the Iroquois Confederacy both mirrored and contributed to the tendency toward Tuscarora autonomy. News traveled quickly along the trails among Iroquois villages in the heartland, which were spread out roughly on an east-west axis with no significant obstacles to travel. But to reach the villages on the Susquehanna River meant traveling through the hilly country of the hunting territory lying between (and shared by) the Oneida and Tuscarora settlement areas at Oneida Lake and Oquaga. For the most part this area was rugged and lacked villages where the traveler could conveniently find shelter and food. Poor communication due to traveling conditions and distance to Onondaga made it difficult for the Tuscaroras and Oneidas at Oquaga to participate in League affairs. The people of the Susquehanna were also remote from other Six Nations settlements in political and religious affinities.

Distance was reflected in attitudes toward competing European powers. During the 1740s and 1750s, the Oneidas and Tuscaroras living in and around Oquaga were decidedly more anti-French and pro-English than most of their counterparts in the Oneida Lake area.[40] One exception might be the Onondaga-Tuscarora community of Ganasaraga. Located on the western edge of the Tuscarora settlements on the trail from Oneida to Onondaga, the people of Ganasaraga more consistently identified themselves with English concerns.[41] The presence of William Printup, an agent and smith who was also married to a Tuscarora (or possibly Onondaga) woman, probably helped encourage this orientation.[42] Other Tuscaroras in the region either tried very hard to be neutral or leaned toward the French.

Friendlier with the English, the Tuscaroras and Oneidas at Oquaga were also more open to the work and message of Protestant missionaries. Community leaders supported Gideon Hawley and Rebecca and Benjamin Ashley after their arrival in 1753. Direct efforts by Protestants to evangelize the Iroquois in the Oneida Lake area came in 1761. The well-known missionary Samuel Kirkland began his work there in 1766, but Tuscarora interest in Christianity emerged more slowly and was never as wholehearted as at Oquaga.[43]

Emerging from such geographical and ideological differences were clear indications of unequal participation in the affairs of the Confederacy. The Tuscaroras at Oquaga were less involved in the life of the Confederacy than those near Oneida Lake. At times they simply refused to attend council meetings at Onondaga; they also were known to ignore Confederacy decisions that related to them.[44] These diverse relationships would have profound importance during the Revolutionary War. The Tuscarora settlements at Oquaga remained loyal to the king and were destroyed by American troops in 1778 and 1779. When neutrality became impossible, the Tuscaroras at Ganasaraga joined the British. On the other hand, Tuscaroras in the Oneida Lake area who had been influenced by Samuel Kirkland tended to cast their lot with the rebellious colonists.[45]

This emphasis on local diversity must not obscure the fact that the Tuscarora emigrants became part of a larger sociopolitical entity. The process by which they were integrated into the Longhouse and their place in that organization remain open to debate. It is generally agreed that those who came north were adopted by the Five Nations around 1722–23 and granted some standing as the sixth nation of the Confederacy.[46] But there is a wide range of opinion about how this adoption took place and what it meant in terms of Tuscarora rights and responsibilities. Perhaps taking their cue from the 1713 Iroquois claim that the Tuscaroras were "no longer a Nation with a name, being once dispersed," some have suggested that the Tuscaroras had a "secondary rank" within the Confederacy, that theirs was a "dependent, child-like status as a relatively powerless, denigrated member of the Iroquois League."[47] A focus on structural distinctions and a static understanding of adoptive status makes such a characterization seem reasonable, for the sachem titles of the Roll Call of the founders were not expanded to include Tuscarora leaders. A nineteenth-century version of the Constitution of the Iroquois League stipulates that

> When any alien nation or individual is admitted into the Five Nations the admission shall be understood only to be a temporary one. . . . No body of alien people who have been adopted temporarily shall have a vote in the council of the Lords of the Confederacy for only they who have been invested with the Lordship titles may vote in the council. Aliens have nothing by blood to make claim to a vote and should they have it, not knowing all the traditions of the Confederacy, might go against its Great Peace. In this manner the Great Peace would be endangered and perhaps destroyed.[48]

These words may reflect concerns that emerged relatively late, after Oneidas reclaimed Tuscarora lands following the American Revolution. In fact, the principles expressed here can also be used to provide support for a different interpretation of Tuscarora participation in the Iroquois Confederacy. It may be inferred that a formerly alien people who have been permanently adopted will be granted fuller rights after they learn and practice the traditions of the Confederacy. Eighty years ago J. N. B. Hewitt claimed that Iroquois adoption of the Tuscaroras involved a process of status changes contingent on their behavior and socialization during successive probationary periods. Hewitt's own Tuscarora family ties might lead some to suspect his objectivity.[49] There is, however, independent evidence that seems to support his processual model. A statement made to the Oneidas in 1753 suggests that the Tuscaroras started as a "nursling still swathed to the cradle-board . . . and hastily [became] a peer, having the right of chiefship in the council on an equal footing with the chiefs of the other tribes."[50] Oral tradition concerning the adoption of another native group from the south, the Tutelos, implies "equal rights" with the Cayugas as council members, rights that were contingent on obeying the "laws of the Six Nations."[51] In 1880, Horatio Hale found references in old Onondaga manuscripts that term the Tuscaroras an added "frame-pole to the great framework" of the Confederacy. A frame-pole of a longhouse was, of course, an "inner one, which is bent to form the frame."[52] Both the socialization of the Tuscaroras and their full incorporation are clearly implied.

A wide range of mid-eighteenth-century references supports this thesis. There are repeated statements identifying the Tuscaroras as a part of the "younger brothers" side or moiety of the Confederacy (with the Oneidas and Cayugas).[53] Sir William Johnson reported in 1763 that the Tuscaroras "now enjoy all privileges with the rest" of the members of the Confederacy.[54] The Tuscaroras at times corrected the Oneidas for what they perceived as inappropriate behavior,[55] and on various occasions the Oneidas asked the Tuscaroras for advice before making political decisions.[56] There were even times when the Tuscaroras "entirely refused" Oneida recommendations.[57] Tuscaroras were also involved in various rituals that lay at the heart of Confederacy life. These included institutional patterns shared by all other members, such as the condolence ceremony and the raising up of new chiefs, adoption of war captives, participation in general councils, and signing land cessions.[58] Even their divided loyalties between France, England, and the rebellious colonists paralleled those of the other Confederacy members.

This is not to deny the existence of differences between the Tuscaroras and the other members of the Confederacy or the variations already noted among Tuscarora communities. These individual histories, cultures, and subcultures were important, and the Tuscaroras were not an original member of the Great League of Peace. Nonetheless, it is strange that scholars sensitive to social and cultural change often talk about the Tuscarora adoptive position in static rather than dynamic terms. In doing so they have imposed a weak, childlike status on the Tuscaroras for all time, when the historical evidence seems to fit Hewitt's processual emphasis far better. Just because the Tuscarora communities in New York after the Revolutionary War were once again virtually landless and powerless, it is a serious mistake to assign them that status for their entire existence in the Iroquois Longhouse.

　　　　While those Tuscaroras who migrated north under the sponsorship of the Five Nations were settling into their new homes, those remaining in the Carolinas and Virginia found themselves in very different — and very difficult — circumstances. Most still in the south were from the upper villages that had benefited from trade with Virginia and had generally remained loyal to the colonists during the war with North Carolina. In spite of the loyalty of these Tuscaroras, the "seek and destroy" operations of South Carolina's forces had driven them into the piedmont looking for safety. Out of these refugees a village headman named Tom Blount emerged as a leader, with colonial help. Provincial officials wanted to control the scattered remaining Tuscaroras; Blount identified closely with the Anglo-Americans and apparently was eager to expand his influence among the Indians. From these mutual needs arose a marriage of convenience, as Blount cooperated with the English in a way that subverted traditional village autonomy. In May 1713, North Carolina Governor Pollock concluded a peace treaty with several Upper Tuscarora villages that had important consequences for all of the Tuscarora people who remained. Under the terms of this agreement, Pollock and Virginia Governor Spotswood recognized Tom Blount as the sole representative of the Tuscaroras; only those Tuscaroras who submitted to Blount's authority would be considered friendly to the colonial governments. Furthermore, Blount had to help round up enemy Indians, deliver all of the Tuscaroras now passing as peaceful who had played any part in the war against the colonies, and use his own men as frontier guards against the incursion of other Indians hostile to North Carolina.[59] Thus all Tuscaroras wishing to return to their North Carolina villages and hamlets had to discard their own village councils and chiefs and become subject to one man, the colonial government's favorite.

Throughout the summer of 1713 Tom Blount and his men brought in prisoners and, to the colonists' satisfaction, pacified much of the frontier.[60] In spite of Blount's insistence that the Upper Tuscaroras in Virginia would soon return to North Carolina to help him, it was nearly a year before they did.[61] In November 1713, Spotswood sent out a band of tributary Indians led by two traders to find these refugees and determine their intentions. Since they had abandoned their villages as much as a year earlier and had been unable to plant crops during the past spring, with winter approaching they were ready to accept almost any proposal. Spotswood's party found a grim scene. Fifteen hundred men, women, and children from five villages were

> dispers'd in small partys upon the head of Roanoake [River], and about the Mountains in very miserable condition, without any habitation or provision of Corne for their Subsistence, but living like wild beasts on what the Woods afforded, in despair whether to return to their old Settlements in North Carolina and run the risque of being knock'd in the head by the English and South Carolina Indians or to submit themselves to the Senecas, who had made them large offers of Assistance to revenge themselves on the English, upon condition of incorporating with them.[62]

Faced with a choice between the Iroquois and the English, these people chose the latter. Representatives from four villages signed a treaty with Virginia in February 1714 in which they agreed to become tributaries of the colony and settle at a designated location to serve as frontier guards. This arrangement apparently had little appeal, however, and by July most had returned to their old territories in North Carolina.[63]

Life would never be quite the same for the Tuscaroras staying in the south. They had refused to help their kinsmen during the war and had spurned the offer to incorporate with the Five Nations. Now they faced the bleak prospect of settling as a dispossessed people, serving the needs and subject to the whims of either North Carolina or Virginia. Gone were their trade advantages and their villages in North Carolina. Since they were no longer needed as border guards, their quality of life and degree of self-determination declined. By 1717 they had moved to Bertie County on the north side of the Roanoke River, an area long reserved for them as a hunting territory, and the North Carolina colonial government had secured the release of all of their other lands in the colony.

Reservation boundaries brought no respite from conflicts with colonial neighbors. Settlers often threatened Tuscaroras for hunting too near their homesteads. Traders plied them with rum and cheated them. Ferry operators either refused them passage or overcharged them. A few colonists conducted unauthorized logging operations; others drove their herds onto Tuscarora lands to graze.[64] Squatters had to be chased off the reservation in 1722, 1732, 1741, and 1757–59, but they kept coming back, defrauding Indians of the land by foreclosing on those with heavy debts. By the time the reservation was finally surveyed properly in 1803, only a small fraction of it was unclaimed by settlers.[65]

In their weakened, disorganized state, the Tuscaroras were easy prey for the continuing raids by the Catawbas and other Indians who had driven them from their homes during the war. Battered by native foes and colonial friends alike, many would simply pack up and leave. One group settled on the headwaters of the Nottoway River in 1715.[66] In the same year another band of as many as seventy headed south to help defend South Carolina against the Yamasees, and after that war most of these were given permission to settle along the coast south of Charleston.[67] The vast majority of emigrants headed toward the Iroquois, until of the twelve hundred or so Tuscaroras initially living on the reservation, only three hundred remained in 1755.[68] During the summer of 1766 about 150 more made the long trek northward,[69] leaving a mere 100 behind in Bertie County.[70]

The following February the recent arrivals told Sir William Johnson: "Although we have lived at a considerable Distance from you, which we have found by travelling it, yet your Name, and Words reached us, as though you was but close by."[71] Their speech indicates that there was regular communication between the Tuscaroras remaining in the south and their northern kinsmen. The Six Nations might have decided to ignore the Tuscaroras in North Carolina or even include them among their other southern enemies such as the Catawbas. In fact, however, the Iroquois chose to establish friendly relations with the North Carolina Tuscaroras, in part at least in order to use their reservation as a southern base of operations. As early as 1717 the Virginia Council reported that Iroquois war parties made "frequent marches to and from the Tuscaroras [and] have occasioned a vast charge and trouble to this Colony in keeping Rangers for its necessary defence."[72] The colonial records of New York, Pennsylvania, Virginia, and North Carolina contain numerous references to the movement of parties from the Six Nations to and from the Tuscarora reservation in Bertie County.[73]

Frequent contact had several consequences for the Tuscaroras remaining in North Carolina. It gave their warriors the opportunity to join larger sorties against Catawbas, Cherokees, and other mutual enemies. In addition, the regular presence of warriors from the Six Nations gave the North Carolina Tuscaroras the opportunity to blame the Six Nations for acts of hostility committed by local Tuscaroras themselves. Most important of all, ongoing contacts with the Six Nations meant that as life on the reservation became unbearable, there was a ready avenue of escape to their kinfolk in the north. Between 1723 and 1803 at least three groups of families elected to do just that.[74]

Even though the Tuscaroras among the Iroquois found themselves embroiled in the Revolutionary War, driven from their villages among the Oneidas and Onondagas, and by 1800 confined to reservations in western New York and Ontario, their circumstances were better than those of their kin in North Carolina. Their new reservations in the north were in sparsely settled frontiers that permitted substantial mobility. They were being treated as important players in the post-war reconstruction and in the ongoing tensions between the newly formed United States and England.[75] In contrast, those remaining in North Carolina had most of their reservation lands tied up in long-term leases to the neighboring settlers who pressed in around them. These Tuscaroras no longer served any desirable purposes for the dominant society, and there is some evidence that they shared in the distrust and hardships that were increasingly imposed on all "free persons of color" in the south.[76]

The eighteenth century was a period of dramatic change for most eastern North American Indian peoples, including the Tuscaroras. During the early part of the century they occupied a contiguous territory with a measure of political and economic power unrivaled by other eastern North Carolina Indians. But their lack of political cohesion, the expansion of colonial settlements, and unstable relations with other native American peoples all seriously damaged their regional standing. As their circumstances deteriorated in North Carolina, relations with the Five Nations improved. The Iroquois rescued them from defeat in 1713, and through mid-century prospects for a better life in the Longhouse seemed assured. However, the failure of the Six Nations to stand united in their relations with the French, English, and rebellious colonies proved to be disastrous. By the end of the century, Tuscarora communities could be found from the Carolinas to New York and Ontario. While uncertainty remains about the precise nature of their social roles and cultural identities, it is clear that the Tuscaroras were creative survivors. Dispersed as the wind scatters the smoke, the Tuscaroras nonetheless remained significant participants in the affairs of Indian North America.

NOTES

ABBREVIATIONS USED in the NOTES

Conn. Recs.: J. H. Turnbull and C. J. Hoadly, eds., *Public Records of the Colony of Connecticut*, 15 vols. (Hartford, Conn., 1850–90).

CRNC: William L. Saunders, ed., *The Colonial Records of North Carolina*, 10 vols. (New York, 1968 [orig. publ. 1886–90]).

CSP: W. Noel Sainsbury, et al., eds., *Calendar of State Papers, Colonial Series, America and the West Indies*, 44 vols. (London, 1860–1969).

CVSP: William P. Palmer, et al., eds., *Calendar of Virginia State Papers and Other Manuscripts . . .* , 11 vols. (Richmond, Va., 1875–93).

DRIA, 1: William L. McDowell, ed., *Documents Relating to Indian Affairs, May 21, 1750–August 7, 1754* (Columbia, S.C., 1958).

DRIA, 2: William L. McDowell, ed., *Documents Relating to Indian Affairs, 1754–1765* (Columbia, S.C., 1970).

HNAI, 15: William C. Sturtevant, gen. ed., *Handbook of North American Indians*, vol. 15: *Northeast*, ed. Bruce G. Trigger (Washington, D.C., 1978).

HSP: Historical Society of Pennsylvania, Philadelphia.

IIDH: Iroquois Indians: A Documentary History of the Diplomacy of the Six Nations and Their League, microfilm ed., 50 reels (Woodbridge, Conn., 1985).

JCHA: J. H. Easterby, et al., eds., *The Journal of the* [South Carolina] *Commons House of Assembly*, 12 vols. to date (Columbia, S.C., 1951–).

JCIT: William L. McDowell, ed., *Journals of the Commissioners of the Indian Trade, September 20, 1710–August 29, 1718* (Columbia, S.C., 1955).

JHB: H. R. McIlwaine, ed., *Journals of the House of Burgesses of Virginia*, 13 vols. (Richmond, Va., 1905–15).

Johnson Papers: James Sullivan, et al., eds., *The Papers of Sir William Johnson*, 14 vols. (Albany, 1921–65).

JR: Reuben Gold Thwaites, ed., *The Jesuit Relations and Allied Documents: Travels and Explorations of the Jesuit Missionaries in New France, 1610–1791*, 73 vols. (Cleveland, 1896–1901).

LIR: Lawrence H. Leder, ed., *The Livingston Indian Records, 1666–1723* (Gettysburg, Pa., 1956).

Mass. Recs.: Nathaniel E. Shurtleff, ed., *Records of the Governor and Company of the Massachusetts Bay in New England,* 5 vols. (Boston, 1853–54).

Md. Archives: William Hand Browne, et al., eds., *Archives of Maryland,* 72 vols. to date (Baltimore, 1883–).

MHSC: Collections of the Massachusetts Historical Society.

NYCD: E. B. O'Callaghan and B. Fernow, eds., *Documents Relative to the Colonial History of the State of New York,* 15 vols. (Albany, N.Y., 1853–87).

NYCM: New York Colonial Manuscripts, New York State Archives, Albany.

NY Council Minutes: New York Council Minutes, 1668–1783, New York State Archives, Albany.

NYDH: E. B. O'Callaghan, ed., *The Documentary History of the State of New York,* small paper ed., 4 vols. (Albany, N.Y., 1849–51).

Pa. Archives: Samuel Hazard, et al., eds., *Pennsylvania Archives,* 9 ser., 138 vols. (Philadelphia, 1852–1949).

Pa. Council Minutes: Samuel Hazard, ed., *Minutes of the Provincial Council of Pennsylvania,* 16 vols. (Harrisburg, 1838–53).

PDT: Alden T. Vaughan, ed., *Early American Indian Documents: Treaties and Laws, 1607–1789,* vol. 1: *Pennsylvania and Delaware Treaties, 1629–1737,* ed. Donald H. Kent (Washington, D.C., 1979).

Plymouth Recs.: Nathaniel B. Shurtleff and David Pulsifer, eds., *Records of New Plymouth,* 12 vols. (Boston, 1855–61).

PROSC: W. Noel Sainsbury, comp., Records in the British Public Record Office Relating to South Carolina, 1663–1782, microfilm ed., 36 vols. (Columbia, S.C., 1955).

Pynchon Papers: Carl Bridenbaugh, ed., *The Pynchon Papers,* 2 vols. (Boston, 1982–84).

R.I. Recs.: John R. Bartlett, ed., *Records of the Colony of Rhode Island and Providence Plantations in New England,* 10 vols. (Providence, 1850–65).

RSUS: Willliam S. Jenkins, comp., Records of the States of the United States, microfilm ed. (Washington, D.C., 1949).

Va. Council Jour.: H. R. McIlwaine, et al., eds., *Executive Journals of the Council of Colonial Virginia,* 6 vols. (Richmond, Va., 1925–66).

VMHB: Virginia Magazine of History and Biography.

WA: Peter Wraxall, *An Abridgement of the Indian Affairs Contained in Four Folio Volumes, Transacted in the Colony of New York, from the Year 1678 to the Year 1751,* ed. C. H. McIlwain (Cambridge, Mass., 1915).

Winthrop Papers: Allyn B. Forbes, ed., *Winthrop Papers,* 5 vols. (Boston, 1929–47).

WMQ: William and Mary Quarterly, 3d ser.

INTRODUCTION

1. *Discourse Delivered before the New-York Historical Society, At Their Anniversary Meeting, 6th December, 1811* (New York, 1812), 8–9, 23.

2. Colden, *The History of the Five Indian Nations Depending on the Province of New-York in America* (New York, 1727); Smith, *The History of the Province of New-York, from the First Discovery to the Year MDCCXXXII* (London, 1757); Morgan, *League of the Ho-dé-no-sau-nee, Iroquois* (Rochester, N.Y., 1851); Parkman, *The Jesuits in North America* (Boston, 1867); Webb, *1676: The End of American Independence* (New York, 1984).

3. The figure represents estimated population after the first wave of epidemic European diseases greatly diminished Iroquois numbers (see Chapter 1). Estimates contained in seventeenth- and eighteenth-century documents usually include only the number of warriors; nearly all the known data are tabulated in Gunther Michelson, "Iroquois Population Statistics," *Man in the Northeast*, no. 14 (Fall 1977), 3–17. Using either a 1:4 or a 1:5 ratio of warriors to total population, most post-1640 warrior counts imply a population of 10,000 or less. For the ratio see Sherburne F. Cook, "Interracial Warfare and Population Decline among the New England Indians," *Ethnohistory* 20 (1973): 13; and Henry F. Dobyns, *Their Number Become Thinned: Native American Population Dynamics in Eastern North America* (Knoxville, Tenn., 1983), 174–75.

4. "The Data and Theory of Restoration Empire," *WMQ* 43 (1986): 450.

5. Anthony F. C. Wallace, "Origins of Iroquois Neutrality: The Grand Settlement of 1701," *Pennsylvania History* 24 (1957): 223–35; Yves F. Zoltvany, "New France and the West, 1701–1713," *Canadian Historical Review* 44 (1965): 301–22; Leroy V. Eid, "The Ojibwa-Iroquois War: The War the Five Nations Did Not Win," *Ethnohistory* 26 (1979): 297–324; Richard Haan, "The Problem of Iroquois Neutrality: Suggestions for Revision," *Ethnohistory* 27 (1980): 317–30; Richard Aquila, *The Iroquois Restoration: Iroquois Diplomacy on the Colonial Frontier, 1701–1754* (Detroit, 1983), Francis Jennings, *The Ambiguous Iroquois Empire: The Covenant Chain Confederation of Indian Tribes with English Colonies from Its Beginnings to the Lancaster Treaty of 1744* (New York, 1984); Daniel K. Richter, "The Ordeal of the Longhouse: Change and Persistence on the Iroquois Frontier, 1609–1720" (Ph.D. diss., Columbia University, 1984).

6. "Rattling the Chains of the Past" (paper presented at the conference on "The 'Imperial' Iroquois," March 1984, Williamsburg, Va.), p. 1. A revised version of this piece appeared as "Francis Parkman: A Brahmin among Untouchables," *WMQ* 42 (1985): 305–28.

7. Elwood Green, quoted in Tim Johnson, "The 'Imperial' Iroquois: The Forty-Fourth Conference on Early American History," *Turtle Quarterly*, Oct. 1984, p. 5.

8. See Robert F. Berkhofer, Jr., "Native Americans and United States History," in William H. Cartwright and Richard L. Watson, Jr., eds., *The Reinterpretation of American History and Culture* (Washington, D.C., 1973), 47–49; Bruce G. Trigger, "Indian and White History: Two Worlds or One?" in Michael K. Foster, Jack Campisi, and Marianne Mithun, eds., *Extending the Rafters: Interdisciplinary Approaches to Iroquoian Studies* (Albany, N.Y., 1984), 17–33; and Bruce G. Trigger, "Ethnohistory: The Unfinished Edifice," *Ethnohistory* 33 (1986): 253–67.

9. The chapters by Boyce, McConnell, Merrell, and Perdue trace their origins to papers delivered at the Williamsburg conference. Those by Druke, Haan, Jennings, and Richter reflect their authors' own movement beyond the Covenant Chain in agreeing to write new essays quite different in focus from their contributions at Williamsburg. (Haan's conference paper was "Iroquois Mystique: The Myth and Reality of the Iroquois League," and Richter's "King William's Other War: The Covenant Chain at Home." For Jennings' paper, see n. 6, above. Druke was a session commentator, along with Richard Aquila, Barbara Graymont, and Charles Hudson.) Other contributors at Williamsburg — whose papers are excluded here not because they lack merit, but because their focus lies elsewhere than on relations

among Indians — were W. J. Eccles ("Franco-Iroquois Attitudes") and William N. Fenton ("Iroquois Political History: An Anthropological View"). Copies of all conference papers are on file at the Institute of Early American History and Culture, Williamsburg. The theme of this volume was further honed in a session at the American Society for Ethnohistory annual meeting, Chicago, November 1985, in which Haan, Jennings, McConnell, Merrell, Perdue, Richter, Salisbury, and Matthew Dennis participated.

1 — ORDEALS of the LONGHOUSE

1. Preliminary versions of this chapter were presented at a colloquium at the Institute of Early American History and Culture, Williamsburg, Va., January 1985; the Conference on Iroquois Research, Rensselaerville, N.Y., October 1985; and the Columbia University Seminar on Early American History and Culture, New York, November 1985. The author thanks Thomas Abler, Mary Druke, Sharon Mead, and William Starna for their comments.

2. On the alien environment that Native Americans faced after European contact see James H. Merrell, "The Indians' New World: The Catawba Experience," *WMQ* 41 (1984): 537-65. On the conservative-as-innovator in Iroquois culture see William N. Fenton, "The Iroquois in History," in Eleanor Burke Leacock and Nancy Oestreich Lurie, eds., *North American Indians in Historical Perspective* (New York, 1971), 129-68, esp. p. 131.

3. Hunter to Lord ?, 12 Mar. 1713, Colonial Office Papers, 5/1085, Public Record Office, London, microfilm copy in IIDH, reel 7.

4. Robert F. Berkhofer, Jr., *The White Man's Indian: Images of the American Indian from Columbus to the Present* (New York, 1978), 62-68; James Axtell, "Ethnohistory: An Historian's Viewpoint," *Ethnohistory* 26 (1979): 1-13; Bruce G. Trigger, "Indian and White History: Two Worlds or One?" in Michael K. Foster, Jack Campisi, and Marianne Mithun, eds., *Extending the Rafters: Interdisciplinary Approaches to Iroquoian Studies* (Albany, N.Y., 1984), 17-33.

5. Fred W. Voget, "Anthropological Theory and Iroquois Ethnography, 1850-1970," in Foster, et al., eds., *Extending the Rafters*, 343-57. Guides to scholarship on the Iroquois may be found in Paul L. Weinman, *A Bibliography of the Iroquoian Literature*, New York State Museum and Science Service Bulletin no. 411 (Albany, 1969); Foster, et al., eds., *Extending the Rafters;* and Francis Jennings, et. al., eds., *The History and Culture of Iroquois Diplomacy: An Interdisciplinary Guide to the Treaties of the Six Nations and Their League* (Syracuse, N.Y., 1985).

6. Morgan, *League of the Ho-dé-no-sau-nee, Iroquois* (Rochester, N.Y., 1851), 62-70. See also idem, *Ancient Society; or Researches in the Lines of Human Progress from Savagery through Barbarism to Civilization,* ed. Eleanor Burke Leacock (Cleveland, 1963), 124-54.

7. W. N. Fenton, ed., "Seneca Indians by Asher Wright (1859)," *Ethnohistory* 4 (1957): 302-21, quotation from pp. 310-11. Despite an extensive correspondence between the two men (for examples see Bernhard J. Stern, ed., "The Letters of Asher Wright to Lewis Henry Morgan," *American Anthropologist* 35 [1933]: 138-45), Morgan was apparently unaware of the document quoted here, which came to light only in the 1940s.

8. Elisabeth Tooker, "The Structure of the Iroquois League: Lewis H. Morgan's Research and Observations," *Ethnohistory* 30 (1983): 141-54; Bernhard J. Stern, *Lewis Henry Morgan: Social Evolutionist* (New York, 1931), 9-19.

9. "We engaged with ardor in the work of studying out the structure and principles of the Ancient League by which they had been united for so many centuries," Morgan later recalled. "We wished to model our organization upon this and to reproduce it with as much fidelity as the nature and objects of our order would permit. This desire on our part, led to the first discovery of the real structure and principles of the League of the Iroquois which up to that time were entirely unknown except in a most general sense" (quoted in Stern, *Lewis Henry Morgan*, 16). In the 1840s, of course, Morgan had not yet developed his elaborate seven-stage evolutionary hierarchy of human societies, which did not receive its full exposition until the publication of *Ancient Society* in 1871. Even at that later date, however, it seems clear that Morgan believed that the Iroquois would be essentially locked in their current evolutionary "ethnical period" until they adopted private property and experienced additional material and social revolutions (*Ancient Society*, 152; see also Morgan's *League of the Iroquois*, 454–56).

10. William N. Fenton, "The Iroquois Confederacy in the Twentieth Century: A Case Study of the Theory of Lewis H. Morgan in 'Ancient Society,'" *Ethnology* 4 (1965): 251–65. On the implications of the encounter between state-organized and nonstate societies see Robert F. Berkhofer, Jr., "The North American Frontier as Process and Context," in Howard Lamar and Leonard Thompson, eds., *The Frontier in History: North America and Southern Africa Compared* (New Haven, 1981), 43–75; Morton H. Fried, *The Evolution of Political Society: An Essay in Political Anthropology* (New York, 1967); and idem, *The Notion of Tribe* (Menlo Park, Calif., 1975).

11. Fenton, ed., "Seneca Indians," 310–11 (quotations); idem, "Toward the Gradual Civilization of the Indian Natives: The Missionary and Linguistic Work of Asher Wright (1803–1875) among the Senecas of Western New York," *Proceedings of the American Philosophical Society* 100 (1956): 567–81; Thomas S. Abler, "Seneca Nation Factionalism: The First Twenty Years," in Elisabeth Tooker, ed., *Iroquois Culture, History, and Prehistory* (Albany, 1967), 25–26; Abler and Tooker, "Seneca," in *HNAI*, 15:511–14.

12. Arthur C. Parker, *The Constitution of the Five Nations; or, the Iroquois Book of the Great Law*, New York State Museum Bulletin 184 (Albany, 1916): 133–36. I am indebted to Thomas Abler for reminding me of this reference.

13. Parker, *Constitution*, 14–60. The text from which Parker worked was produced in the late 19th century by Seth Newhouse, an Onondaga of the Six Nations Reserve in Ontario. See also the version compiled in reaction to Newhouse's by the chiefs of the Reserve (ibid., 61–113; and Duncan C. Scott, ed., "Traditional History of the Confederacy of the Six Nations, Prepared by a Committee of the Chiefs," *Transactions of the Royal Society of Canada* 3d ser., 5 [1912]: 195–246). Some of the political and scholarly turmoil surrounding the efforts of the giants of early Iroquoian studies may be followed in J. N. B. Hewitt, Review Essay, *American Anthropologist*, n.s., 19 (1917): 429–38; William N. Fenton, "Seth Newhouse's Traditional History and Constitution of the Iroquois Confederacy," *Procs. Am. Phil. Soc.* 93 (1949): 141–58; Fenton, "Introduction," in idem, ed., *Parker on the Iroquois* (Syracuse, N.Y., 1968), 38–46; Mary W. Fleming Mathur, "The Iroquois in Ethnography: A Time-Space Concept," *Indian Historian* 2, no. 3 (1969): 12–18; and Sally M. Weaver, "Seth Newhouse and the Grand River Confederacy at Mid-Nineteenth Century," in Foster, et. al., eds., *Extending the Rafters*, 165–82.

14. See, among other works, Francis Parkman, *The Jesuits in North America* (Boston, 1867), 44–60; Allen W. Trelease, *Indian Affairs in Colonial New York: The Seventeenth Century* (Ithaca, N.Y., 1960), 20–24; Gary B. Nash, *Red, White, and Black: The Peo-*

ples of Early America (Englewood Cliffs., N.J., 1974), 18; and Elisabeth Tooker, "The League of the Iroquois: Its History, Politics, and Ritual," in *HNAI* 15:418–41.

15. Hunter to Lord ?, 12 Mar. 1713.

16. See, among others, the following ethnographically rich sources which contain scant or no discussions of the Grand Council: [Harmen Meyndertsz van den Bogaert,] "Narrative of a Journey into the Mohawk and Oneida Country, 1634–1635," in J. Franklin Jameson, ed., *Narratives of New Netherland, 1609–1664* (New York, 1909), 139–62; Joseph-François Lafitau, *Customs of the American Indians Compared with the Customs of Primitive Times,* ed. and trans. William N. Fenton and Elizabeth L. Moore, 2 vols. (Toronto, 1974, 1977 [orig. publ. 1724]); Carl F. Klinck and James J. Talman, eds., *The Journal of Major John Norton, 1816* (Toronto, 1970); "Account of the descriptions, given by Mr. [John] Norton Concerning his Country customs and Manners, Cambridge, 12 March 1805," Manuscript Item 13350, New York State Library, Albany; Douglas W. Boyce, ed., "A Glimpse of Iroquois Culture History Through the Eyes of Joseph Brant and John Norton," *Procs. Am. Phil. Soc.* 107 (1973): 286–94; and William N. Fenton, ed., "The Hyde Manuscript: Captain William Hyde's Observations of the 5 Nations of Indians at New York, 1698," *American Scene Magazine* 6 (1965): n.p. On the absence of sachem titles from diplomatic records, see William A. Starna, "Seventeenth-Century Dutch-Indian Trade: A Perspective from Iroquoia," *de Halve Maen* 69, no. 3 (1984): 7.

17. *JR,* passim, esp. 43:161–79, 47:77–81, 51:237; *Johnson Papers,* 4:56, 10:663–64, and passim.

18. William N. Fenton, "Locality as a Basic Factor in the Development of Iroquois Social Structure," in idem, ed., *Symposium on Local Diversity in Iroquois Culture,* Bureau of American Ethnology Bulletin 149 (Washington, D.C., 1951), 39–54; idem, "Factionalism in American Indian Society," in *Actes des IVᵉ Congrès International des Sciences Anthropologiques et Ethnologiques,* 3 vols. (Vienna, 1954–56), 2:330–40; Laurence M. Hauptman, "Refugee Havens: The Iroquois Villages of the Eighteenth Century," in Christopher Vecsey and Robert W. Venables, eds., *American Indian Environments: Ecological Issues in Native American History* (Syracuse, N.Y., 1980), 128–39.

19. ? to Thomas, Lord Culpeper, 26 July 1681, *CSP, 1681–85,* no. 185.

20. Treaty minutes, 12 July 1697, NYCM, 41: 93. On patterns of leadership among the Iroquois, see chapter 2, below.

21. "Structure, Continuity, and Change in the Process of Iroquois Treaty Making," in Jennings, et al., eds., *History and Culture of Iroquois Diplomacy,* 3–36, quotation from p. 5.

22. The following analysis is based upon Parker, *Constitution;* Scott, "Traditional History"; Paul A. W. Wallace, *The White Roots of Peace* (Philadelphia, 1949); Anthony F. C. Wallace, "The Dekanawideh Myth Analyzed as the Record of a Revitalization Movement," *Ethnohistory* 5 (1958): 129–39; and William N. Fenton, "The Lore of the Longhouse: Myth, Ritual and Red Power," *Anthropological Quarterly* 48 (1975): 131–47. The most recent attempt to systematize and interpret the many oral traditions is by Christopher Vecsey, "The Story and Structure of the Iroquois Confederacy," *Journal of the American Academy of Religion* 54 (1986): 79–106.

23. Parker, *Constitution,* 17. For archaeological evidence of this period of warfare, see John Witthoft, "Ancestry of the Susquehannocks," in idem and W. Fred Kinsey, III, eds., *Susquehannock Miscellany* (Harrisburg, Pa., 1959), 32–36; James A. Tuck, *Onondaga Iroquois Prehistory: A Study in Settlement Archaeology* (Syracuse, N.Y., 1971), 207–25;

Bruce G. Trigger, "Prehistoric Social and Political Organization: An Iroquoian Case Study," in Dean R. Snow, ed., *Foundations of Northeast Archaeology* (New York, 1981), 33–35; and idem, "Iroquois Prehistory," in Foster, et al., eds., *Extending the Rafters*, 254–57.

24. Daniel K. Richter, "War and Culture: The Iroquois Experience," *WMQ* 40 (1983): 537–44.

25. Wallace, *White Roots of Peace*, 18.

26. *JR*, 51:237 (quotation); Tooker, "League of the Iroquois," 418–29.

27. William M. Beauchamp, *Civil, Religious and Mourning Councils and Ceremonies of Adoption of the New York Indians*, N.Y. St. Mus. Bull. 113 (Albany, 1907), 351–97; William N. Fenton, "An Iroquois Condolence Council for Installing Cayuga Chiefs in 1945," *Journal of the Washington Academy of Sciences* 36 (1946): 110–27.

28. George S. Snyderman, "Behind the Tree of Peace: A Sociological Analysis of Iroquois Warfare," *Pa. Archaeol.* 18, nos. 3–4 (1948): 24–29; James Wesley Bradley, "The Onondaga Iroquois, 1500–1655: A Study in Acculturative Change and Its Consequences" (Ph.D. diss., Syracuse University, 1979), 394–406; Jack Campisi, "The Iroquois and the Euro-American Concept of Tribe," *New York History* 63 (1982): 165–82; William Engelbrecht, "New York Iroquois Political Development," in William W. Fitzhugh, ed., *Cultures in Contact: The European Impact on Native Cultural Institutions in Eastern North America, AD 1000–1800* (Washington, D.C. 1985), 163–83.

29. *JR*, 51:237.

30. John Phillip Reid, *A Better Kind of Hatchet: Law, Trade, and Diplomacy in the Cherokee Nation during the Early Years of European Contact* (University Park, Pa., 1976), 9–17, quotation from p. 16.

31. James H. Coyne, ed. and trans., "Exploration of the Great Lakes, 1660–1670, by Dollier de Casson and de Bréhant de Galinée," *Ontario Historical Society Papers and Records* 4 (1903): 17.

32. Parker, *Constitution*, 37 (quotation); Anthony F. C. Wallace, *The Death and Rebirth of the Seneca* (New York, 1969), 30–44.

33. Quoted in Fenton, "Lore of the Longhouse," 131.

34. Tuck, *Onondaga Prehistory*, 202–4; Donald Lenig, "Of Dutchmen, Beaver Hats and Iroquois," *Researches and Transactions of the New York State Archaeological Association* 17, no. 1 (1977): 71–84.

35. Van den Bogaert, "Journal," 140–41; *JR*, 21:211; Bruce G. Trigger, *The Children of Aataentsic: A History of the Huron People to 1660*, 2 vols. (Montreal, 1976), 2:602; idem, "Ontario Native People and the Epidemics of 1634–1640," in Shepard Krech, III, ed., *Indians, Animals, and the Fur Trade: A Critique of "Keepers of the Game"* (Athens, Ga., 1981), 21–38. Population losses much in excess of 50 percent are suggested by one recent study of archaeological and documentary evidence (William A. Starna, "Mohawk Iroquois Population: A Revision," *Ethnohistory* 27 [1980]: 371–82). On the general issue of economic and epidemiological change as a result of European contact see Richard White, *The Roots of Dependency: Subsistence, Environment, and Social Change among the Choctaws, Pawnees, and Navajos* (Lincoln, Neb., 1983).

36. H. P. Biggar, gen. ed. and trans., *The Works of Samuel de Champlain*, 6 vols. (Toronto, 1922–36), 1:98–109, 141, 178–79, 2:90–91, 3:171–72; Léo-Paul Desrosiers, *Iroquoisie* (Montreal, 1947), 21–90.

37. Nicholaes van Wassenaer, "Historisch Verhael," in Jameson, ed., *Narratives of New Netherland*, 84–89; Bruce G. Trigger, "The Mohawk-Mahican War: The Establishment of a Pattern," *Canadian Historical Review* 52 (1971): 276–86.

38. Biggar, ed., *Works of Champlain*, 5:214–32, 264–66, 308–12; Desrosiers, *Iroquoisie*, 91–343; Trigger, *Children of Aataentsic*, 1:464–98.

39. George T. Hunt, *The Wars of the Iroquois: A Study in Intertribal Trade Relations* (Madison, Wis., 1940), passim; Daniel K. Richter, "The Ordeal of the Longhouse: Change and Persistence on the Iroquois Frontier, 1609–1720" (Ph.D. diss., Columbia University, 1984), 75–126.

40. *JR*, 45:207.

41. Richter, "War and Culture," 537–44.

42. See chapters 5–6, below.

43. *JR*, 50:127–47, 181–205, 51:81–85, 57:25–27; *NYCD*, 3:118–35, 146–54; A. J. F. van Laer, trans. and ed., *Correspondence of Jeremias van Rensselaer, 1651–1674* (Albany, N.Y., 1932), 325–32, 345–46, 358–71, 412–13, 440–49; Lynn Ceci, "The First Fiscal Crisis in New York," *Economic Development and Cultural Change* 28 (1980): 839–47; Daniel K. Richter, "New York, New France, and the Five Nations Iroquois: The 1660s as Turning Point," paper presented at the Annual Meeting of the Organization of American Historians, New York, April 1986. The economic impact of the English conquest is questioned in Jan Kupp, "Aspects of New York–Dutch Trade under the English, 1670–1674," *New-York Historical Society Quarterly* 57 (1974): 139–47.

44. Lafitau, *Customs of American Indians*, 1:294–97; Fenton, "Locality as a Basic Factor," 50–51.

45. On Garakontié (whose Christian name was Daniel) see William M. Beauchamp, *A History of the New York Iroquois, Now Commonly Called the Six Nations*, N.Y. St. Mus. Bull. 78 (Albany, 1905), 200–222; Bruce G. Trigger, "Garakontié," in George W. Brown, et al., eds., *Dictionary of Canadian Biography*, 9 vols. to date (Toronto, 1966–), 1:322–23; Daniel K. Richter, "Iroquois versus Iroquois: Jesuit Missions and Christianity in Village Politics, 1642–1686," *Ethnohistory* 32 (1985): 4–5; and Stephen Saunders Webb, *1676: The End of American Independence* (New York, 1984), 251–302.

46. See chapter 2, below.

47. Michael K. Foster, "On Who Spoke First at Iroquois-White Councils: An Exercise in the Method of Upstreaming," in idem, et al., eds., *Extending the Rafters*, 183–207; Mary A. Druke, "Iroquois Treaties: Common Forms, Varying Interpretations," in Jennings, et al., eds., *History and Culture of Iroquois Diplomacy*, 85–98; "The Earliest Recorded Description: The Mohawk Treaty with New France at Three Rivers, 1645," ibid., 127–53.

48. *JR*, 43:127–85, quotations from pp. 167–69.

49. Ibid., 47:69–83, quotations from pp. 77–79.

50. See, for example, ibid., 53:231–33.

51. *NYCD*, 3:126–35; Nicholas Perrot, "Memoir on the Manners, Customs, and Religion of the Savages of North America," in Emma Helen Blair, trans. and ed., *The Indian Tribes of the Mississippi Valley and Region of the Great Lakes . . .* , 2 vols. (Cleveland, 1911), 1:199–203.

52. Tooker, "League of the Iroquois," 429; Elwood Green, comment from the floor, conference on "The 'Imperial' Iroquois," Williamsburg, Va., March 1984.

53. *NYCD*, 4:39 (quotation); Leroy V. Eid, "The Ojibwa-Iroquois War: The War

the Five Nations Did Not Win," *Ethnohistory* 26 (1979): 297–324; Richter, "Iroquois versus Iroquois," 1–16; idem, "King William's Other War: The Covenant Chain at Home," paper presented at conference on "The 'Imperial' Iroquois"; idem, "Cultural Brokers and Intercultural Politics: New York–Iroquois Relations during King William's War," paper presented to the American Society for Ethnohistory Annual Meeting, New Orleans, November 1984. See also chapter 3, below.

54. *JR*, 64:243–49; Chevalier de Baugy, "Journal of the Expedition of Marquis de Denonville against the Iroquois, 1687," trans. and ed. Nathaniel Shurtleff Olds, Rochester Historical Society, *Publication Fund Series* 9 (1931): 1–56. On Leisler's Rebellion and its impact on Albany, see Charles Howard McCormick, "Leisler's Rebellion" (Ph.D. diss., American Univ., 1971), esp. 297–302; David S. Lovejoy, *The Glorious Revolution in America* (New York, 1972), 98–121, 312–24; and Robert C. Ritchie, *The Duke's Province: A Study of New York Politics and Society, 1664–1691* (Chapel Hill, N.C., 1977), esp. 205–11.

55. *JR*, 64:59–61. See also Treaty minutes, 20 Sept. 1688, NYCM, 35:174. Garakontié died during the winter of 1677–78 (*JR*, 59:21–33). Otreouti's name last appears in Euro-American records in 1688 (Thomas Grassman, "Otreouti," in Brown, et al., eds., *Dictionary of Canadian Biography*, 1:525–26). Tahiadoris died in 1691, on the eve of an Anglo-Iroquois invasion of Canada in which he was to play a leading role. His inopportune demise led Albany magistrate Dirck Wesselse to call Tahiadoris "a Sachim who never did good in his Lifetime and his death it self was prejudicial to a good Design" (Wesselse to Henry Sloughter, 2 July 1691, NYCM, 27:176).

56. *LIR*, 103 (quotations), 133, 148.

57. Treaty minutes, 3 Feb. 1690, Untitled Notebook, Indians of North America, Miscellaneous Papers, 1620–1895, American Antiquarian Society, Worcester, Mass.; *WA*, 14–16; Cadwallader Colden, *The History of the Five Indian Nations of Canada, Which are Dependent on the Province of New-York in America, and Are the Barrier between the English and French in that Part of the World* (London, 1747), 105–13.

58. When wampum belts signifying peace with the Ottawas were distributed, "a large Belt was given also to the Albany Messengers as their Share" (Colden, *History*, 109). The lone identifiable League sachem was Jesuit missionary Pierre Millet, whom Oneidas had adopted and given the Sachem title *Odatshedeh*. Millet, however, was in no position to wield much influence in the 1690 council: his Oneida and Mohawk enemies planned to expose to the gathering his supposed treacheries through a public reading of a packet of his letters that they had intercepted. Alas—apart from some suspicious black powder (probably ink)—the paper contained "nothing but common News and Compliments" (ibid., 112 [quotation]; Treaty minutes, 3 Feb. 1690, Notebook, Am. Antiq. Soc.).

59. See, for example, the intricate maneuvering that preceded the 1690 meeting discussed in the previous paragraph: *JR*, 64:91; *NYDH*, 2:137–44; Treaty minutes, 27 Dec. 1689, 4, 6 Jan., 3 Feb. 1690, Notebook, Am. Antiq. Soc.

60. Anthony F. C. Wallace, "Origins of Iroquois Neutrality: The Grand Settlement of 1701," *Pennsylvania History* 24 (1957): 223–35.

61. Richter, "Ordeal of the Longhouse," 289–437. On the redefinition of the Covenant Chain with New York see also chapter 3, below.

62. The political divisions and the delicate factional balance achieved in 1701 persisted. Factional leaders continued to be the most visible characters in intercultural diplomacy, and for much of the 18th century the Five Nations functioned less as a single league than as a congeries of several factional confederacies united by the common ceremonies and

unbroken traditions of the Grand Council of the Great League of Peace. See chapter 3, below; Richard Haan, "'Indian Metaphors Have a Logic of Their Own': The Iroquois and Pennsylvania, 1725–45," paper presented at the American Society for Ethnohistory Annual Meeting, New Orleans, November 1984; Francis Jennings, "Iroquois Alliances in American History," in idem, et al., eds., *History and Culture of Iroquois Diplomacy*, 41; and Richter, "Ordeal of the Longhouse," 438–572.

63. On Iroquois experiences during the American War for Independence, see Barbara Graymont, *The Iroquois in the American Revolution* (Syracuse, N.Y., 1972), passim. On the New Religion of Handsome Lake see Wallace, *Death and Rebirth of the Seneca*, 239–337.

2–LINKING ARMS

1. *JR*, 27:261. For assistance in research for this chapter, I am indebted to the Philips Fund of the American Philosophical Society, which funded archival study in Great Britain, and to the Newberry Library for a pre-doctoral fellowship.

2. Names of nations with whom the Iroquois negotiated from the early 17th to the mid-19th centuries can be found in the index in the printed guide to IIDH. For lists of some Indian allies of the Iroquois during the mid-18th century, see *Johnson Papers*, 3:273n, 9:493, 560–61. See also Dorothy V. Jones, *License for Empire: Colonialism by Treaty in Early America* (Chicago, 1982), 21–35.

3. William N. Fenton, "Masked Medicine Societies of the Iroquois," in *Annual Report of the Smithsonian Institution for 1940* (Washington, D.C., 1941), 397–429; A. C. Parker, "Secret Medicine Societies of the Seneca," *American Anthropologist*, n.s., 11 (1909): 161–85; Morris Wolf, *Iroquois Religion and Its Relation to Their Morals* (New York, 1919), 26, 57.

4. J. N. B. Hewitt, "Iroquoian Cosmology (Second Part)," in *Forty-Third Annual Report of the Bureau of American Ethnology* (Washington, D.C., 1928), 485–90.

5. Idem, "Orenda and a Definition of Religion," *American Anthropologist*, n.s., 4 (1902): 41; Mary A. Druke, "The Concept of Personhood in Seventeenth and Eighteenth Century Iroquois Ethno Personality," in Nancy Bonvillain, ed., *Studies on Iroquois Culture* (Rindge, N.H., 1980), 66–67.

6. Council in Philadelphia, 27 Mar.–10 Apr. 1756, p. 15, American Philosophical Society Library, Philadelphia; *Johnson Papers*, 2:773, 4:56, 7:186–87, 11:41, 13:206; Joseph François Lafitau, *Customs of the American Indians Compared with the Customs of Primitive Times*, ed. and trans. William N. Fenton and Elizabeth L. Moore, 2 vols. (Toronto, 1974, 1977 [orig. publ. 1724]), 1:291, 293, 364; *NYCD*, 4:271; Richard Smith, *A Tour of Four Great Rivers: The Hudson, Mohawk, Susquehanna and Delaware in 1769* (New York, 1906), 157–58. For an extensive study of Iroquois leadership, see Mary A. Druke, "Structure and Meanings of Leadership Among the Mohawk and Oneida During the Mid-Eighteenth Century" (Ph.D. diss., University of Chicago, 1982), esp. chs. 4–5.

7. Lafitau, *Customs of American Indians*, 2:54–56.

8. *Johnson Papers*, 2:700, 9:18, 20, 10:227, 11:29, 31; *NYCD*, 8:505; Walter Pilkington, ed., *The Journals of Samuel Kirkland: 18th-Century Missionary to the Iroquois, Government Agent, Father of Hamilton College* (Clinton, N.Y., 1980), 107, 306. For information on Iroquois kinship, see William N. Fenton, "Northern Iroquoian Culture Patterns," in *HNAI*, 15:296–321.

9. Lafitau, *Customs of American Indians*, 1:xxxi, 2:99. See also Fenton, "Northern Iroquoian Culture Patterns," 315–16; J. N. B. Hewitt, "The Requickening Address of the Iroquois Condolence," ed. William N. Fenton, *Journal of the Washington Academy of Sciences* 34 (1944): 65–85; and Elizabeth Tooker, "The League of the Iroquois: Its History, Politics and Ritual," in *HNAI*, 15:418–41.

10. *Johnson Papers*, 11:41, 158, emphasis added.

11. Ibid., 4:274, 9:452, 10:280–85; Weiser Correspondence, 33, HSP.

12. The classic study of Iroquois kinship is Lewis H. Morgan, *League of the Ho-dé-no-sau-nee, Iroquois* (Rochester, N.Y., 1851), esp. ch. 4.

13. *Johnson Papers*, 1:737.

14. Haldimand Papers, Add. Mss. Coll., 21775:62, Brit. Mus.; Anthony F. C. Wallace, *The Death and Rebirth of the Seneca* (New York, 1969), 30–39.

15. Unlike the acephalous political structure of segmentary lineages among the Nuer, so brilliantly analyzed in 1940 by E. E. Evans-Pritchard (*The Nuer* [Oxford, 1940]), the Iroquois political structure was polycephalous.

16. *Johnson Papers*, 12:533.

17. Haldimand Papers, Add. Mss. Coll., 29237:14, Brit. Mus. See also ibid., 21771:213; and *NYCD*, 8:548.

18. *Johnson Papers*, 2:821.

19. Ibid., 128; *WA*, 36; William N. Fenton, "Locality as a Basic Factor in the Development of Iroquois Social Structure," in idem, ed., *Symposium on Local Diversity in Iroquois Culture*, Bureau of American Ethnology Bulletin 149 (Washington, D.C., 1951), 39–54.

20. *Johnson Papers*, 12:801. See also Lafitau, *Customs of American Indians*, 1:341.

21. Peter Force, ed., *American Archives: Consisting of a Collection of Authentick Records, State Papers, Debates and Letters and Other Notices of Publick Affairs* (Washington, D.C., 1837–53), 5th ser., 1:1045. For similar wording, see Account of a Conference in 1677, Colonial Office Papers, 1/40, fol. 82v, Public Record Office, London.

22. Wilbur Jacobs, *Diplomacy and Indian Gifts: Anglo-French Rivalry along the Ohio and Northwest Frontiers, 1748–1763* (Stanford, Calif., 1950).

23. Newcastle Papers, Add. Mss. Coll., 32833:404, Brit. Mus. Documents that provide data about renewal of alliances abound; see IIDH, passim.

24. *WA*, 125; *NYCD*, 5:669.

25. Council at Chote [Chota], 25 Aug. 1776, C.O. 5/77, PRO; *Johnson Papers*, 9:841, 847, 561. Aspiring Euro-American officials often took credit for peaceful negotiations between tribes, when it was to their advantage. Extensive reading of historical documents, however, indicates that many of these attempts to make peace were Indian-inspired. See Indian Records, RC10, ser. 2, 2:61, 78, 123, Public Archives of Canada, Ottawa.

26. William N. Fenton, "Structure, Continuity, and Change in the Process of Iroquois Treaty Making," in Francis Jennings, et al., eds., *The History and Culture of Iroquois Diplomacy* (Syracuse, N.Y., 1985), 21–22. See also "Names by Which Different Indian Nations Address Each Other in Public Conferences," MG19, Ser. F11, Item no. 1, Publ. Arch. Canada. Within matrilineal Iroquois society, a person would be of the same matrilineage as one's "brother" or one's "uncle" or "nephew." "Cousins" (father's sister's children) were members of one's father's line, one's *agadoni*. Unfortunately, in dealing with 17th- and 18th-century data we have mainly translations of speeches to work with in trying to decipher

council rhetoric. With very few exceptions, speeches are not available in Iroquoian languages. It is hoped, however, that research into use of kinship terms in modern-day Iroquois council speeches will someday be of benefit in analyzing data from the past.

27. *Johnson Papers*, 7:379, 10:635, 902, 969, 11:139, 12:272; *NYCD*, 8:527.

28. Bouquet Papers, Add. Mss. Coll., 21265:126–27, Brit. Mus.

29. *NYCD*, 4:59–63.

30. Lafitau, *Customs of American Indians*, 1:295–97.

31. Claude Charles le Roy de Bacqueville de La Potherie, *Histoire de l'Amérique Septentrionale* (Paris, 1722), 1:362; Fenton, "Locality as a Basic Factor," passim.

32. *JR*, 51:237; *Johnson Papers*, 2:686; W. N. Fenton, ed., "Seneca Indians by Asher Wright (1859)," *Ethnohistory* 4 (1957): 310–12.

33. *Johnson Papers*, 12:458.

34. Haldimand Papers, 21670:21, 21760:95; *Johnson Papers*, 3:707–9, 711, 7:852, 9:559, 10:87.

35. Penn Manuscripts, Indian Affairs, 1687–1753, 1:49, HSP.

36. *Johnson Papers*, 2:415, 9:860, 12:256–57, 321; Haldimand Papers, 21670:24.

37. *Johnson Papers*, 2:822ff, 8:884, 12:688. Excellent sources of information about details of council procedure may be found in Fenton, "Structure, Continuity, and Change," 3–36; and Michael K. Foster, "Another Look at the Function of Wampum in Iroquois-White Councils," in Jennings, et al., eds., *History and Culture of Iroquois Diplomacy*, 99–114.

38. Council at Chote, 25 Aug. 1776; Michael K. Foster, "On Who Spoke First at Iroquois-White Councils: An Exercise in the Method of Upstreaming," in Michael K. Foster, Jack Campisi, and Marianne Mithun, eds., *Extending the Rafters: Interdisciplinary Approaches to Iroquoian Studies* (Albany, N.Y., 1984), 183–207.

39. *Johnson Papers*, 2:686, 9:455–57; *JR*, 27:247–305; Council at Chote, 25 Aug. 1776. For other locations of councils, see index of printed guide to IIDH.

40. *JR*, 27:247–305; Lafitau, *Customs of American Indians*, 2:174; *NYCD*, 7:133–34; *Johnson Papers*, 1:125–26.

41. *Johnson Papers*, 1:126–27, 3:475; Newcastle Papers, 32833:404; Journal of George Croghan of Meeting with Indians in Philadelphia on the Ohio (Fort Pitt), 1759, Mss., Class 970.5, M665:29, Am. Phil. Soc.; Treaty with the Ohio Indians at Carlisle, Oct. 1753, Mss., Class 970.5, No. T716, FL.D, p. 2, ibid.

42. Foster, "Another Look at Wampum," 103.

43. Lafitau, *Customs of American Indians*, 2:296–97. See also Bouquet Papers, 21655:124–25; Council at Chote, 25 Aug. 1776; Penn Mss., Indian Affairs, 1689–1783, 1:49, HSP; *Johnson Papers*, 2:686; Pilkington, ed., *Journals of Kirkland*, 25, 29.

44. Bouquet Papers, 21655:23; *Johnson Papers*, 9:115; *NYCD*, 8:606; Pilkington, ed., *Journals of Kirkland*, 6.

45. Mary A. Druke, "Iroquois Treaties: Common Forms, Varying Interpretations," in Jennings, et al., eds., *History and Culture of Iroquois Diplomacy*, 88–90. See also Council at Chote, 25 Aug. 1776; and Jacobs, *Diplomacy and Indian Gifts*, 22–23.

46. Haldimand Papers, 21670:28; *NYCD*, 8:519, 527.

47. *Johnson Papers*, 4:57, 9:736, 11:59; *NYCD*, 4:271, 6:974; Haldimand Papers, 21670:95; Smith, *Tour of Four Rivers*, 85.

48. *Johnson Papers,* 9:706. See also ibid., 2:699, 4:56, 7:993, 8:950, 9:115, 10:87, 11:231–32, 12:369, 458; Haldimand Papers, 21670:24; Force, ed., *American Archives,* 4th ser., 5:1104; Papers of the Continental Congress, i153, 3:59–60, 72, National Archives, Washington, D.C.

49. Bouquet Papers, 21655:126–27.

50. *NYCD,* 8:527. See also ibid., 499–500, 507–9, 525–26; *Johnson Papers,* 13:701.

51. *NYCD,* 8:527.

52. Ibid., 111–34; Pilkington, ed., *Journals of Kirkland,* 25, 29.

53. For information on other symbols of alliance, see Fenton, "Structure, Continuity, and Change," in Jennings, et al., eds., *History and Culture of Iroquois Diplomacy,* 22; and "Glossary of Figures of Speech in Iroquois Political Rhetoric," in ibid., 115–24.

3 – COVENANT and CONSENSUS

1. Francis Jennings, *The Ambiguous Iroquois Empire: The Covenant Chain Confederation of Indian Tribes with English Colonies from Its Beginnings to the Lancaster Treaty of 1744* (New York, 1984).

2. For other recent work developing these themes see Richard Aquila, *The Iroquois Restoration: Iroquois Diplomacy on the Colonial Frontier, 1701–1754* (Detroit, 1983); Stephen Saunders Webb, *1676: The End of American Independence* (New York, 1985). Compare Lewis H. Morgan, *League of the Ho-dé-no-sau-nee, Iroquois* (Rochester, N.Y., 1851).

3. Jennings, *Ambiguous Empire,* 149. See also his use of the term "constitutional" (pp. 162, 165).

4. Lawrence H. Leder, *Robert Livingston, 1654–1728, and the Politics of Colonial New York* (Chapel Hill, N.C., 1961); Stanley N. Katz, *Newcastle's New York: Anglo-American Politics, 1732–1753* (Cambridge, Mass., 1968). For further discussion of the roots of European misperceptions, see chapter 1 above.

5. Jennings, *Ambiguous Empire,* 145–67; Stephen Saunders Webb, *The Governors-General: The English Army and the Definition of the Empire, 1569–1681* (Chapel Hill, N.C., 1979), 422–25, 445–59, 491, 498, 510. See also Francis Jennings, "Iroquois Alliances in American History," in idem, et al., eds., *The History and Culture of Iroquois Diplomacy: An Interdisciplinary Guide to the Treaties of the Six Nations and Their League* (Syracuse, N.Y., 1985), 37–65.

6. *NYCD* 3:254–59; Jennings, *Ambiguous Empire,* 145–85, esp. 148–49, 170, 185; Webb, *1676,* 299, 355–404.

7. "Propositions made by Col. Henry Courcy . . ." [1677], Colonial Office Papers, 1/40, Public Record Office, London, copy in IIDH, reel 2; "Instructions For Col. Henry Coursey . . . ," 30 Apr. 1677, ibid.; Coursey to ?, 22 May 1677, ibid.; ? to Coursey, 2 June 1677, ibid.; Webb, *1676,* 297–99.

8. For general comments on these meetings see NY Council Minutes, vol. 3, pt. 2, 144; and *NYCD,* 3:254–57. Neither source mentions a "silver" chain, despite the comments in Webb, *1676,* 299; and Jennings, et al., eds., *History and Culture of Iroquois Diplomacy,* 160. On Iroquois protocol, see Mary A. Druke, "Structure and Meanings of Leadership Among the Oneida Indians During the Mid-Eighteenth Century" (Ph.D. diss., Univ. of Chicago, 1982), 22–23, 193–99, 217–19; Michael K. Foster, "On Who Spoke First at Iroquois-White Councils:

An Exercise in the Method of Upstreaming," in Michael K. Foster, Jack Campisi, and Marianne Mithun, eds., *Extending the Rafters: Interdisciplinary Approaches to Iroquoian Studies*, (Albany, 1984), 183–207; and Michael K. Foster, "Another Look at the Function of Wampum in Iroquois-White Councils," in Jennings, et al., eds. *History and Culture of Iroquois Diplomacy*, 99–114.

9. On the pattern of the 1677 meetings with Maryland, see *LIR*, 43–48; and Treaty minutes, 20–21 July 1677, C.O. 1/40, copy in IIDH, reel 2. In 1762 the Mohawk orator Cayenquiragoa, when asked if he spoke for all his people, replied "I speak for the Whole; All those who are of a different way of thinking, don't chuse to make their Appearance" (*Johnson Papers*, 4:56). See also Druke's discussion of leaders not responsible for the acts of their followers ("Structure and Meanings of Leadership," 144–46, 162–63); and Foster, "Who Spoke First," 182–84, 202–3.

10. Foster, "Another Look," 110, 116. The Mohawks used the "clasped hands" metaphor rather steadily ("Propositions of 3 Mohawk Castles," 25 Feb. 1690, NYCM, 36:30).

11. *LIR*, 49–55, 60–62.

12. Ibid., 68–69.

13. Ibid., 71–74; Treaty Minutes, 30 July 1684, C.O. 5/1407, copy in IIDH, reel 3; Treaty minutes, 31 July–6 Aug. 1684, Colonial Papers, folder 4, item 2a, Virginia State Library, Richmond, copy in IIDH, reel 3; Jennings, *Ambiguous Empire*, 178–85.

14. *LIR*, 73–74; Treaty Minutes, 31 July–6 Aug. 1684.

15. *LIR*, 80–81; Treaty Minutes, 31 July–6 Aug. 1684. This seems to be the first appearance of the term "silver" in the written record. Jennings relies much too heavily on Canasetego's 1742 rendition of the Covenant Chain's origins (*Ambiguous Empire*, 167). No other recitation is as precise, raising suspicions that Pennsylvania officials provided the phrasing to confirm, as Jennings has shown, that colony's claims to a long-standing relationship with the Five Nations. Compare Canasetego's version (reprinted in Jennings, *Ambiguous Empire*, 357–59) with the 1694 version that makes no mention of the "silver" chain with New York, until New York reinstates the simile "shines like Silver" (Treaty minutes, 15–20 Aug. 1694, NYCM, 39:184). Jennings implies that a 1683 Mohawk-Albany meeting refers to the Silver Covenant Chain (*Ambiguous Empire*, 149n). It does not. It refers to the earlier trading alliance that Jennings describes as one of iron. Even though the Mohawks refer to the chain as being "of the most precious metal," which they promise to keep "bright and shining," the speech also refers to this agreement as "the ancient covenant made between us in the presence of Major Pynshon." Pynchon, whose trading post was situated at Springfield, did not attend the Albany meetings of either 1676 or 1677. (A. J. F. van Laer, trans. and ed., *Minutes of the Court of Albany, Rensselaerswyck and Schenectady, 1668–1685*, 3 vols. [Albany, 1926–32], 3:362–64).

16. *LIR*, 93–97. Jennings provides a summary chronology in *Ambiguous Empire*, 187–91.

17. Jennings, *Ambiguous Empire*, 173–80; W. J. Eccles, *Frontenac: The Courtier Governor* (Toronto, 1959), 103–26. Anthony F. C. Wallace, "Origins of Iroquois Neutrality: The Grand Settlement of 1701," *Pennsylvania History* 24 (1957): 223–35.

18. Jennings, *Ambiguous Empire*, 186–91.

19. *LIR*, 71–77; Treaty minutes, 31 July–6 Aug. 1684; Cadwallader Colden, *The History of the Five Indian Nations Depending on the Province of New-York in America* (Ithaca, N.Y., 1958), 46–57.

20. Colden, *History*, 51, quoted in Jennings, *Ambiguous Empire*, 183.

21. *LIR*, 95; *NYCD*, 9:297–98. Denonville's concern related to the recent activities of Albany merchants to penetrate the Great Lakes trade. See *NYCD*, 9:287–88; Allen W. Trelease, *Indian Affairs in Colonial New York: The Seventeenth Century* (Ithaca, N.Y., 1960), 269–70; Jennings, *Ambiguous Empire*, 188–90; Thomas Elliot Norton, *The Fur Trade in Colonial New York, 1686–1776* (Madison, Wis., 1974), 153; and Eccles, *Frontenac*, 177–80.

22. On Dongan's first proposals, actually delivered by the Albany Commissioners in November, see *LIR*, 94. The May meeting is recorded in ibid., 99–100; see too ibid., 97–98; and Norton, *Fur Trade*, 47–49. That even the Mohawks saw these as separate chains is seen in the Mohawk observation in July 1684 that "There are three things we must all observe. *First*, the Covenant with Corlaer. *Secondly* The Covenant with Virginia and Maryland. *Thirdly*, The Covenant with Boston" (Treaty minutes, 31 July–6 Aug. 1684).

23. *LIR*, 100.

24. Ibid. On the western trade, see Norton, *Fur Trade*, 47–49, 152–54; and Helen Broshar, "The First Push Westward of the Albany Traders," *Mississippi Valley Historical Review* 7 (1920): 233–35.

25. *LIR*, 114, 102–3, 109. On Iroquois factionalism and the goals of war at the end of the seventeenth century, see Daniel K. Richter, "War and Culture: The Iroquois Experience," *WMQ* 40 (1983): 528–59. On kinship see Druke, "Structure and Meanings of Leadership," 163–67; and Joseph François Lafitau, *Customs of the American Indians Compared with the Customs of Primitive Times*, ed. and trans. William N. Fenton and Elizabeth L. Moore, 2 vols. (Toronto, 1974, 1977), 1:334–39, 2:99n, 152.

26. Jennings, *Ambiguous Empire*, 189–91; Eccles, *Frontenac*, 180–85, 196–97, 207.

27. Trelease, *Indian Affairs*, 281–83, 295–331; Aquila, *Iroquois Restoration*, 42–46. On the 1687 meeting see *NYCD*, 3:438–44; and "Diary of Proceedings at Councils at Albany," 6 Aug.–15 Sept. 1687, Gwynn Mss., Thomas Gilcrease Institute of American History and Art, Tulsa, Okla.

28. *Propositions Made by the Five Nations of Indians . . . to His Excellency Richard Earl of Bellomont . . . the 10th of July Anno Dom. 1698* (New York, 1698).

29. Richard L. Haan, "The Covenant Chain: Iroquois Diplomacy on the Niagara Frontier, 1687–1730" (Ph.D. diss., Univ. of California, Santa Barbara, 1976).

30. Haan, "Covenant Chain," 128–42; Aquila, *Iroquois Restoration*, 78–81; Wallace "Origins," 223–35. See also chapter 1, above.

31. Haan, "Covenant Chain," 131–37.

32. Richard Haan, "'Indian Metaphors Have a Logic of Their Own': The Iroquois and Pennsylvania, 1725–45," paper presented at the American Society for Ethnohistory Annual Meeting, New Orleans, November 1984.

33. Aquila, *Iroquois Restoration*, 205–32, offers the fullest argument for a "policy" in the south. On the linkages between the Iroquois and the Susquehanna region, see Barry C. Kent, *Susquehanna's Indians* (Harrisburg, 1984), 14–24, 53–70. On face-to-face meetings see, for example, *NYCD*, 9:1062–63.

34. See chapter 6, below.

35. Richard Haan, "The Problem of Iroquois Neutrality: Suggestions for Revision," *Ethnohistory* 27 (1980): 324–25.

36. On Johnson, see, for example, *NYCD*, 6:614–39, for the debate between Governor Clinton and the Assembly, where Johnson was charged with having "invented" a chain

of 1,000 Iroquois. See, too, Johnson's Census of 1763, where he includes "in Alliance with the Six Nations" the Caughnawagas of Canada as well as the Ohio nations under the leadership of the Iroquois of New York (*NYDH*, 1:26–30). This, in spite of New York's earlier recognition of how unlikely was this unity (*NYCD*, 6:602–3).

4–TOWARD the COVENANT CHAIN

1. I wish to thank Gordon Day, Francis Jennings, Dean Snow, and especially Peter Thomas — as well as the editors — for their comments on earlier versions of this chapter.

2. Esp. Francis Jennings, *The Invasion of America: Indians, Colonialism, and the Cant of Conquest* (New York, 1975), ch. 18; and Stephen Saunders Webb, *1676: The End of American Independence* (New York, 1984), 355–404.

3. For important exceptions, see Gordon M. Day, "The Ouragie War: A Case History in Iroquois–New England Indian Relations," in Michael K. Foster, Jack Campisi, and Marianne Mithun, eds., *Extending the Rafters: Interdisciplinary Approaches to Iroquoian Studies* (Albany, 1984), 35–50; and esp. Peter Allen Thomas, "In the Maelstrom of Change: The Indian Trade and Cultural Process in the Middle Connecticut Valley, 1635–1665" (Ph.D. diss., Univ. of Massachusetts, Amherst, 1979).

4. Elisabeth Tooker, "The League of the Iroquois: Its History, Politics, and Ritual," in *HNAI*, 15:423–24; Mary A. Druke, "Iroquois Treaties: Common Forms, Varying Interpretations," in Francis Jennings, et al., eds., *The History and Culture of Iroquois Diplomacy: An Interdisciplinary Guide to the Treaties of the Six Nations and Their League* (Syracuse, N.Y., 1985), 85–98; Michael K. Foster, "Another Look at the Function of Wampum in Iroquois-White Councils," in ibid., 99–114; "The Earliest Recorded Description: The Mohawk Treaty With New France at Three Rivers, 1645," in ibid., 127–53; Daniel Karl Richter, "The Ordeal of the Longhouse: Change and Persistence on the Iroquois Frontier, 1609–1720" (Ph.D. diss., Columbia Univ., 1984), 21–26, 31–33. See also Charles F. Wray and Harry L. Schoff, "A Preliminary Report on the Seneca Sequence in Western New York, 1550–1687," *Pennsylvania Archaeologist* 23 (1953): 57–59; William M. Beauchamp, *Wampum and Shell Articles Used by the New York Indians*, New York State Museum Bulletin 41 (Albany, 1901), 329–44, 350–403, 430–62; James Wesley Bradley, "The Onondaga Iroquois, 1500–1655: A Study in Acculturative Change and Its Consequences" (Ph.D. diss., Syracuse Univ., 1979), 254–55, 273–74; George R. Hamell, "Life's Immortal Shell: Wampum Among the Iroquois" (unpublished paper in author's possession, 1984); idem, "Trading in Metaphors: The Magic of Beads," in Charles F. Hayes, gen. ed., *Proceedings of the 1982 Glass Trade Bead Conference* (Rochester, N.Y., 1982), 5–28, esp. 25.

5. Neal Salisbury, *Manitou and Providence: Indians, Europeans, and the Making of New England, 1500–1643* (New York, 1982), 147–52, 203–15.

6. *Winthrop Papers*, 3:427, 431, 434–38, 441, 446, 448, 451–54, 456–58, 490–91; John Winthrop, *Winthrop's Journal: "History of New England," 1630–1649*, ed. James K. Hosmer, 2 vols. (New York, 1908), 1:226–28, 229; William Bradford, *Of Plymouth Plantation*, ed. Samuel Eliot Morison (New York, 1967), 297.

7. Bradford, *Of Plymouth Plantation*, 297; *Winthrop Papers*, 4:258–59, 418, 419, 427–28, 431–33, 435, 443, 507; *R.I. Recs.*, 1:139–40; Winthrop, *Journal*, 2:6–7; J. Franklin Jameson, ed., *Narratives of New Netherland, 1609–1664* (New York, 1909), 276; *Plymouth Recs.*, 9:11, 19, 30; Salisbury, *Manitou and Providence*, 231; Thomas, "Maelstrom of Change,"

71–74. Dean Snow has found that the first tubular beads in 17th-century Mohawk village sites do not appear until after 1635 and, in most villages, only after 1645 (Snow, personal communication, 13 June 1985). These dates are consistent with English accounts of large wampum presents from the Narragansetts and other New England Algonquians to the Mohawks, and underscore the critical role which this wampum played in Iroquois life—and particularly in the rise of the Mohawks—during the seventeenth century.

8. *Plymouth Recs.*, 9:116–17; *Winthrop Papers*, 4:441–42, 5:249–51, 267–68. The only firmly documented record of overt Mohawk military activity in southern New England during this period is of a small party unsuccessfully attacking the pro-Mohegan, pro-English Weepawaugs of New Haven colony (John W. DeForest, *History of the Indians of Connecticut* [Hartford, 1851], 223–24).

9. *JR*, 36:101–5; Thomas, "Maelstrom of Change," 209–10; Day, "Ouragie War," 40–41. On Druillettes' work among the Kennebec Abenakis, see Kenneth M. Morrison, *The Embattled Northeast: The Elusive Ideal of Alliance in Abenaki-Euramerican Relations* (Berkeley, 1984), 80–86.

10. *JR*, 36:79–101, 105–11; *NYCD*, 9:5–7; *Plymouth Recs.*, 9:199–203.

11. *R.I. Recs.*, 1:295–96; *Mass. Recs.*, 3:436–37.

12. *Plymouth Recs.*, 9:202.

13. Thomas, "Maelstrom of Change," chs. 4–6; Howard Millar Chapin, *The Trading Post of Roger Williams, With Those of John Wilcox and Richard Smith* (Providence, 1933), passim; Francis X. Moloney, *The Fur Trade in New England, 1620–1676* (Cambridge, Mass., 1931), 43–44; Neal Salisbury, "Social Relations on a Moving Frontier: Natives and Settlers in Southern New England, 1640–1675," *Man in the Northeast*, no. 33 (forthcoming, 1987).

14. A. J. F. van Laer, trans. and ed., *Van Rensselaer Bowier Manuscripts* (Albany, 1908), 483–84, 526; *Plymouth Recs.*, 9:172–73; Thomas, "Maelstrom of Change," 178–80. See also Robert Hassenstab, "The Role of the Connecticut Valley Indians in the Fur Trade" (unpublished paper in author's possession, 1978), 16.

15. Chapin, *Trading Post*, 22–23.

16. Alden T. Vaughan, *New England Frontier: Puritans and Indians, 1620–1675*, rev. ed. (New York, 1979), esp. ch. 6; Jennings, *Invasion of America*, ch. 15.

17. Salisbury, "Social Relations on a Moving Frontier."

18. *NYCD*, 14:108, 169, 372, 386–87, 400, 450–51, 481, 503–4; Lynn Ceci, "The First Fiscal Crisis in New York," *Economic Development and Cultural Change* 28 (1979–80): 846–47; Richter, "Ordeal of the Longhouse," 120.

19. *NYCD*, 13:101, 107, 150, 162–63, 240, 14:446–47, 465–67; Arthur H. Buffinton, "New England and the Western Fur Trade," *Publications of the Colonial Society of Massachusetts* 18 (1915–16): 177–83.

20. *NYCD* 13:355–56; *JR*, 49:139–41, 53:141–45; Thomas, "Maelstrom of Change," 245–51.

21. *JR*, 48:61; Thomas, "Maelstrom of Change," 251–52; Gordon M. Day, *The Identity of the Saint Francis Indians* (Ottawa, 1981), 13.

22. *Pynchon Papers*, 1:50; *MHSC*, 5th ser., 3 (1871): 399–400, 8 (1882): 88–90; A. J. F. van Laer, trans. and ed., *Correspondence of Jeremias van Rensselaer, 1651–1674* (Albany, 1932), 358; *NYCD* 2:371, 13:381; Thomas, "Maelstrom of Change," 253–55.

23. Francis Jennings, *The Ambiguous Iroquois Empire: The Covenant Chain Confederation of Indian Tribes with English Colonies From Its Beginnings to the Lancaster Treaty

of 1744 (New York, 1984), 129–30. One indication of the Iroquois' growing isolation is the use of the term *Loup* in the French documents. Applied before 1660 to the Mahicans alone, the term thereafter referred to the Mahican-led, anti-Iroquois alliance. Extended to the Sokokis in 1662, it gradually encompassed most of the other New England Algonquian groups by the later part of the decade; see Gordon M. Day, *The "Mots Loups" of Father Mathevet* (Ottawa, 1975), 35–44.

24. *NYCD*, 3:67–68; *MHSC*, 4th ser., 6 (1863): 531–32; Thomas, "Maelstrom of Change," 258–59.

25. *Pynchon Papers*, 1:56; Allen W. Trelease, *Indian Affairs in Colonial New York: The Seventeenth Century* (Ithaca, N.Y., 1960), 242–45; Richter, "Ordeal of the Longhouse," 123–25.

26. *LIR*, 29–31.

27. Van Laer, trans. and ed., *Correspondence of van Rensselaer*, 413; *Pynchon Papers*, 1:55–58; *NYCD*, 3:117.

28. *LIR*, 33–35.

29. *JR*, 51:81–83, 243, 249, 52:135–37; Richter, "Ordeal of the Longhouse," 125–26.

30. *Pynchon Papers*, 1:54, 71–72, 80; Connecticut Archives, Indians, 1:8, 9, Connecticut State Library, Hartford.

31. *Plymouth Recs.*, 9:137–38; Photostats, 28 April 1653, Massachusetts Historical Society; John W. Ford, *Some Correspondence Between the Governors and Treasurers of the New England Company in London and the Commissioners of the United Colonies in America* (London, 1896), 20; William Kellaway, *The New England Company, 1649–1776: Missionary Society to the American Indians* (London, 1961), 118.

32. Daniel Gookin, *Historical Collections of the Indians in New England* (1674), ed. Jeffrey H. Fiske (n.p., 1970), 40–42; *JR*, 53:137–53.

33. *NYCD*, 13:427, 439–40; van Laer, ed. and trans., *Correspondence of van Rensselaer*, 449; *Pynchon Papers*, 1:102–7. On the Mohawk-Mahican agreement, see *JR*, 52:137; 55:59–61; and Richter, "Ordeal of the Longhouse," 206–7. The Massachusett delegation arrived three days after the ceremonies had ended, bearing Bibles rather than wampum as its peace offering. Though the Bibles must have been in either English or in John Eliot's Algonquian translation, the New York authorities were uncertain whether to pass them on, fearing that the books would offend not only the many Iroquois Catholics but their French Jesuit instructors (*Pynchon Papers*, 1:102).

34. *Pynchon Papers*, 1:57; Day, "Ouragie War," 43–44.

35. The best account of the war is Bruce G. Trigger, "The Mohawk-Mahican War (1624–28): The Establishment of a Pattern," *Canadian Historical Review* 52 (1971): 276–86; but on the settlement see Ted J. Brasser, *Riding on the Frontier's Crest: Mahican Indian Culture and Culture Change* (Ottawa, 1974), 14–19; and Jennings, *Ambiguous Iroquois Empire*, 49–50.

36. *LIR*, 35–37.

37. *Pynchon Papers*, 1:124; *NYCD*, 4:715, 743–44, 902, 991; Cadwallader Colden, *The History of the Five Indian Nations Depending on the Province of New-York in America* (Ithaca, N.Y., 1958 [orig. publ. 1727, 1747]), 84; Day, *Identity of St. Francis Indians*, 19.

38. *LIR*, 37–38; Brasser, *Riding on Frontier's Crest*, 23. In addition, the recent death of the Mahicans' patron, Jeremias van Rensselaer, had left them without an effective spokesman in Albany (*LIR*, 38).

39. Salisbury, "Social Relations on a Moving Frontier."

40. *NYCD*, 3:254; *Conn. Recs.*, 2:377–78; *Plymouth Recs.*, 10:453; *Pynchon Papers*, 1:150–52; Trelease, *Indian Affairs*, 230–33; Jennings, *Invasion of America*, 300–302; Webb, *1676*, 360–63. Webb does not demonstrate his more specific contention that this meeting launched the Covenant Chain and the diplomatic career of the Onondaga leader Garakontié.

41. *NYCD*, 3:255, 265, 13:528, 14:715–16; *Conn. Recs.*, 2:397–98, 404, 406–7; A. J. F. van Laer, ed., *Minutes of the Court of Albany, Rensselaerswyck and Schenectady*, 3 vols. (Albany, 1926–32), 2:48–49; Charles H. Lincoln, ed., *Narratives of the Indian Wars, 1675–1699* (New York, 1913), 68, 87–88, 97; Jennings, *Invasion of America*, 313–16; Webb, *1676*, 367–71. Increase Mather's suggestion that the Algonquians attacked the Mohawks and then tried to pin the blame on the English in order to obtain Mohawk backing is not only unlikely but is contradicted by the New York records cited above; see Mather, "A Brief History of the Warr with the Indians in New-England" (1676), in Richard Slotkin and James K. Folsom, eds., *So Dreadfull a Judgment: Puritan Responses to King Philip's War, 1676–1677* (Middletown, Conn., 1978), 128–29. Nevertheless, Mather's version has been accepted by some historians writing from a strictly New England perspective; see the qualified acceptance of Douglas Edward Leach, *Flintlock and Tomahawk: New England in King Philip's War* (New York, 1958), 142; and Richard Irwin Melvoin, "New England Outpost: War and Society in Colonial Frontier Deerfield, Massachusetts" (Ph.D. diss., Univ. of Michigan, 1983), 201–2.

42. George Madison Bodge, *Soldiers in King Philip's War*, 3d ed. (Boston, 1906), 242; *Conn. Recs.*, 2:461–62. Although misreading some of the evidence, Melvoin offers the fullest account of the Mohawks' military role in King Philip's War ("New England Outpost," 196–206).

43. *NYCD*, 13:497; William Hubbard, *The History of the Indian Wars in New England*, ed. Samuel G. Drake (2 vols.; Roxbury, Mass., 1865 [orig. publ. 1677]), 1:279–82; Trelease, *Indian Affairs*, 234–35.

44. *Conn. Recs.*, 2:466–67, 469–70, 477–78, 480, 492–95; *Pynchon Papers*, 1:168–69; *NYCD*, 13:502; Trelease, *Indian Affairs*, 235–36; Jennings, *Ambiguous Empire*, 148.

45. *Conn. Recs.*, 2:443, 480, 485, 488, 492–93; Conn. Archives, Indians, 1:37; *NYCD*, 13:504.

46. *CSP, 1677–1680*, 295; Jennings, *Ambiguous Empire*, 148. The Mahican agreement is in *LIR*, 39–40. No record of the Mohawk treaty survives, but the contents were referred to at a Massachusett-Mohawk conference the following year (*NYCD*, 13:528–29; see also pp. 529–30; A. J. F. van Laer, trans. and ed., *Minutes of Court of Albany*, 3:363; and *Wyllys Papers, Connecticut Historical Society Collections* 21 [1924]: 268.

47. The term *Covenant Chain* first appears in the Maryland-Mohawk agreement of July 1677 (*LIR*, 45–46). For varying perspectives on the Covenant Chain, see Francis Jennings, "The Constitutional Evolution of the Covenant Chain," *Proceedings of the American Philosophical Society* 115 (1971), 88–96; idem, *Ambiguous Empire*, 148–71; Webb, *1676*, 355–404; and chapter 3, above.

48. On the Mohegans, see *NYCD*, 3:271, 275, 13:508, 509, 517; *Conn. Recs.*, 2:495, 499, 502; and *LIR*, 40n. On the Natick and other "praying" Indians, see *NYCD*, 13:513–14, 517, 519–30; Daniel Gookin, "An Historical Account of the Doings and Sufferings of the Christian Indians in New England [1678]," *Transactions and Collections of the American Antiquarian Society* 1 (1836): 519–20; Daniel K. Richter, "Rediscovered Links in the Covenant

Chain: Previously Unpublished Transcripts of New York Indian Treaty Minutes, 1677–1691," *Proceedings of the American Antiquarian Society* 92 (1982): 76; and *Plymouth Recs.*, 10:366–67, 390–92, 395–96.

49. *Plymouth Recs.*, 10:398; *Mass. Recs.*, 5:299–300, 319–20, 461–62; *Pynchon Papers*, 1:179–83.

5 —"PENNSYLVANIA INDIANS" and the IROQUOIS

1. Francis Jennings, *The Ambiguous Iroquois Empire: The Covenant Chain Confederation of Indian Tribes With English Colonies From Its Beginnings to The Lancaster Treaty of 1744* (New York, 1984), ch. 2. See also idem, "Francis Parkman: A Brahmin among Untouchables," *WMQ* 42 (1985): 305–28; Lewis Henry Morgan, *League of the Ho-dé-no-sau-nee, Iroquois* (New York, 1962) [orig. publ. 1851]), 442–43.

2. Jennings, *Ambiguous Empire*, chs. 3–10; Richard Aquila, *The Iroquois Restoration: Iroquois Diplomacy on the Colonial Frontier, 1701–1754* (Detroit, 1983); Dorothy V. Jones, *License for Empire: Colonialism by Treaty in Early America* (Chicago, 1982), ch. 2. See also chapter 6, below.

3. John Heckewelder, *An Account of the History, Manners, and Customs of the Indian Nations, Who Once Inhabited Pennsylvania and the Neighbouring States* [1819], ed. William C. Reichel, *Memoirs of the Historical Society of Pennsylvania* 12 (1876): 47–50.

4. A *tribe*, in my lexicon, is a coherent and self-conscious political entity integrated by kinship rather than bureaucracy and coercion; it functions as a nation in external affairs and as a family internally.

5. Francis Jennings, "Glory, Death, and Transfiguration: The Susquehannock Indians in the Seventeenth Century," *Proceedings of the American Philosophical Society* 112 (1968): 17–20, 50–53.

6. Barry C. Kent, *Susquehanna's Indians*, Anthropological Series 6 (Harrisburg, Pa., 1984), 95.

7. For the Maryland connection, see the documentation in Francis Jennings, "Indians and Frontiers in Seventeenth-Century Maryland," in David B. Quinn, ed., *Early Maryland in a Wider World* (Detroit, 1982), 216–41.

8. Jennings, "Glory, Death, and Transfiguration," 28–29.

9. John Romeyn Brodhead, *History of the State of New York*, 2 vols. (New York, 1853–71), 1:735–45; *NYCD*, 3:67–68.

10. *NYCD*, 9:52–54, 60; W. J. Eccles, *The Canadian Frontier, 1534–1760* (New York, 1969), 62–63.

11. *LIR*, 30, 36; *NYCD*, 3:172; 13:439; 9:110; *JR*, 51:241–43.

12. Jennings, "Glory, Death, and Transfiguration," 29–30.

13. Ibid., 33.

14. Wilcomb E. Washburn, *The Governor and the Rebel: A History of Bacon's Rebellion in Virginia* (Chapel Hill, N.C., 1957), 20–23, 40–48. Washburn's account has been criticized recently from two sides. Stephen Saunders Webb presents a different story of Susquehannock involvement in *1676: The End of American Independence* (New York, 1984), passim; and Elisabeth Tooker insists that the Susquehannocks were conquered by the Iroquois ("The Demise of the Susquehannocks: A 17th Century Mystery," *Pennsylvania Ar-*

chaeologist 54 [1984]: 1–10). Tooker's article takes issue with my earlier accounts, which have been based on Washburn's pioneering work. Having reviewed all the source materials, I have confirmed Washburn's findings and adopted them as my own. Dr. Tooker has not consulted the explicit statements by eyewitnesses in the Virginia and Maryland sources or the Coventry Papers at Longleat House, but has rested her case on rumors reaching Canadian Jesuits far distant from the events. Professor Webb is so angry at the Virginia aristocrats (probably rightly) that he has reverted (I think, wrongly) to a long discredited notion of Nathaniel Bacon being a champion of the people. Clearly, he has studied the sources; I differ with his interpretation of Indian affairs.

15. Jennings, *Ambiguous Empire*, ch. 8; see also chapter 4, above. An alternate interpretation which seems to me to be at odds with the sources is in Webb, *1676*, passim. My view is also at variance with Richard Haan's (chapter 3, above).

16. Heckewelder, *Account of the Indian Nations*, xxv–xxix; Morgan, *League*, 14–15; Horatio Hale, ed., *The Iroquois Book of Rites*, reprint ed. William N. Fenton (Toronto, 1963 [orig. publ. 1883]), 92–93.

17. Purchases are itemized in Samuel Hazard, *Annals of Pennsylvania From the Discovery of the Delaware, 1609–1682* (Philadelphia, 1850), 420, 437, 443, 461, 465. See also *NYCD*, 12:523, 542; C. A. Weslager, in collaboration with A. R. Dunlap, *Dutch Explorers, Traders, and Settlers in the Delaware Valley, 1609–1664* (Philadelphia, 1961), 307; Jennings, "Glory, Death, and Transfiguration," 50–53.

18. Cayuga chief Jacob E. Thomas recited his tribe's tradition at the Newberry Library, 22 May 1980.

19. *Md. Archives*, 5:269.

20. Draft minutes of Indian conference, 15 Sept. 1718, Logan Papers, 11:7, HSP. Sassoonan added, "but those [Iroquois] Nations have their own Lands and Countrey and these here have theirs, and each of them are to Manage their own concerns."

21. See the list of deeds in *Pa. Council Minutes*, 13:462–67.

22. Richard S. Dunn and Mary Maples Dunn, et al., eds. *The Papers of William Penn*, 2 vols. to date (Philadelphia, 1981–), 2:260 and passim.

23. *Pa. Council Minutes*, 13:464; *Md. Archives*, 5:402; *NYCD*, 3:417–18.

24. Gary B. Nash, "The Quest for the Susquehanna Valley: New York, Pennsylvania, and the Seventeenth-Century Fur Trade," *New York History* 48 (1967): 3–27; Dunn, et al., eds., *Papers of William Penn*, 2:467–68.

25. Jennings, *Ambiguous Empire*, 228–30, 235, 357–58.

26. Ibid., 232–33; text reconstituted from NY Council Minutes, 5:163, 169 (mutilated by fire); and *NYDH*, 1:403–5 (extracts). Copies of the unique, reconstituted text—reproduced in IIDH, reel 3—are on file in the New York State Archives, Albany, and the Newberry Library, Chicago.

27. Aquila, *Iroquois Restoration*, chs. 2–3.

28. *LIR*, 128.

29. *Pa. Council Minutes*, 1:447–49 (italics added).

30. Kent, *Susquehanna's Indians*, 56–58; *NYCD*, 4:648.

31. Deed, Dongan to Penn, 12 Jan. 1696, Gratz Collection, Governors of Pennsylvania, Case 2, Box 33-a, HSP.

32. Deed, 13 Sept. 1700, Cadwallader Collection, Box 12, Fol. Penn Indian Deeds,

HSP; copy in Philadelphia Deed Book F-8:242, Philadelphia City Hall; printed in *Pa. Archives*, 1st ser., 1:133; Treaty, 3 Apr. 1701, Penn Papers, Indian Affairs, 1:45, HSP; printed in *Pa. Council Minutes*, 2:14–18.

33. *WA*, 33; NY Council Minutes, 30 Aug. 1699, 8:131.

34. J. N. B. Hewitt, "Tuscarora," in F. W. Hodge, ed., *Handbook of American Indians North of Mexico*, 2 vols. (Washington, D.C., 1907), 2:843; *Pa. Council Minutes*, 16 June 1710, 2:511–12.

35. Conestoga meeting, 8 June 1710, reported in *Pa. Council Minutes*, 16 June 1710, 2:511. French agreed with "our Seneques" at Conestoga to send the Tuscarora belt to the Five Nations. On arriving, the Iroquois spokesman pronounced "the message sent us *from Philadelphia*" as "verry acceptable" (Minutes, 31 July 1710, mss., Penn Papers, Indian Affairs, 1:34 [italics added]).

36. Loc. cit. Note that Teganissorens had been the chief rebuked by New York in 1699 for seeking rapprochement with Pennsylvania at that time. See n. 33, above. New York records spell his name as it sounded to English ears: *Decanisora*. In the 1710 mss., he is spelled *Connessoa*.

37. Paul A. W. Wallace, *Indians in Pennsylvania* (Harrisburg, Pa., 1961), ch. 14, quotation on p. 105.

38. Jennings, *Ambiguous Empire*, 196–201.

39. NY Council Minutes, 10:602; *NYCM*, 55:73, 83; *Pa. Council Minutes*, 1 Aug. 1711, 2:537.

40. *NYCD*, 5:270, 272. My understanding of this event is altered from that published in "The Constitutional Evolution of the Covenant Chain," *Procs. Am. Phil. Soc.*, 115 (1971): 91–92.

41. *Pa. Council Minutes*, 1 Oct. 1714, 2:573–74.

42. *NYCD*, 5:675–76.

43. For detailed analysis, see William A. Hunter, "Documented Subdivisions of the Delaware Indians," *Bulletin of the Archaeological Society of New Jersey* 20 (1978): 20–40. Note especially that "the Delaware River was not a boundary to these people [the 'Jersey' Delawares] who clearly had ties on both sides of it" (p. 26).

44. Ibid., p. 23.

45. Compare *Pa. Council Minutes*, 19 May 1712, 2:546, with photostat of mss. of same document in Society Collection, HSP, and with formal mss. record at Pennsylvania Historical and Museum Commission, Harrisburg. (Italics added.)

46. See Jennings, "The Indian Trade of the Susquehanna Valley," *Procs. Am. Phil. Soc.* 110 (1966): 406–24.

47. *Pa. Council Minutes*, 18 May 1704, 2:145, 28 Aug. 1704, 2:159.

48. Jennings, *Ambiguous Empire*, 169, 264.

49. *Pa. Archives*, 1st ser., 1:329; Sylvester K. Stevens and Donald H. Kent, eds., *Wilderness Chronicles of Northwestern Pennsylvania* (Harrisburg, Pa., 1941), 6–7.

50. C. A. Weslager, *Red Men on the Brandywine* (Wilmington, Del., 1953); Francis Paul Jennings, "Miquon's Passing: Indian-European Relations in Colonial Pennsylvania, 1674–1755" (Ph.D. diss., University of Pennsylvania, 1965), 107–14, 235–45, 290–91.

51. Jennings, "Incident at Tulpehocken," *Pennsylvania History* 35 (1968), 335–55.

52. *Pa. Archives*, 1st ser., 1:329.

53. Stevens and Kent, eds., *Wilderness Chronicles*, 3–4, 9.

54. Jennings, *Ambiguous Empire*, 302n, 306, 312n.

55. *Pa. Council Minutes*, 4–5 June 1728, 3:316–26; same with an appendix, Penn-Physick Mss., 6:25, HSP.

56. See Jennings, "The Delaware Interregnum," *Pennsylvania Magazine of History and Biography* 89 (Apr. 1965): 174–98.

57. Jennings, *Ambiguous Empire*, 314–16; see also chapter 6, below.

58. Ethnologists have long studied religious syncretism to good effect, but they have neglected political syncretism. The reordering of the Covenant Chain displays the capability of tribal peoples for innovation in politics.

59. *Pa. Council Minutes*, 4:80–85, 90–95; Logan to Weiser, Oct. 1736, Logan Papers, 11:26, HSP; same to same, 18 Oct. 1736, ibid., 10:64; same to same, 27 Oct. 1736, ibid., 10:65.

60. Jennings, *Ambiguous Empire*, ch. 18.

61. Sassoonan's speech, 7 Aug. 1741, Records of the Provincial Council and Other Papers from the Numismatic and Antiquarian Society (boxed), fol. 1740–49, HSP.

62. *Pa. Council Minutes* 4:575–80.

63. See Anthony F. C. Wallace, *King of the Delawares: Teedyuscung, 1700–1763* (Philadelphia, 1949); Paul A. W. Wallace, *Conrad Weiser, 1696–1760, Friend of Colonist and Mohawk* (Philadelphia, 1945); Theodore Thayer, *Israel Pemberton: King of the Quakers* (Philadelphia, 1943). To be discussed in detail in Francis Jennings, *Empire of Fortune: Crowns, Colonies, and Tribes in the Seven Years War in America* (in press).

64. P. A. W. Wallace, *Indians in Pennsylvania*, 153–62.

65. The migrations can be followed in C. A. Weslager, *The Delaware Indians: A History* (New Brunswick, N.J., 1972); and idem, *The Delaware Indian Westward Migration* (Wallingford, Pa., 1978).

6 – PEOPLES "IN BETWEEN"

1. *NYCD*, 7:573.

2. Cadwallader Colden, *The History of the Five Indian Nations Depending on the Province of New-York in America* (Ithaca, N.Y., 1958 [orig. published 1727, 1747]). The most recent reinterpretation of British-Iroquois relations is found in Francis Jennings, *The Ambiguous Iroquois Empire: The Covenant Chain Confederation of Indian Tribes With English Colonies From Its Beginnings to the Lancaster Treaty of 1744* (New York, 1984).

3. See, for example, Randolph C. Downes, *Council Fires on the Upper Ohio: A Narrative of Indian Affairs in the Upper Ohio Valley until 1795* (Pittsburgh, 1940); and C. A. Weslager, *The Delaware Indians: A History* (New Brunswick, N.J., 1972). Recent ethnohistorical studies of the region and period have provided useful correctives to earlier interpretations: Jennings, *Ambiguous Empire*; Richard Aquila, *The Iroquois Restoration: Iroquois Diplomacy on the Colonial Frontier, 1701–1744* (Detroit, 1983); and Dorothy V. Jones, *License For Empire: Colonialism by Treaty in Early America* (Chicago, 1982).

4. James B. Griffin, "Late Prehistory of the Ohio Valley," *HNAI*, 15:547–59; Marian C. White, "Erie," ibid., 412–17. See also William J. Mayer-Oakes, *Prehistory of the Upper Ohio Valley*, Annals of the Carnegie Museum 34 (Pittsburgh, 1955); and David S. Brose,

ed., *The Late Prehistory of the Lake Erie Drainage Basin: A 1972 Symposium Revised* (Cleveland, Ohio, 1976).

5. William A. Hunter, "History of the Ohio Valley," *HNAI*, 15:588–93; Charles Callendar, "Shawnee," ibid., 630–31; Barry C. Kent, Janet Rice, and Kakuko Ota, "A Map of 18th Century Indian Towns in Pennsylvania," *Pennsylvania Archaeologist* 51 (1981): 1–19; William N. Fenton, "Problems Arising from the Historic Northeastern Position of the Iroquois," *Smithsonian Miscellaneous Collections* 100 (1940): 159–252, esp. 241–42.

6. Elizabeth Tooker, "Wyandot," *HNAI*, 15:400.

7. Thomas Abler and Elizabeth Tooker, "Seneca," ibid., 506–7.

8. *PDT*, 451; *Pa. Archives*, 1st ser., 1:329–30; *Pa. Council Minutes* 3:112.

9. *Pa. Archives*, 1st ser., 1:243, 299–301.

10. Ibid., 299–300.

11. William A. Hunter, "Traders on the Ohio, 1730," *Western Pennsylvania Historical Magazine* 35 (1952): 85–92.

12. I am indebted to Dr. Barry Kent of the Pennsylvania Historical and Museum Commission and his associates at the William Penn Memorial Museum, Harrisburg, Pennsylvania, for sharing the archaeological information on the upper Ohio Valley upon which this summary is based and especially for the use of: Marco M. Hervatin, "Refuge[e] Wyandot Town of 1748," Beaver Valley Chapter, Society for Pennsylvania Archaeology *Newsletter* 7 (Jan.–Feb., 1958); and John A. Zakucia, "Chambers Site, 36Lall," 1957 (unpublished artifact inventory and field notes on file with the Pennsylvania Historical and Museum Commission, Harrisburg). Illustrations of maskettes similar to those found at Wyandotte Town appear in Richard Rose, *Face to Face: Encounters with Identity* (Rochester, N.Y., 1983), 6–7.

13. *Pa. Archives*, 1st ser., 1:299–301; *Pa. Council Minutes*, 5:351.

14. *JR*, 8:302, 44:49, 62:191–99.

15. *Pa. Archives*, 1st ser., 1:329.

16. *PDT*, 347–48; see also *Pa. Archives*, 1st ser., 1:243–45, 254–55, 261, 2:16–17.

17. *PDT*, 346, 349. The Senecas did, however, make at least one unsuccessful effort to persuade the Delawares and Shawnees to return to the East (ibid., 406; *Pa. Archives*, 1st ser., 1:454).

18. On the evolution of the Chain in eastern Pennsylvania see Jennings, *Ambiguous Empire*, chs. 8, 12–17.

19. *Pa. Archives*, 1st. ser., 1:340; William A. Hunter, "Documented Sub-Divisions of the Delaware Indians," New Jersey Archaeological Association *Bulletin* 35 (1978): 34.

20. Hunter, "Traders on the Ohio," passim.

21. Not all the news was encouraging, however. Another expression of a developing regional interest came again from the Shawnees, who sent messages on behalf of their neighbors to the French, British, and eastern Indians asking that no liquor be carried to the Ohio (*Pa. Archives*, 1st ser., 1:551–52).

22. Reuben Gold Thwaites, ed., *Collections of the State Historical Society of Wisconsin*, vol. 17: *The French Regime in Wisconsin, 1727–1748* (Madison, Wis., 1906), 131, 186, 230–31, 281, 350.

23. Ibid., 458–62, 479–80.

24. *Pa. Archives*, 1st ser., 1:737, 741–42.

25. [Julian P. Boyd, ed.,] *Indian Treaties Printed by Benjamin Franklin, 1736–1762* (Philadelphia, 1938), 103–5.

26. *Pa. Council Minutes*, 5:478–79.

27. On the development and meaning of the "Iroquois mystique" see Jones, *License for Empire*, ch. 2.

28. *Pa. Council Minutes*, 5:480.

29. *NYCD*, 6:593–94.

30. On the influence of locality in Iroquois society see William N. Fenton, "Locality as a Basic Factor in the Development of Iroquois Social Structure," in idem, ed., *Symposium on Local Diversity in Iroquois Culture*, Bureau of American Ethnology Bulletin 149 (Washington, D.C., 1951), 35–54; George S. Snyderman, "Concepts of Land Ownership Among the Iroquois and Their Neighbors," ibid., 13–34.

31. Note, for example, the mixed ethnic background of well-known Mingo leader Tanaghrisson (discussed below) (Sylvester K. Stevens and Donald H. Kent, eds., *Journal of Chaussegros de Léry* [Harrisburg, Pa., 1940], 19).

32. Boyd, ed., *Indian Treaties*, 104.

33. Sylvester K. Stevens and Donald H. Kent, eds., *Wilderness Chronicles of Northwestern Pennsylvania* (Harrisburg, Pa., 1941), 50–51; Donald H. Kent, *The French Invasion of Western Pennsylvania, 1753* (Harrisburg, Pa., 1954), 49, 51.

34. *Pa. Council Minutes*, 5:438–39 (emphasis added); see also Snyderman, "Concepts of Land Ownership," 25.

35. Quoted in [Julian P. Boyd,] "Indian Affairs in Pennsylvania," in idem, ed., *Indian Treaties*, lxiii.

36. *Johnson Papers*, 4:244.

37. *Pa. Archives*, 1st ser., 1:737; William A. Hunter, "Tanaghrisson," in George W. Brown, et al., eds., *Dictionary of Canadian Biography*, 9 vols. to date (Toronto, 1966–   ), 3:613–15.

38. Theodore Calvin Pease, ed., *Collections of the Illinois State Historical Library*, vol. 29: *Illinois on the Eve of the Seven Years' War, 1747–1755* (Springfield, Ill., 1940), 919.

39. Boyd, ed., *Indian Treaties*, 113–20.

40. *Pa. Council Minutes*, 5:357–58.

41. A. A. Lambing, ed., "Celoron's Journal," *Ohio Archaeological and Historical Quarterly* 29 (1920): 343, 346, 354.

42. "Treaty of Logg's Town, 1752," *Virginia Historical Magazine* 13 (1913): 171–72.

43. *Pa. Council Minutes*, 5:533, 536.

44. "Treaty of Logg's Town," 167–68.

45. Scarouady quoted in Lawrence Henry Gipson, *The British Empire Before the American Revolution*, vol. 4: *Zones of International Friction: North America South of the Great Lakes Region, 1748–1754* (New York, 1967), 284; Tanaghrisson quoted in "The Case of the Ohio Company," in Lois Mulkearn, comp. and ed., *George Mercer Papers Relating to the Ohio Company of Virginia* (Pittsburgh, 1954), 23.

46. Kent, *French Invasion of Western Pennsylvania*, esp. 27–68; W. J. Eccles, "The Fur Trade and Eighteenth-Century Imperialism," *WMQ* 40 (1983): 341–62, esp. 356–62.

47. On Tanaghrisson's declining influence see Donald Jackson and Dorothy Two-

hig, eds., *The Diaries of George Washington,* 6 vols. (Charlottesville, Va., 1976–80) 1:140–42. On Ohio Indian assistance to the French see Stevens and Kent, eds., *Wilderness Chronicles,* 51–52; and Kent, *French Invasion of Western Pennsylvania,* 46–49.

48. *Diaries of Washington,* 1:205; Boyd, ed., *Indian Treaties,* 125.

49. *NYCD,* 6:779–80, 796–97.

50. Ibid., 785–88, esp. 788.

51. Stevens and Kent, eds., *Wilderness Chronicles,* 50–51.

52. Hunter, "Tanaghrisson," 614.

53. "Two Journals of Western Tours by Charles Frederick Post," in Reuben Gold Thwaites, ed., *Early Western Travels, 1748-1846* (Cleveland, Ohio, 1904), 1:281.

54. Beverly W. Bond, Jr., ed., "The Captivity of Charles Stuart, 1755–1757," *Mississippi Valley Historical Review* 13 (1926–27): 63–65; William A. Hunter, "Provincial Negotiations with the Western Indians, 1754–1758," *Pennsylvania History* 18 (1951): 213–19.

55. For details concerning Post's two missions see "Two Journals of Western Tours," 176–291; and *Pa. Archives,* 2d ser., 3:520–44.

56. On the Delawares as "women" see John Heckewelder, *An Account of the History, Manners, and Customs of the Indian Nations Who Once Inhabited Pennsylvania and the Neighboring States* [1819], ed. William C. Reichel, *Memoirs of the Historical Society of Pennsylvania* 12 (1876): 58–59; Jennings, *Ambiguous Empire,* 301–2; Jay Miller, "The Delaware as Women: A Symbolic Solution," *American Ethnologist* 1 (1974): 507–14.

57. *Pa. Archives,* 2d ser., 3:539; "Two Journals of Western Tours," 278.

58. *Johnson Papers,* 2:664; Boyd, ed., *Indian Treaties,* 174–75, 186–87.

59. "Two Journals of Western Tours," 273.

60. Ibid., 273–74.

61. *Johnson Papers,* 4:296, 308, 368.

62. Ibid., 243–44; *NYCD,* 7:603; Jones, *License for Empire,* 33–34, 68–92.

63. Nicholas B. Wainwright, ed., "George Croghan's Journals, 1759–1763," *Pennsylvania Magazine of History and Biography* 71 (1947): 345.

64. *Johnson Papers,* 13:444.

65. *Pa. Archives,* 1st ser., 3:148–49, 305–8; *Pa. Council Minutes,* 7:341–43.

66. Wainwright, ed. "Croghan's Journals," 403, 410; *Johnson Papers,* 10:321–22. On the general subject of diplomacy and gift-giving see Wilbur R. Jacobs, *Wilderness Politics and Indian Gifts: The Northern Colonial Frontier, 1748-1763* (Lincoln, Neb., 1967).

67. Louis M. Waddell, et al., eds., *The Papers of Henry Bouquet,* 5 vols. to date (Harrisburg, Pa., 1958–   ), 5:32; Sylvester K. Stevens and Donald H. Kent, eds., *The Papers of Colonel Henry Bouquet,* 19 vols. (Harrisburg, Pa., 1940–42), series 21634: 81–83, series 21648: 3, 4, 20–21, 45; *Johnson Papers,* 3:387, 515, 10:265–66.

68. *Johnson Papers,* 3:444, 456, 460, 462–67, 521, 629–30.

69. Charles E. Hunter, "The Delaware Nativist Revival of the Mid-Eighteenth Century," *Ethnohistory* 19 (1971): 39–49; Anthony F. C. Wallace, "New Religious Beliefs Among the Delaware Indians, 1600–1900," *Southwestern Journal of Anthropology* 12 (1956): 1–21.

70. Wainwright, ed., "Croghan's Journals," 438.

71. Jones, *License for Empire,* 68–74. For a general history of the war see Howard H. Peckham, *Pontiac and the Indian Uprising* (New York, 1970).

72. Boyd, ed., *Indian Treaties*, 293–94; *Johnson Papers*, 4:504; *NYCD*, 7:583; Clarence Walworth Alvord and Clarence Edwin Carter, eds., *Collections of the Illinois State Historical Library*, vol. 10: *The Critical Period, 1763–1765* (Springfield, Ill., 1915), 306; Stevens and Kent, eds., *Papers of Bouquet*, ser. 21655: 235.

73. Alvord and Carter, eds., *Collections*, 12:89; *Johnson Papers*, 11:328–33; Jones, *License for Empire*, 91.

74. For the most recent discussions of the events surrounding the Fort Stanwix Treaty see Jones, *License for Empire*, ch. 4; and Peter Marshall, "Sir William Johnson and the Treaty of Fort Stanwix, 1768," *Journal of American Studies* 1 (1967): 149–79.

75. Jones, *License for Empire*, 89–92. The text of the treaty is found in *NYCD*, 8:111–37.

76. *Johnson Papers*, 12:366–67; Clarence Walworth Alvord and Clarence Edwin Carter, eds., *Collections of the Illinois State Historical Library*, vol. 12: *Trade and Politics, 1767–1769* (Springfield, Ill., 1921), 75; Jones, *License for Empire*, 75–86.

77. *NYCD*, 8:111–37. The names of Benevissica, a Shawnee, and of Killbuck and Turtle Heart, two Delawares, were appended to the treaty below those of the Six Nations chiefs. None of these men participated in the proceedings, and the extent to which they represented significant numbers of Ohio Indians is unclear.

78. Marshall, "Johnson and Fort Stanwix," 177–79.

79. K. G. Davies, ed., *Documents of the American Revolution, 1770–1783*, Colonial Office Series, 21 vols. (Shannon, Ireland, 1972–81), 2:21–22; *Johnson Papers*, 7:184.

80. Snyderman, "Concepts of Land Ownership," 25.

81. On the history of the Ohio Country and Ohio Indians from the 1770s through 1794 see Jones, *License for Empire*, chs. 6–7; Downes, *Council Fires on the Upper Ohio*, chs. 7–13; and Anthony F. C. Wallace, *The Death and Rebirth of the Seneca* (New York, 1969), chs. 5–6.

7—"THEIR VERY BONES SHALL FIGHT"

1. *DRIA*, 1:95.

2. *Pa. Council Minutes*, 5:473; Catawba Nation to the Iroquois, 11 Nov. 1752, George Clinton Papers, William L. Clements Library, Ann Arbor, Mich.

3. John Lawson, *A New Voyage to Carolina*, ed. Hugh T. Lefler (Chapel Hill, N.C., 1967), 207, 53.

4. James Mooney, *The Siouan Tribes of the East*, Bureau of American Ethnology Bulletin 22 (Washington, D.C., 1894), 12, 14. For a fuller and more balanced account of Catawba warfare, see Douglas Summers Brown, *The Catawba Indians: The People of the River* (Columbia, S.C., 1966), ch. 8.

5. *CVSP*, 1:179; William W. Hening, ed., *The Statutes at Large; Being a Collection of the Laws of Virginia . . .* , 13 vols. (Richmond, Va., 1816–23), 4:103; Samuel C. Williams, ed., *Adair's History of the American Indians* (New York, 1974 [rpt. of 1930 ed.]), 235.

6. *NYCD*, 5:444; "Continuation of Colden's History of the Five Indian Nations, for the Years 1707 through 1720," *Collections of the New-York Historical Society* 68 (1935): 423.

7. *JHB*, 1:15–16; *JR*, 47:143, 145.

8. I suggest—from the absence of complaints about them, even by explorers of

the interior – that these northern intruders were not a menace until the late 1670s (see Clarence W. Alvord and Lee Bidgood, eds., *The First Explorations of the Trans-Allegheny Region by the Virginians, 1650-1674* [Cleveland, 1912]). The Susquehannocks' story is traced in Francis Jennings, "Glory, Death, and Transfiguration: The Susquehannock Indians in the Seventeenth Century," *Proceedings of the American Philosophical Society* 112 (1968): 15–53; in chapter 5 of this volume; and in Stephen Saunders Webb, *1676: The End of American Independence* (New York, 1984). For the Occaneechis' response, see Wilcomb E. Washburn, *The Governor and the Rebel: A History of Bacon's Rebellion in Virginia* (Chapel Hill, N.C., 1957), 43. For the Susquehannock role in the later raids on Virginia, see *CSP, 1681-85*, 92–94.

9. Joseph Ewan and Nesta Ewan, eds., *John Banister and His Natural History of Virginia, 1678-1692* (Urbana, Ill., 1970), 38. For other raids on Virginia during this period, see ibid., 39–40; Cornelius Dabney to Francis Moryson, 29 June 1678, Colonial Office Papers, 1/42, 277, Public Record Office, London, copy in Virginia Colonial Records Project, Microfilm M-319, Colonial Williamsburg Archives, Williamsburg, Va.; Nicholas Spencer to ?, 23 Nov. 1683, C.O. 1/53, 183, copy in ibid., M-327; *LIR*, 54–55, 61, 85, 87, 125–26, 135–36, 138–39; *JHB*, 1:147, 159, 162; "Virginia in 1681," *VMHB* 25 (1917): 369; Cadwallader Colden, *The History of the Five Indian Nations Depending on the Province of New-York in America* (Ithaca, N.Y., 1973; orig. pub. 1727, 1747), 20–45, 69.

10. Cadwallader Jones to Lord Baltimore, 6 Feb. 1682, C.O. 1/48, 115, copy in Va. Col. Rec. Proj., M-327. For other evidence that war parties were going south beyond Virginia, see *LIR*, 70–71; and *Va. Council Jour.*, 1:253.

11. William P. Cumming, ed., *The Discoveries of John Lederer* (Charlottesville, Va., 1958), 41–42; *NYDH*, 1:13; and "Virginia in 1681," 369.

12. Some scholars have argued that Iroquois expeditions southward halted during the 1690s, when the Five Nations were occupied elsewhere (Richard Aquila, "Down the Warriors' Path: The Causes of the Southern Wars of the Iroquois," *American Indian Quarterly* 4 [1978]: 211; Daniel K. Richter, "War and Culture: The Iroquois Experience," *WMQ* 40 [1983]: 557–58). Evidence from the southern colonies suggests that expeditions never altogether ceased. See Francis Nicholson to the Committee, 26 Jan. 1691, C.O. 5/1306, 43, Library of Congress transcripts, Washington, D.C.; "Notes from the Records of Stafford County, Virginia, Order Books," *VMHB* 45 (1937): 376–79; *Va. Council Jour.*, 1:253; "Queries Sent by the Lords of the Councell of trade and Plantations to be Ansered by the Govern[o]r of Virginia," C.O. 5/1309, 57, Lib. Cong. trans.; and *CSP, 1700*, 309.

13. Lawson, *New Voyage*, 50–59.

14. Ibid., 38.

15. *Pa. Council Minutes*, 2:138.

16. Aquila, "Warriors' Path," 211; Richter, "War and Culture," 552–59.

17. For the occasional talk of peace, see *NYCD*, 4:918, 5:221; and *WA*, 52, 60–61, 191.

18. For the Tuscaroras, see chapter 9, below. The Savannahs' story is told in James H. Merrell, "Natives in a New World: The Catawba Indians of Carolina, 1650-1800" (Ph.D. diss., Johns Hopkins Univ., 1982), 148–55.

19. For examples of these Indians heading north, see *Pa. Archives*, 1:238–39; and *Pa. Council Minutes*, 3:327.

20. Ewan and Ewan, eds., *Banister and His Natural History*, 38; *JHB*, 1:147.

21. Spencer to ?, 23 Nov. 1683; Williams, ed., *Adair's History*, 158; Report of Joshua Fry to Lewis Burwell, 8 May 1751, C.O. 5/1327, 373–74, Lib. Cong. trans.

22. Report of Fry, 370.

23. *Pa. Council Minutes*, 3:124.

24. PROSC, 16:4.

25. *NYCD*, 9:1098.

26. *JR*, 47:143.

27. See *JHB*, 1:15; and "Notes from Stafford County," *VMHB*, 45 (1937): 378–79. For later reports of Iroquois hunting in the south, see *CRNC*, 2:24; William Byrd, "The History of the Dividing Line," in Louis B. Wright, ed., *The Prose Works of William Byrd of Westover: Narratives of a Colonial Virginian* (Cambridge, Mass., 1966), 258.

28. Williams, ed., *Adair's History*, 158–59.

29. Aquila, "Warriors' Path," 218–19; Richter, "War and Culture," 528–59; Anthony F. C. Wallace, *The Death and Rebirth of the Seneca* (New York, 1969), 39–48, 101–3; and see above, chapter 1. In 1741 a missionary among the Iroquois observed that the Indians "esteem It the greater Honour, the farther distant they seek an Enemy from their own Country" ("Continuation of Colden's History," 280).

30. Lawson, *New Voyage*, 207.

31. Williams, ed., *Adair's History*, 158–59.

32. "A Treaty Between Virginia and the Catawbas and Cherokees, 1756," *VMHB* 13 (1906): 241.

33. "A Coppy of a Paper from O Tassity, commonly called Judge Freind, to Connecotte, called Old Hop, May 26th, 1757," encl. in Raymond Demere to William Henry Lyttelton, 4 July 1757, William Henry Lyttelton Papers, Clements Library. For a good summary of the many functions warfare served, see Williams, ed., *Adair's History*, 406.

34. *NYCD*, 5:793; South Carolina Upper House Journals, 1 Nov. 1725, in RSUS, S.C. A.1a, reel 1; Upper House of Assembly Journals, 9 Sept. 1727, C.O. 5/429, 176–77, microfilm copy in Lester K. Born, *British Manuscripts Project: A Checklist of the Microfilm Prepared in England and Wales for the American Council of Learned Societies, 1941–1945* (Washington, D.C., 1955), D 491.

35. *DRIA*, 1:362.

36. Williams, ed., *Adair's History*, 235.

37. Hugh Jones, *The Present State of Virginia . . .* , ed. Richard L. Morton (Chapel Hill, N.C., 1956), 57; *JHB*, 4:197; *Pa. Council Minutes*, 3:11; South Carolina Council Journals, 27 Apr. 1748, RSUS, S.C. E.1p, reel 3. See also Williams, ed., *Adair's History*, 421–23. Warfare may have served the same function among the Iroquois; see Aquila, "Warriors' Path," 215–16.

38. John P. Reid, *A Law of Blood: The Primitive Law of the Cherokee Nation* (New York, 1970), 8.

39. Thomas Lee to Board of Trade, 29 Sept. 1750, C.O. 5/1327, 244, Lib. of Cong. trans.

40. PROSC, 23:74; Wilbur R. Jacobs, ed., *Indians of the Southern Colonial Frontier: The Edmond Atkin Report and Plan of 1755* (Columbia, S.C., 1954), 47; Williams, ed., *Adair's History*, 235.

41. *Pa. Archives*, 1st ser., 1:671; *DRIA*, 2:107; see also S.C. Council Journals, 27 May 1758, RSUS, S.C. E.1p, reel 8.

42. Reid, *Law of Blood*, 5; Jacobs, ed., *Atkin Report*, 49.

43. Charles M. Hudson, *The Catawba Nation*, University of Georgia Monographs 18 (Athens, Ga., 1970), 11–17, 26–27; Joffre L. Coe, "The Cultural Sequence of the Carolina Piedmont," in James B. Griffin, ed., *Archeology of Eastern United States* (Chicago, 1952), 308–9; Leland G. Ferguson, "South Appalachian Mississippian" (Ph.D. diss., Univ. North Carolina, 1971), esp. 214–16, 243–47; Steven G. Baker, "Cofitachique: Fair Province of Carolina" (M.A. thesis, Univ. South Carolina, 1974); George E. Stuart, "Post-Archaic Occupation of Central South Carolina" (Ph.D. diss., Univ. North Carolina, 1975), esp. 153.

44. PROSC, 25:324.

45. Paul A. W. Wallace, *Conrad Weiser, 1696–1760, Friend of Colonist and Mohawk* (Philadelphia, 1945), 220.

46. *South Carolina Gazette*, 20 Aug. 1753.

47. Williams, ed., *Adair's History*, 133.

48. *DRIA*, 1:218.

49. S.C. Commons House Journals, 25 Jan. 1733, RSUS, S.C. A.1b, reel 4; *Va. Council Jour.*, 5:198, 311; *S.C. Gazette*, 9 June 1746; *CVSP*, 1:239; *JCHA*, 9:209; Lee to Board of Trade, 11 May 1750, C.O. 5/1327, 179–80, Lib. Cong. trans.; *DRIA*, 1:47; PROSC, 25:130, 304; *NYCD*, 9:884; *JCHA*, 6:140; S.C. Council Journals, 28 Mar. 1750, RSUS, S.C. E.1p, reel 4.

50. *DRIA*, 1:101. See also p. 47.

51. *Pa. Council Minutes*, 4:721, 733 (quotation), 668; *DRIA*, 1:47; Williams, ed., *Adair's History*, 143. For the "double Men" theme, see also Wallace, *Conrad Weiser*, 92.

52. James Logan to Gov. Clarke, 6 Dec. 1740, James Logan Papers, 4:21, American Philosophical Society, Philadelphia; *Pa. Archives*, 1:671; *Pa. Council Minutes*, 4:721, 5:402; For examples of treachery, see *NYCD*, 5:483; "Continuation of Colden's History," 429; *Md. Archives*, 25:362, 367, 369; and *Pa. Council Minutes*, 5:473.

53. *WA*, 177–79; *Va. Council Jour.*, 4:209; *Pa. Archives*, 1:241–42, 671; *Pa. Council Minutes*, 5:473; *DRIA*, 1:95; Carl F. Klinck and James J. Talman, eds., *The Journal of Major John Norton, 1816* (Toronto, 1970), 262–63.

54. *DRIA*, 1:95.

55. Wallace, *Conrad Weiser*, 165. See also *Pa. Council Minutes*, 4:668.

56. *CSP, 1681–85*, 93. See also pp. 91–92; and Colden, *History*, 33. On the "ungoverned" Five Nations, see chapter 1, above, at n. 19.

57. *Pa. Council Minutes*, 3:12.

58. Jacobs, ed., *Atkin Report*, 47.

59. *Pa. Council Minutes*, 3:9–12, 86–87, 89–90, 4:234–35, 336–37, 447; *WA*, 225–26; Jacobs, ed., *Atkin Report*, 4–5, 47; PROSC, 22:151, 23:110; *DRIA*, 1:53. The Shawnee and Cherokee stories may also be followed in chapter 6, above, and chapter 8, below.

60. Jacobs, ed., *Atkin Report*, 47.

61. PROSC, 24:414–15; *JCHA*, 1:335.

62. S.C. Council Journals, 22 May 1750, RSUS, S.C. E.1p, reel 4. See also ibid., 27 Apr. 1748, reel 3.

63. Glen to Clinton, 7 July 1750, Clinton Papers.

64. Logan to Gooch, 2 Feb. 1738, Logan Papers, 4:11.

65. *WA*, 191–96.

66. *Va. Council Jour.*, 3:446; R. A. Brock, ed., *The Official Letters of Alexander*

Spotswood, Lieutenant-Governor of the Colony of Virginia, 1710-1722, Collections of the Virginia Historical Society, n.s., 2 (Richmond, 1885): 252.

67. PROSC, 16:3. See also *NYCD*, 5:549.

68. PROSC, 16:19; *DRIA*, 1:432. See also *CVSP*, 1:215.

69. For incidents see *Va. Council Jour.*, 4:368, 370, 383; *Virginia Gazette*, 3 Nov. 1738; *JHB*, 5:320-21; *JCHA*, 8:171-72, 10:338-39, 353-54.

70. PROSC, 20:572. See also *NYCD*, 6:137-38; *Pa. Council Minutes*, 5:27.

71. *Pa. Council Minutes*, 4:245, 776, 5:24, 402; *CRNC*, 4:822; *WA*, 188, 199; Logan to Six Nations, 27 Sept. 1737, Logan Papers, 4:67-68.

72. *WA*, 210; see also pp. 60-61.

73. *DRIA*, 1:467. *Va. Council Jour.*, 5:62-63, 171, 188; *Pa. Council Minutes*, 5:5; *NYCD*, 6:208, 210-11; *JCHA*, 3:366; *Pa. Archives*, 1:664; Gooch to George Thomas, 12 Sept. 1745, Logan Papers, 4:119.

74. *NYCD*, 9:1063. See also S.C. Council Journals, 12 Jan. 1743, RSUS, S.C. E.1p, reel 1.

75. *WA*, 199; *Pa. Council Minutes*, 4:779.

76. *Va. Council Jour.*, 5:188; *Pa. Council Minutes*, 4:781.

77. *Pa. Council Minutes*, 4:781.

78. S.C. Council Journals, 25 Aug. 1750, RSUS, S.C. E.1p, reel 4.

79. For the Catawbas' plight see Merrell, "Natives in a New World," 349-67. Their departure date is noted in *S.C. Gazette*, 27 May 1751.

80. *Va. Gazette*, 4 July 1751.

81. *DRIA*, 1:92. This was Bull's assessment. That Catawbas would have agreed can be inferred from *JCHA*, 10:382; *DRIA*, 1:34.

82. *DRIA*, 1:34.

83. Ibid., 92.

84. Ibid., 92-93.

85. Ibid., 110; see also p. 111.

86. Wallace, *Conrad Weiser*, 326-28; *DRIA*, 1:92-97, 105-7, 138-46; "At a Meeting of the Indians to give their Answer to his Exellency 8 July 1751," Clinton Papers.

87. *DRIA*, 1:108, 95.

88. Ibid., 108; S.C. Council Journals, 18 Nov. 1751, RSUS, S.C. E.1p, reel 5.

89. "10 July [1751]," untitled ms., Clinton Papers; Wallace, *Conrad Weiser*, 329; *DRIA*, 1:95-96, 144-45 (quotations).

90. S.C. Council Journals, 16, 17, 26 Aug. 1751, RSUS, S.C. E.1p, reel 5; *JCHA*, 11:19.

91. *DRIA*, 1:168.

92. Ibid., 98; see also p. 99.

93. S.C. Council Journals, 26 Aug. 1751, RSUS, S.C. E.1p, reel 5.

94. *DRIA*, 1:167.

95. See ibid., 167, 205; Catawbas to Six Nations, 22 Sept. 1751, in S.C. Council Journals, 4 Oct. 1751, RSUS, S.C. E.1p, reel 5; and Glen to Clinton, 15 Oct. 1751, Clinton Papers.

96. *DRIA*, 1:167.

97. Ibid., 167–68; Catawbas to Six Nations, 22 Sept. 1751; Glen to Clinton, 15 Oct. 1751. The Iroquois examined the evidence that Catawbas sent—arrows, a hatchet, and a pipe—and denied the charge (*DRIA*, 1:202).

98. *DRIA*, 1:99.

99. Ibid., 167.

100. Ibid., 213–14; *JCHA*, 11:346.

101. S.C. Council Journals, 5 Mar., 7 May 1752, RSUS, S.C. E.1p, reel 5; *JCHA*, 11:154–55, 156, 180; *DRIA*, 1:212–13.

102. *DRIA*, 1:167, 201, 212–13; Catawbas to Iroquois, 11 Nov. 1752; S.C. Council Journals, 7–8 May 1752, RSUS, S.C. E.1p, reel 5; *JCHA*, 11:156.

103. *DRIA*, 1:354–56, quotation on p. 355.

104. Ibid., 358, 360.

105. Catawbas to Iroquois, 11 Nov. 1752.

106. *DRIA*, 1:357–58.

107. Ibid., 1:363.

108. Ibid., 373, 454, 457, 463.

109. Ibid., 456–57.

110. *Johnson Papers*, 9:114, 118.

111. *DRIA*, 2:27–28 (quotation); S.C. Council Journals, 16 Dec. 1754, RSUS, S.C. E.1p, reel 7.

112. *DRIA*, 2:48–49. See also S.C. Council Journals, 30 Apr., 29 Aug. 1755, RSUS, S.C. E.1p, reel 7.

113. PROSC, 26:212–14, quotation on p. 214.

114. *NYCD*, 7:23.

115. *Johnson Papers*, 9:834–35.

116. Sylvester K. Stevens and Donald H. Kent, eds., *The Papers of Col. Henry Bouquet* (Harrisburg, Pa., 1943), ser. 21655: 47.

117. *Johnson Papers*, 10:951.

118. Gage to Stuart, 27 Jan. 1764, Thomas Gage Papers, American Series, 1755–75, p. 13, Clements Library.

119. *NYCD*, 7:777–78. See also *Johnson Papers*, 4:279–80, 296; 12:21. *Md. Archives*, 32:57.

120. John C. Fitzpatrick, ed., *The Diaries of George Washington, 1748–1799*, 4 vols. (Boston, 1925), 1:415. See also *Johnson Papers*, 12:344–45; 6:665, 7:84, 89; 8:6–8.

121. S.C. Council Journals, 16 Aug. 1771, RSUS, S.C. E.1p, reel 10; *Johnson Papers*, 8:247–48; *South Carolina and American General Gazette*, 26 Aug. 1771; *S.C. Gazette*, 12 Sept. 1771.

122. For example, see *DRIA*, 2:92.

123. Rowan County, North Carolina, Minutes of the Court of Pleas and Quarter Sessions, 2:72, North Carolina State Archives, Raleigh; Atkin to Hagler, 17 Dec. 1757, encl. in Atkin to Lyttelton, 6 Jan. 1758, Lyttelton Papers; *DRIA*, 1:370–71, 2:36, 92; S.C. Council Journals, 2, 4 Mar. 1761, RSUS, S.C. E.1p, reel 8; *S.C. Gazette*, 12 Sept. 1771.

124. S.C. Council Journals, 4 Mar. 1761, RSUS, S.C. E.1p, reel 8; PROSC, 25:326; *DRIA* 1:370, 463; Christofer French, Journals, vol. 1: Expedition to South Carolina, 22 Dec.

1760–14 Nov. 1761, pp. 89, 134, Library of Congress, photostatic copy in York County (S.C.) Public Library, Rock Hill.

125. S.C. Council Journals, 2 Mar. 1761, RSUS, S.C. E.1p, reel 8.

126. *Johnson Papers*, 9:886–87, 951, 959–61.

127. For examples of confusion, see ibid., 94; 1:369; S.C. Council Journals, 30 Apr., 29 Aug. 1755, RSUS, S.C. E.1p, reel 7; *Johnson Papers*, 8:247; *S.C. Gazette*, 12 Sept. 1771.

128. Thomas Coke, *Extracts of the Journals of the Rev. Dr. Coke's Five Visits to America* (London, 1793), 149–50.

129. H. Lewis Scaife, *History and Condition of the Catawba Indians of South Carolina* (Philadelphia, Pa., 1896), 20.

130. *DRIA*, 1:358; see also p. 371.

131. Catawbas to Iroquois, 11 Nov. 1752.

132. For Catawbas as slavecatchers, see James H. Merrell, "The Racial Education of the Catawba Indians," *Journal of Southern History* 50 (1984): 371. Catawba participation in the patriot cause during the American Revolution is surveyed in Brown, *Catawba Indians*, 260–71. For the British theater tour, see ibid., 273–74.

133. Scaife, *Catawba Indians*, 20.

8 – CHEROKEE RELATIONS with the IROQUOIS in the EIGHTEENTH CENTURY

1. Alexander Hewatt, *An Historical Account of the Rise and Progress of the Colonies of South Carolina and Georgia, 1779*, 2 vols. (London, 1779), 2:4.

2. Among the many surveys of Cherokee history are John P. Brown, *Old Frontiers: The Story of the Cherokee Indians From the Earliest Times to the Date of Their Removal to the West, 1838* (Kingsport, Tenn., 1938); and Grace Steele Woodward, *The Cherokees* (Norman, Okla., 1963).

3. For the importance of the Cherokee trade to Carolinians, see Verner W. Crane, *The Southern Frontier, 1670–1732* (Durham, N.C., 1928); and for the impact on Cherokee society, see John Phillip Reid, *A Better Kind of Hatchet: Law, Trade, and Diplomacy in the Cherokee Nation during the Early Years of European Contact* (University Park, Pa., 1976). The best primary sources for the Cherokee trade are *JCIT; DRIA*, 1; and *DRIA*, 2.

4. *NYCD*, 5:611; *DRIA*, 2:74. For studies that emphasize warfare on the southern colonial frontier, see David H. Corkran, *The Cherokee Frontier: Conflict and Survival, 1740–62* (Norman, Okla., 1962); and John Richard Alden, *John Stuart and the Southern Colonial Frontier: A Study of Indian Relations, War, Trade, and Land Problems in the Southern Wilderness, 1754–1775* (New York, 1966).

5. *JCIT*, 215; *DRIA*, 2:22, 518; *NYCD*, 10:974.

6. Carl F. Klinck and James J. Talman, eds., *The Journal of Major John Norton, 1816* (Toronto, 1970), 262; *Johnson Papers*, 3:988, 4:848–49.

7. Richard Aquila, *The Iroquois Restoration: Iroquois Diplomacy on the Colonial Frontier, 1701–1754* (Detroit, 1983), 227–32; *DRIA*, 2:19–20.

8. "War and Culture: The Iroquois Experience," *WMQ* 40 (1983): 557–59.

9. *DRIA*, 2:348; Klinck and Talman, eds., *Journal of Norton*, 263.

10. *NYCD*, 6:137, 211, 10:242–45; *DRIA*, 2:85–106.

11. *WA*, 60–61; Klinck and Talman, eds., *Journal of Norton*, 263.

12. *Pa. Archives*, 1st ser., 1:544; *WA*, 209–10.

13. *WA*, 210–11.

14. Ibid.; *NYCD*, 6:137, 148.

15. *NYCD*, 6:172–79.

16. Ibid., 210–11.

17. Ibid., 216–19; Cadwallader Colden, *The History of the Five Indian Nations of Canada*, 2 vols. (New York, 1922), 2:168–69.

18. *DRIA*, 2:347; *Pa. Council Minutes*, 7:553–56; *NYCD*, 7:227, 281–83.

19. *NYCD*, 7:324–28.

20. *Pa. Council Minutes*, 8:124–25, 129, 135–37; *Johnson Papers*, 2:258–62.

21. Jeremiah Curtin and J. N. B. Hewitt, "Seneca Fiction, Legends, and Myths," *Thirty-Second Annual Report of the Bureau of American Ethnology* (Washington, D.C., 1918), 428–32.

22. *DRIA*, 2:15, 18, 44.

23. Klinck and Talman, eds., *Journal of Norton*, 264.

24. *DRIA*, 1:35.

25. Ibid., 224; *DRIA*, 2:474.

26. Aquila, *Iroquois Restoration*, 221–22; *NYCD*, 6:241, 9:1092; Klinck and Talman, eds., *Journal of Norton*, 264.

27. *NYCD*, 10:233, 237, 242–45; *DRIA*, 2:19–20.

28. *DRIA*, 2:44, 50–51.

29. *NYCD*, 7:219, 10:262–64, 540, 555–63; *DRIA*, 2:122, 333, 391, 393.

30. *Pa. Council Minutes*, 7:31; Alden, *John Stuart*, 57–60; Corkran, *Cherokee Frontier*, 104.

31. *Johnson Papers*, 4:62, 10:190, 196, 543, 548–49, 573–74, 576, 605, 13:246; *Pa. Council Minutes*, 8:755, 779–80.

32. *Johnson Papers*, 10:635, 12:315; *NYCD*, 7:542.

33. In 1763, Virginians complained to New York officials about ninety-four Iroquois discovered on the frontier. The Indians had neither prisoners nor scalps but wampum belts, which led the Virginians to conclude that they had been seeking an alliance with the Cherokees. The Virginians assumed that such an alliance could only spell trouble for them, so they attacked the Iroquois (*Johnson Papers*, 10:908–9). Evidence of Cherokee suffering comes from ibid., 5:31, 12:56–57.

34. Ibid., 4:848–49, 5:449, 828, 10:755, 908–9, 942–43; *NYCD*, 7:778.

35. *Johnson Papers*, 3:988, 4:848–49; see also *NYCD*, 7:778. W. J. Eccles has pointed out: "The policy of the Indian nations was always to play the French off against the English using the fur trade as an instrument of their own foreign policy. Their tragedy was not to have foreseen the consequences were the French to be eliminated from the equation" ("The Fur Trade and Eighteenth-Century Imperialism," *WMQ* 40 [1983]: 341–62, quotation from p. 362).

36. *Johnson Papers*, 12:21; *NYCD*, 8:42; James C. Kelly, "Oconostota," *Journal of Cherokee Studies* 3 (1979): 221–38.

37. *NYCD*, 8:38–53.

38. Alden, *John Stuart*, 270–81; Ray A. Billington, "The Ft. Stanwix Treaty of 1768," *New York History* 25 (1944): 182–94; Jack M. Sosin, *Whitehall and the Wilderness: The Middle West in British Colonial Policy, 1760–1775* (Lincoln, Neb., 1961), 165–80.

39. Alden, *John Stuart*, 280; *Johnson Papers*, 7:328, 332, 525.

40. *NYCD*, 8:203–4, 227–44, emphasis in original.

41. *Johnson Papers*, 7:993, 1016, 8:70.

42. Ibid., 9:560–61.

43. See chapter 7, above.

9—"AS the WIND SCATTERS the SMOKE"

1. Adelaide L. Fries, et al., eds., *The Records of the Moravians in North Carolina*, 11 vols. (Raleigh, N.C., 1922–68), 1:41–53.

2. Floyd G. Lounsbury, "Iroquoian Languages," in *HNAI*, 15:334–35.

3. David Sutton Phelps, "Archaeology of the North Carolina Coast and Coastal Plain: Problems and Hypotheses," in Mark A. Mathis and Jeffrey J. Crowe, eds., *The Prehistory of North Carolina: An Archaeological Symposium* (Raleigh, N.C., 1983), 1–51; Joffre Lanning Coe, "The Formative Cultures of the Carolina Piedmont," *Transactions of the American Philosophical Society*, n.s., 1, pt. 5 (1964): 101–5, 119.

4. For summaries of a broad range of population data, see Douglas W. Boyce, "Iroquoian Tribes of the Virginia-North Carolina Coastal Plain," in *HNAI*, 15:288; and idem, "Notes on Tuscarora Political Organization, 1650–1713" (Master's thesis, Univ. North Carolina, Chapel Hill, 1971), 13–15.

5. Idem, "Did A Tuscarora Confederacy Exist?" in Charles M. Hudson, ed., *Four Centuries of Southern Indians* (Athens, Ga., 1975), 28–45.

6. John Lederer, "Discoveries of John Lederer," in Clarence Walworth Alvord and Lee Bidgood, eds., *First Explorations of the Trans-Allegheny Region by the Virginians, 1650–1674* (Cleveland, 1912), 162.

7. Vincent H. Todd, ed., *Christoph von Graffenried's Account of the Founding of New Bern* (Raleigh, N.C., 1920), 276; Fairfax Harrison, "Western Explorations in Virginia Between Lederer and Spotswood," *VMHB* 30 (1922): 326.

8. William Stanard, ed., "Letters of William Byrd, First," *VMHB* 28 (1920): 23.

9. *JHB*, 2:23, 454; Stanard, ed., "Letters of Byrd," *VMHB* 26 (1918): 29; *Va. Council Jour.*, 1:147.

10. Seneca warfare with Hurons, apparently waged even before new pressures were produced by the fur trade, serves as one of several analogies to explode such a belief (Conrad E. Heidenreich, "Huron," in *HNAI*, 15:385–86).

11. See chapter 5, above; and Francis Jennings, "Glory, Death, and Transfiguration: The Susquehannock Indians in the Seventeenth Century," *Proceedings of the American Philosophical Society* 112 (1968): 15–53.

12. John R. Swanton, *The Indians of the Southeastern United States*, Bureau of American Ethnology Bulletin 137 (Washington, D.C., 1946), 149; Jennings, "Glory, Death, and Transfiguration," passim.

13. "Bacon's Rebellion," *William and Mary College Quarterly Historical Maga-*

zine, 1st ser., 9 (1900): 7; Wilcomb E. Washburn, *The Governor and the Rebel: A History of Bacon's Rebellion in Virginia* (Chapel Hill, N.C., 1957), 193; W. Stitt Robinson, "Tributary Indians in Colonial Virginia," *VMHB* 67 (1959): 60.

14. *Va. Council Jour.*, 1:117, 262, 2:331.

15. Ibid., 2:380.

16. *CVSP*, 1:114.

17. John Lawson, *A New Voyage to Carolina*, ed. Hugh Talmage Lefler (Chapel Hill, N.C., 1967), 174–75.

18. Ibid., 207.

19. *Pa. Council Minutes*, 2:511–12. See also chapter 5.

20. Conference proceedings, 31 July 1710, Penn MSS, Indian Affairs, vol. 1, HSP, copy in RSUS, Pa. M.1a, reel 1.

21. *Pa. Council Minutes*, 2:533.

22. *CRNC*, 1:828; Verner W. Crane, *The Southern Frontier, 1670–1732*, rev. ed. (Ann Arbor, Mich., 1956), 157–58.

23. More in-depth treatment of these events can be found in Thomas C. Parramore, "The Tuscarora Ascendancy," *North Carolina Historical Review* 59 (1982): 322–26; and Douglas W. Boyce, "Tuscarora Political Organization, Ethnic Identity, and Sociohistorical Demography, 1711–1825" (Ph.D. diss., Univ. North Carolina, Chapel Hill, 1973), 17–21.

24. Joseph Barnwell, ed., "The Tuscarora Expedition: Letters of Colonel John Barnwell," *South Carolina Historical and Genealogical Magazine* 9 (1908): 35.

25. R. A. Brock, ed., *The Official Letters of Alexander Spotswood, Lieutenant-Governor of the Colony of Virginia, 1710–1722*, 2 vols. (Richmond, Va., 1887), 1:141; *NYCD*, 5:343.

26. *CRNC*, 2:1–2, 23–24.

27. "Extracts from Letters of Ramezay and Began to the French Minister, Dated September 13, 16, 1714," *Collections of the State Historical Society of Wisconsin* 16 (1902): 321.

28. John Wolfe Lydekker, *The Faithful Mohawks* (New York, 1938), 49.

29. "New York and the New Hampshire Grants," *Collections of the New-York Historical Society* 2 (1869): 463.

30. *NYCD*, 5:371.

31. Ibid., 376.

32. *WA*, 96.

33. *NYCD*, 5:387.

34. Elias Johnson, *Legends, Traditions, and Laws of the Iroquois, or Six Nations, and a History of the Tuscarora Indians* (Lockport, N.Y., 1881), 68.

35. Hawley to Cooper, 25 Dec. 1770, Gideon Hawley Papers, Congregational Library, Boston, Mass. The Oquaga (Onoghoquaga) settlement appears in English records as early as 1712; see *LIR*, 221.

36. Pomroy Jones, *Annals and Recollections of Oneida County* (Rome, N.Y., 1851), 660.

37. Lydekker, *Faithful Mohawks*, 49.

38. David Humphreys, *An Historical Account of the Incorporated Society for the Propagation of the Gospel in Foreign Parts* (London, 1730), 305–6.

39. William N. Fenton, "Locality as a Basic Factor in the Development of Iroquois Social Structure," in idem, ed., *Symposium on Local Diversity in Iroquois Culture*, Bureau of American Ethnology Bulletin 149 (Washington, D.C., 1951), 35–54. See also chapter 1, above.

40. *Johnson Papers*, 11:827, 903–4; "Answer from the Indians. . . ," 9 Sept. 1746, George Clinton Papers, vol. 14, William L. Clements Library, Ann Arbor, Mich.

41. Charles M. Johnston, ed., *The Valley of the Six Nations* (Toronto, 1964), 281, 307; Journal of Samuel Kirkland, Jan.–Apr. 1804, Samuel Kirkland Papers, Hamilton College Library, Clinton, N.Y.; "A Journal of the Proceedings of Conrad Weiser on his Journey to Onontaga. . . ," Aug.–Sept., 1750, Penn Mss., Ind. Aff., copy in RSUS, Pa. M.1a., reel 1; *Johnson Papers*, 10:92–94.

42. *Johnson Papers*, 9:585, 624–25.

43. Hawley to Belknap, n.d., Hawley Papers; Electa F. Jones, *Stockbridge, Past and Present; or Records of an Old Mission Station* (Springfield, Mass., 1854), 74–75; Barbara Graymont, *The Iroquois in the American Revolution* (Syracuse, N.Y., 1972), 34–35; Boyce, "Tuscarora Political Organization," 58–63.

44. *Johnson Papers*, 9:714–15; *NYCD*, 6:811; Journal of Gideon Hawley, Jan.–May 1754, Hawley Papers.

45. *Pa. Archives*, 2d ser., 15:232–33, 291; Hugh Hastings, comp., *Public Papers of George Clinton*, 10 vols. (Albany, N.Y., 1899–1914), 4:185, 222–31, 492–93, 529, 568; "Journal of Lieutenant Robert Parker, 1779," *Pennsylvania Magazine of History and Biography* 27 (1903): 412, 28 (1904): 19; "A Speech of the Oneida Chiefs to Lieut. Colonel Van Dyck. . . . ," 18 June 1780, Indian Miscellaneous Manuscripts, New-York Historical Society, New York.

46. David Landy, "Tuscarora Among the Iroquois," in *HNAI*, 15:519.

47. Ibid., 520; idem, "Tuscarora Tribalism and National Identity," *Ethnohistory* 5 (1958): 278.

48. Arthur C. Parker, *The Constitution of the Five Nations; or, The Iroquois Book of the Great Law*, New York State Museum Bulletin 184 (Albany, 1916), 50–51.

49. It should be added, however, that his reputation as a researcher was one of balance, caution, and careful documentation of findings; he was probably "the leading authority on the organization of the Iroquois League" (John R. Swanton, "John Napoleon Brinton Hewitt," *American Anthropologist* 40 [1938]: 286–90).

50. J. N. B. Hewitt, "Adoption," in Frederick Webb Hodge, ed., *Handbook of American Indians North of Mexico*, 2 vols., Bureau of American Ethnology Bulletin 30 (Washington, D.C., 1907–10), 1:15–16. The allusion to the cradleboard status was made by Sir William Johnson (*Johnson Papers*, 9:113).

51. John Buck, Jr., "The Tutelo" (1918), recorded in Onondaga by J. N. B. Hewitt, Eng. trans. by W. N. Fenton with the assistance of A. General (1945), J. N. B. Hewitt Papers, no. 1364, National Anthropological Archives, Smithsonian Institution, Washington, D.C.

52. Horatio Hale, *The Iroquois Book of Rites* (Philadelphia, 1883) 152–53.

53. Conrad Weiser, "An Account of the first Confederacy of the Six Nations, their present Tributaries, Dependents, and Allies, and of their Religion, and Form of Government," *American Magazine and Historical Chronicle*, Dec. 1744, p. 666; "A Journal of the Proceedings of Conrad Weiser. . . ," Aug.–Sept. 1750, Penn Mss., Ind. Aff., vol. 1, copy in RSUS, Pa. M.1a, reel 1; *Johnson Papers*, 2:375, 9:880, 10:902–4.

54. *NYCD*, 7:582.

55. *Johnson Papers*, 9:332–33.

56. Ibid., 852.

57. Ibid., 44.

58. Proceedings of the Fort Herkimer Conference, June 1785, O'Rielly Collections, New-York Hist. Soc.; Pickering to Jay, 15 Mar. 1798, Timothy Pickering Papers, vol. 8, Massachusetts Historical Society, Boston; Jay to Pickering, 10 Apr. 1798, ibid., vol. 22.

59. *CRNC*, 2:39, 52; Brock, ed., *Letters of Spotswood*, 2:18.

60. *CRNC*, 2:60.

61. Ibid., 74.

62. Brock, ed., *Letters of Spotswood*, 2:42.

63. *CVSP*, 1:173; *Va. Council Jour.*, 3:364–65; William Stanard, ed., "Examination of Indians, 1713(?)," *VMHB* 19 (1911): 273; "Treaty of Peace . . . 27th day of February 1713 [i.e. 1714]," Fulham Palace Papers Relating to the American Colonies, 1626–1824, 14: 192–95 (microfilm, Southern Historical Collection, University of North Carolina, Chapel Hill); Brock, ed., *Letters of Spotswood*, 2:70.

64. *CRNC*, 2:458, 4:45, 224, 5:155, 785.

65. Ibid., 2:428–29, 456; 3:404, 4:345, 5:785, 994–95, 1082, 6:100; "A Correct Plan of the Lands Alloted to Tuscarora Nation of Indians" (1803), Governor James Turner Letter Book, North Carolina Department of Archives and History, Raleigh.

66. *Va. Council Jour.*, 3:397; Alexander Spotswood, "Journal of the Lieut. Governor's Travels and Expeditions Undertaken For the Public Service of Virginia," *Wm. Mary Coll. Qtly. Hist. Mag.* 2d ser., 3 (1923): 42.

67. *CRNC*, 2:60; Urmstone to Taylor, 12 June 1715, and Hassell to Taylor, 1 Dec. 1715, Society for the Propagation of the Gospel Records, British Library, London (microfilm, Southern Hist. Coll.), reel 3, nos. 21a, 33.

68. *CRNC*, 2:168, 283, 295; Newman to Secretary of the SPG, 29 June 1722, Soc. Prop. Gospel Rec., reel 3, no. 9.

69. *CRNC*, 7:431.

70. Ibid., 5:321, 7:218, 249.

71. *Johnson Papers*, 12:273–74.

72. Council Proceedings, 4 May 1717, Ludwell Papers, Virginia Historical Society, Richmond.

73. For example *NYCD*, 5:660; *Va. Council Jour.*, 3:126, 4:365; *CRNC*, 2:304–5, 11:10–15; *Pa. Council Minutes*, 4:734; *CVSP*, 1:210.

74. *CRNC*, 2:496, 3:153, 7:218–20, 249, 431.

75. Boyce, "Tuscarora Political Organization," 85–143.

76. Idem, *Our Time Here: Adaptive Responses and Changing Identities, Eastern North Carolina Indians to 1835* (Pembroke, N.C., 1984), 111–46.

INDEX

Abenakis, 63–64, 66
Adair, James, 119–21, 123
Adam, 38
Adoption, 140–41, 158–60. *See also* Prisoners
Albany: fur trade, 42, 47, 50, 53–54, 67–70, 81, 84, 179; import of, 25, 36, 69, 71, 108; Iroquois-New England Algonquian meeting (1671), 68–69; Iroquois-Catawba meeting (1751), 115–16, 127–28; Mohawk-Mahican meeting (1677), 71–73, 182. *See also* Fort Orange
Algonquians: of New England, 21, 61–73, 181–82; of St. Lawrence region, 19–20
Algonquins, 22, 36
Allegheny Mountains, 44, 100
Allegheny River, 75, 87, 94–95, 105, 111
Alumapees, 97
American Revolution, 12, 27, 57, 82, 95, 158–60, 163
Andrews, William, 156
Andros, Gov. Edmund: Covenant Chain and, 24, 43–44, 69, 72, 79; Mohawks and, 43–44, 70–72, 80
Anontagketa, 122
Appalachian Mountains, 75, 111, 136
Aquila, Richard, 81, 84
Aradgi, 26
Ashley, Benjamin and Rebecca, 157
Atkin, Edmond, 121, 124, 148
Attakullakulla, 145

Bacon, Nathaniel, 185
Bacon's Rebellion, 78, 184–85

Baltimore, Lord, 47, 76–78
Barnwell, John, 154
Beaver River, 94, 98, 109
Beaver Wars, 20–24, 41, 61, 64–65, 78
Bellomont, Earl of, 52
Benevissica, 191
Blount, Tom, 160–61
Blue Mountain, 89
Braddock, Gen. Edward, 106, 130
Bradstreet, Col. John, 110
Bull, William, 127–29
Burnet, Gov. William, 84

Canadagaye, 35
Canasetego, 55, 90, 99, 178
Caninda, 51
Captain Plans, 129
Carondawana, 85
Cartier, Jacques, 48
Catawba River, 120
Catawbas, 83, 115–33, 141, 143, 162; diplomacy and, 120–21; French and, 125; location of, 116; refugees and, 120–21, 127; unity of, 120–21, 124; Virginia and, 126–27
Catholicism, 7, 24, 48, 63, 182. *See also* Jesuits
Caughnawaga: village in Mohawk country, 68; on St. Lawrence, 7
Caughnawagas, 7, 24, 127, 180
Cayenquiragoa, 178
Cayugas: Cherokees and, 35, 138–39; Choctaws and, 147; French and, 21, 25, 143; Ohio Country and, 96, 107; Pennsylvania and, 88; Susquehannocks and, 55, 77–78; Tutelos and,

Cayugas (*cont.*)
159; Virginia and, 144; as Younger
Brother, 17, 34, 159
Céloron de Blainville, Capt. Pierre-
Joseph, 102–4
Charleston, 139
Cheraws, 120–21
Cherokees, 135–49; Catawbas and, 121–
22, 162; Choctaws and, 146–47; di-
plomacy of, 35, 36, 125, 137–42,
145–49; English and, 135–49; French
and, 136–37, 140, 143; leadership
and, 135; Lower, 136; Middle town,
136; Overhill, 136, 142; Pennsylvania
and, 140; Shawnees and, 143; South
Carolina and, 136–37; Spanish and,
138; town structure, 136; trade and,
136–37; unity of, xiv, 121, 147–48;
Valley towns, 136; Virginia and, 138
Cherokee War (1760), 136, 144–46
Chesapeake Bay, 82, 117; islands, 76
Chickasaws, 36, 121, 141, 147
Chickataubut, Josias, 68
Choctaws, 146–47
Chota, 36, 139, 141–43, 145
Christianity, 7, 24, 48, 63, 156–57, 182
Claessen, Laurence, 126
Claiborne, William, 76
Clan: defined, 30–31; import of, 12–13,
30–31
Clarke, Gov. George, 139, 142
Clinton, DeWitt, 5–6
Clinton, Gov. George, 35, 127–28
Colden, Cadwallader, 5, 93
Communitarianism, 148–49
Condolence ceremony, 140; sachems
and, 17–19, 22–23; wampum and, 17,
61–62; Words of Condolence, 17–18,
25, 34. *See also* Iroquois diplomacy
Conestogas, 82–86
Connecticut, 62–63, 67–68
Connecticut River, 62, 64–71, 77
Connessoa. *See* Teganissorens
Conoys. *See* Piscataway-Conoys
Constitution of the Five Nations, 14,
158–59, 169
Councils: clan, 34; general, 35; hierarchy
of, 34–35; import of, 34–39; private,
35; protocol and, 35–37, 44–45, 55;

Councils (*cont.*)
unanimity and, 38; village, 12, 21–
22, 34. *See also* Grand Council; Iroquois Confederacy Council
Coursey, Henry, 44–45
Covenant Chain: Connecticut and, 79;
creation of, 24–25, 42–54, 61, 183;
English and, 5, 24, 26, 41–43, 50, 54,
142; Iron, 42–43, 54; Maryland and,
43–47, 51, 79–80; Massachusetts and,
71–73, 79; multiple nature of, xiii,
41–57, 179; New France and, 43, 51–
52; New Netherlands and, 42–43;
New York and, 5, 24, 43–55, 71–73,
79, 83, 105, 178; Ohio Country and,
55–57, 97, 105–8, 180; Pennsylvania
and, 54–56, 80–91, 178; political
power and, 43, 72–73, 97; Silver, 43–
57, 178; structure of, xiii–xiv, 5, 7,
89, 119, 125, 187; trade and, 42–43;
Virginia and, 43–47, 50–52, 55, 79–80
Cowetas, 142
Creeks, 29, 142, 144, 147
Croghan, George, 97, 103, 105, 111
Cultural adaptation, 7–8, 11–12, 19–20,
22, 26–27
Cuming, Sir Alexander, 135, 147
Currundawawnah, 124, 128
Curtin, Jeremiah, 140–41

Day, Gordon, 69
Decanisora. *See* Teganissorens
Deganawidah, 17–20
Deganawidah epic, 16–17, 62. *See also*
Condolence ceremony, Hiawatha
Delaware Bay, 76–78
Delaware River, 75–76, 81, 86, 94, 186
Delawares, 36, 153; Brandywine, 86–87,
94; French and, 104–6; Germans
and, 87; Jersey, 86, 88, 90, 186;
Minisinks and, 76; Mingos and, 102–
5; New York and, 79–80; Ohio
Country and, 91–98, 104–6, 109–12,
146, 191; Pennsylvania and, 55, 76,
80–91, 106–7; Quakers and, 90;
Shawnees and, 87–88; Susquehan-
nocks and, 76–77; Tulpehocken

Delawares (*cont.*)
(Schuylkill), 86–88, 94; unity of,
109; "as women," 75, 79–82, 86–90
Denonville, Marquis de, 49, 51, 179
Detroit, 34, 36, 38, 53, 57, 98, 107–9
Diseases: Catawbas and, 120, 127, 132;
Cherokees and, 138, 144; Eries and,
94; influenza, 48; Iroquois and, 19–
20, 26, 78, 82, 167; smallpox, 78,
138; Tuscaroras and, 152
Dongan, Gov. Thomas, 81; Covenant
Chain and, 24, 43, 47–52, 179; New
France and, 25, 50–52
Druillettes, Gabriel, 63–64
Dunmore, Lord, 39, 112
Duquesne, Marquis, 104

Effingham, Lord Howard of, 43, 46–48,
51–52
Elder Brothers, 17, 25, 34
Eliot, John, 68, 182
England: military support and, 25; New
Netherlands and, 21, 66, 78; Ohio
Country and, 107–12; sovereignty,
43, 50–51, 93, 107–12, 135, 149. *See
also* Covenant Chain
Eries, 94, 96
"Ethnographic present," 12–14
Ethnohistory, 12–15; upstreaming and,
16

Fallen Timbers, Battle of (1794), 112
False Face. *See* Hadu'i'
Fenton, William, 16
Finger Lakes, 76
"Five Nations of Scioto," 110
"Flatheads," 116. *See also* Catawbas
Forbes, Gen. John, 90
Fort Cumberland, 130
Fort Duquesne, 90, 106–7
Fort Frontenac, 25, 47–48, 51
Fort Le Boeuf, 104
Fort Loudoun, 143
Fort Niagara, 34, 50, 53–54, 109
Fort Orange, 19–20, 42–43, 65–67. *See
also* Albany

Fort Oswego, 54
Fort Pitt, 108–9
Fort Pontchartrain, 94
Fort Presqu'Ile, 104
Fort Prince George, 143
Fort St. Louis, 85
Foster, Michael, 36
Foxes, 100
Frontenac, Gov. Louis de Buade de, 25,
47–48

Gage, Gen. Thomas, 131, 144, 147
Ganasaraga, 157
Gannentaha, 22
Garakontié, 22–25, 43, 45, 48, 173, 183
Georgia, 136
German Flats Conference (1770), 146–47
Glen, Gov. James, 121–30, 132
Gookin, Daniel, 68, 83
Gordon, Gov. Patrick, 96–97
Grand Council: functions of, 12, 17–19,
22–23, 174; majority rule and, 14;
peace and, 17–19; powers of, 15, 27;
structure of, 12–13, 17, 32; unani-
mous consent and, 13–14. *See also*
Great League of Peace
Grand Settlement of 1701, 26–27, 118;
Covenant Chain and, 52–54; English
and, 53, 137; French and, 5–6, 53,
82; trade and, 53–54
Grant, Ludovic, 141–43
Great Lakes, 53, 56, 93, 95, 179
Great League of Peace: antiquity of, 11,
15–16; as central government, xiv,
14–19, 27; foundation of, 16–17; Iroquois Confederacy and, xiv, 11–16,
21–27; tradition and, 11–12, 23–27,
160. *See also* Deganawidah epic;
Grand Council
Great Meadows, Battle of (1754), 105

Hadu'i', 29–30
Hagler (King Hagler), 115–16, 120, 122,
125–32
Hale, Horatio, 159

Hamilton, Gov. James, 99–100, 112
Handsome Lake, 27
Hans, 31
Hawley, Gideon, 156–57
Headmen: of villages, 18, 21–22, 24. See also Sachems
Hendrick, 56, 127–28
Hewitt, J. N. B., 14, 159, 160, 201
Hiawatha, 16–17, 62
Hithquoquean, 82
Hiwassee River, 136
Holston River, 146
Hoosic River, 69
Howard, Lord. See Lord Howard of Effingham
Hudson River, 20–21, 64, 66–67, 71, 76
Hunter, Gov. Robert, 11, 15, 85, 154–55
Hurons, 20, 22, 36, 63, 199

Illinois, 47
Illinois River, 85
Iroquois alliances: concepts of, 29–33, 36, 45; dynamism and, xiv, 33, 52, 54; hierarchical, 32; intertribal, 7–8, 29–39, 116, 119; kinship and, 29–34; marriage and, 31; moieties and, 33–34. See also Covenant Chain; Iroquois diplomacy
Iroquois Confederacy: American Revolution and, 12, 27, 57, 82, 158–60; as central government, 23; functions, xiv, 11–16; influence, 5, 8, 57, 84–86; leadership in, 12, 21–27, 32, 34, 99; power in, 6, 38, 52, 56, 69–70, 93–103, 107–11; structure of, 15, 116, 136, 159; unity of, xiv, 7, 22–27, 32, 44–45, 52, 54, 57, 99, 124, 131–32, 147–48, 156–60, 163, 173–74; warfare and, 24–26, 50–52, 55, 64, 77, 95–98, 115–17, 191–93. See also Great League of Peace; Iroquois Confederacy Council
Iroquois Confederacy Council, 12, 25–26, 34–35, 45, 55–56
Iroquois diplomacy: Algonquins and, 22, 36; basis of, 29–39, 45; Catawbas and, 115, 125–33; Cherokees and,

Iroquois diplomacy (cont.)
35, 125, 135, 139–48, 198; complexity, xiii; Condolence ceremony and, 22–23, 36; Delawares and, 79–82, 86–87, 96–97, 109–12; effectiveness, 5–6, 11, 29, 52; Maryland and, 43–47, 78–80; New England Algonquians and, 61–73; New England colonies and, 68–73; New France and, 21, 24, 67; New York and, 24–27, 42, 53, 55, 67–73; Ohio Country and, 38, 55–56, 87–88, 93–112; Pennsylvania and, 55–56, 80–91; Shawnees and, 38–39, 96–97, 110–12; southern Indians and, 55–56, 139, 152–55, 162–63; Virginia and, 43–47. See also Covenant Chain
Iroquois "empire": as myth, xiii, 5–6, 41, 52, 75, 78
Iroquois politics: central government and, 11–19, 23–24, 56, 148; change in, 11–14; factionalism and, 13–14, 24, 26–27, 50–53, 56–57, 99, 107, 156–59, 173–74; kinship and, 24, 29–31, 175–76; leadership and, 12, 19–27, 30–34, 37, 44–45, 178

Jennings, Francis, 41–43, 57
Jesuit Relations, 15
Jesuits, 63, 182; Iroquois and, 24, 50, 67, 119; Mohawks and, 22; Oneidas and, 173; Onondagas and, 22–23, 48
Johnson, John, 32
Johnson, Gov. Robert, 125–26
Johnson, Sir William, 31–38, 130–31, 159, 162, 201; Cherokees and, 137, 140, 144–47; Covenant Chain and, 56, 179–80; Grand Council and, 15; Mohawks and, 108; Ohio Country and, 57, 93, 101, 107–11; Senecas and, 109
Juniata River, 156

Kanadacta (Black Kettle), 100–102, 111
Kanawha River, 146

Katearas, 152
Keith, Gov. William, 118
Kennebec River, 64
Keyauwees, 117, 121
Kiashuta, 109
Killbuck, 191
King George's War, 97–98
King Philip's War, 43–44, 61, 70–73, 79.
    See also Metacom
King, Thomas, 35
King William's War, 24, 26, 51–52. See
    also Grand Settlement of 1701
Kinship: bilateral ties and, 31; import
    of, 30–34, 184; nonbiological, 31,
    140–41; obligations, 18, 31, 55. See
    also Clan; Matrilineality
Kirkland, Rev. Samuel, 157–58
Kiskiminetas River, 94
Kittanning, 94, 97
Klock, George, 32
Kuskuskies, 102

La Barre, Gov. Joseph-Antoine le Febvre
    de, 48–49
Lafitau, Joseph-François, 22, 34, 37
Lake Champlain, 20
Lake Erie, 47, 97, 104
Lake George, 20
Lake Ontario, 47, 53, 76
Lamberville, Jean de, 25
La Salle, Robert Cavelier de, 47–48, 85
Lawson, John, 115, 117, 119, 153
Leisler's Rebellion, 25
Le Mercier, François, 17–18
Le Moyne, Simon, 22–23
Lenni Lenape. See Delawares
Little Tennessee River, 136
Livingston, Robert, 42
Logan, James, 55, 86–90
Logstown, 97, 101–6
Long Island, 62, 64
Louisiana, 137, 143

Mahicans, 20–21, 36, 64–65, 67–72, 78–
    79, 100, 127, 182

Maine, 63
Marin de la Malgue, Paul, 104–5
Maryland, 43–47, 50, 76–80, 87, 117, 153
Massachusetts, 62–64, 67–68, 70–73, 78
Mather, Increase, 183
Matrilineality, 30–31, 175–76
Maumee River, 95
Metacom ("King Philip"), 43–44, 71
Miamis, 98
Michilimackinac, 108
Millet, Pierre, 173
Mingos: ethnic groups and, 100, 189;
    French and, 98, 100, 102–6; Iroquois
    Confederacy and, 85, 98–102; Mi-
    amis and, 98; Pennsylvania and, 98–
    103; Wyandots and, 97–98
Minisinks, 76, 88–89
Mississaugas, 33
Mississippi River, 48
Mohawk River Valley, 42, 66
Mohawks: Algonquins and, 19–20, 22,
    36; Catawbas and, 128–32; Chero-
    kees and, 139–40; Covenant Chain
    and, 56, 105; Delawares and, 79–80;
    diplomacy and, 22, 68–72, 178;
    Dutch and, 19–21, 42–43, 65–66; as
    Elder Brother, 17, 25, 34; English
    and, 43–44, 64–70; French and, 19–
    22, 36, 48, 66–67, 78; Hurons and,
    22, 36; Iroquois Confederacy and,
    23, 32, 44, 105; Mahicans and, 20,
    67–72, 182; Mohegans and, 63–64,
    67–68, 72; Narragansetts and, 63–65,
    72, 181; New England Algonquians
    and, 61, 67–73, 181, 183; Ohio
    Country and, 107; Pennsylvania and,
    88–89; Pequots and, 62; Pocumtucks
    and, 67, 72; Protestants and, 156;
    Puritans and, 61, 72; Senecas and,
    22; Sokokis and, 66, 77; Susquehan-
    nocks and, 66–67; Wampanoags and,
    70–71; wampum and, 62–65; warfare
    and, 19–20, 44, 48, 63, 67–72, 181
Mohegans, 62–72
Mohocksey, 82
Moieties, 17, 33–34, 159. See also Elder
    Brothers; Younger Brothers
Monongahela River, 75
Monongahelans, 96

Montagnais, 64, 66
Montour, Andrew, 103
Montreal, 26, 53
Mooney, James, 115–16
Moore, James, 154
Moravians, 151
Morgan, Lewis Henry, 5–6, 27, 75; Iroquois government and, 12–15, 18–19, 25, 41, 169; kinship and, 13; *League of the Iroquois*, 13
Mourning process. *See* Condolence ceremony
Mourning war, 16–22, 31, 61–62, 119–21, 132–33, 137, 148
Moytoy, 135, 147
Munsees, 110
Muskingum River, 98, 109
Muskogean, 136
Mystic River, 62

Nanticokes, 35
Narragansett Bay, 62, 65, 70
Narragansetts, 29, 62–67, 72, 181
Neolin, 109
Netawatwees, 110
Neutrality, 32, 53, 99, 107, 136, 141–42, 156–57, 198
New Amsterdam, 65
New England, 61–73
New France, 78, 84, 125; conquest of, 107–8; military force and, 20–21, 24–26, 47–54, 67, 81–82, 88, 97–98, 100, 104–6, 136; New England and, 63–68; Ohio Country and, 94–95, 102–5
New Haven, 63, 181
Newhouse, Seth, 169
New Netherlands, 21, 62, 65–66, 69, 77, 78. *See also* Covenant Chain; England
New Sweden, 76–77
New York: Dutch and, 69; New England and, 68–73; New France and, 47–53; North Carolina and, 155–56; Pennsylvania and, 80–84. *See also* Covenant Chain
New York Commissioners of Indian Affairs, 138–39

North Carolina, 83–84, 136, 151–56, 160–63
Norton, Major John, 137–38, 141–42
Norwottuck, 69
Nottoway River, 162
Nottoways, 153
Nutamis, 90

Oconaluftee River, 136
Oconostota, 145
Ohio Company, 103–4
Ohio Country, 55–57, 85, 87; migrations, 94–100; native alliances and, 110–12; Pennsylvania and, 55–56, 94–107, 124–25; settlement of, 109–12; United States and, 112; Virginia and, 101–6, 109, 112
Ohio Iroquois. *See* Mingos; Ohio Senecas
Ohio River Valley, 75, 93, 111
Ohio Senecas, 104–6, 109–12
Ojibwas, 34, 38
Old Hop, 143
Oneida Lake, 157–58
Oneidas: Catawbas and, 123–24, 128; Cherokees and, 35, 146; Chickasaws and, 36; English and, 157; French and, 21, 25, 173; Mahicans and, 36; Ohio Country and, 96; Pennsylvania and, 88; Protestants and, 157; Shawnees and, 36, 87–88; Sokokis and, 77; Tuscaroras and, 156–60; as Younger Brother, 17, 34, 45, 159
Onondaga, 14–15, 22–23, 34–36, 98–99, 108
Onondagas: Catawbas and, 130; Covenant Chain and, 56; Delawares and, 81–82; as Elder Brother, 17, 34; as "firekeepers," 25, 34; French and, 21–25, 48–53, 99, 143; Mingos and, 98–99; Mohawks and, 22, 84; Oneidas and, 45; Senecas and, 49; Shawnees and, 86–87; Sokokis and, 77; Susquehannocks and, 77–78; Tuscaroras and, 153, 157, 159
Opessa, 85
Oquaga, 31, 35, 38, 156–58

Oratory, 21–22, 45
Orontony, Nicholas, 98
Otreouti ("Big Mouth"), 25, 173
Otsiningo, 36
Ottawas, 25, 34, 38, 47, 97, 173
Ottrawana, 33

Parker, Arthur C., 14, 169
Parkman, Francis, 5–6, 75
Peace: Indian concepts of, 18; protocol
    and, 126–29, 148
Penn, Thomas, 82, 88–90; Ohio Coun-
    try and, 96–97; Shawnees and, 96–97
Penn, William, 80–82, 86
Pennacooks, 64
Pennsylvania, 54–56, 75–91, 94–103,
    124–26, 138, 140, 151, 153, 156
Penobscots, 29
Pequots, 62, 67, 70
Pequot War, 61–62, 64
Peters, Richard, 101
Petuns, 20
Philadelphia, 126, 140
Piscataway-Conoys, 77, 83
Plymouth, 62–64, 67–68
Pocumtuck, 66–67
Pocumtucks, 63–64, 67, 69–72
Pojassick, 69
Political organization: nonstate, 13–15,
    18, 41, 56, 89, 148–49; polycepha-
    lous, 175; tribal, 76, 184, 187. See
    also Great League of Peace; Iroquois
    Confederacy
Pollock, Gov. Thomas, 154, 160
Population: Catawba, 116, 132; Chero-
    kee, 138, 144; disease and, 19–21,
    78, 82, 108, 120, 127, 138, 167; Iro-
    quois, 5, 19–21, 78, 82, 107, 167,
    171; Ohio Country, 95; Tuscarora,
    152
Post, Christian Frederick, 106
Potawatomis, 34, 38
Potomac River, 77, 83, 118
Printup, William, 157
Prisoners: adoption of, 15, 20–21, 61,
    129, 137, 141, 159; exchange of, 128–
    29, 139, 143

Proclamation of 1763, 90, 146
Puritans, 61, 72
Pynchon, John, 64–69, 178

Quakers, 90, 103
Quebec Act (1774), 90

Rappahannock River, 152
Reciprocity, 33–34, 55, 126. See also Iro-
    quois alliances
Richelieu River, 19
"River Indians," 67, 69–71
Roanoke River, 161

Sachems: characteristics of, 18–19; 147–
    48; Great League of Peace and, 12–
    14, 17–19, 32, 158; Iroquois Confed-
    eracy and, 23–24; moieties and, 17;
    power of, 12–15, 45; warriors versus,
    147–48. See also Condolence cere-
    mony; Headmen
Sadekanaktie, 26
Saint Augustine, 138
Saint Lawrence River, 19–20, 64
Salisbury, Neal, 79
Saponis, 121
Sassacus, 62
Sassoonan, 80, 87–90, 185
Sauks, 29
Savannahs. See Shawnees
Scarouady, 104–5
Schaghticoke, 69, 71, 79
Schollitchy, 86
Scioto River, 94
Senecas: Cherokees and, 138–44; Chick-
    asaws and, 141; Choctaws and, 147;
    Delawares and, 81–82; as Elder
    Brother, 17, 25, 34; English and, 38,
    44, 48; factionalism and, 13–14;
    French and, 21, 25, 47–48, 51, 53; as
    general term for Iroquois, 116;
    Hurons and, 199; Ohio Country
    and, 34, 93–97, 105; Pennsylvania

Senecas (*cont.*)
and, 83–84, 88, 186; Shawnees and,
85, 96; Susquehannocks and, 44, 55,
77–78, 82, 153; Tuscaroras and, 153–
55; Virginia and, 48, 144, 198. *See
also* Mingos; Ohio Senecas
Seven Years' War, 32, 41, 90, 104, 109,
136, 142, 148
Shamokin, 87–89
Shawnees, 36, 85–86, 93–98, 110–12,
124–25, 143, 146, 153, 188, 191; Ca-
tawbas and, 118, 124; French and,
87–88, 94–95, 105–6, 143; Mingos
and, 102–4; Pennsylvania and, 83–
84, 88, 125; Virginia and, 38–39
Shickellamy, 88
Shingas, 103, 106
Shirley, Major Gen. William, 31
Sixth Nation. *See* Tuscaroras
Smith, John, 116
Smith, Richard, 65
Smith, William, 5
Sokokis, 64, 66, 77, 182
South Carolina, 83–84, 115–29, 136–37,
141, 143, 154, 160–62
Spain, 138
Spangenberg, Bishop August, 151
Spotswood, Lt. Gov. Alexander, 154,
160
Squakheag. *See* Sokokis
Stuart, John, 144, 146
Susquehanna River, 36, 50, 55, 75–76,
82–87, 90, 94, 96, 100, 109, 156–57
Susquehannocks, 20–21, 55, 66–67; de-
cline of, 78–80, 82, 184–85; Dutch
and, 77; French and, 153; Maryland
and, 44, 76–79, 117, 153; New Swe-
den and, 76–77; New York and, 79;
Virginia and, 44, 76, 78, 117, 153
Syncretism, 187

Tahiadoris, 25, 173
Tamaqua, 106–7
Tamaqua (Pa.), 156
Tammany, 82
Tanaghrisson (Half-king), 101–6, 189
Tawiskaron, 30

Teedyuscung, 90–91
Teganissorens, 26–27, 53–56, 83–84, 186
Teharonghyawagon, 30
Tennessee, 136
Thames River (Conn.), 62
Thomas, Gov. George, 90
Tooker, Elisabeth, 184–85
Toole, Matthew, 127–29
Trade: Dutch, 19–21, 42–43, 65–66, 76–
77; effects of, 26, 95; English, 42, 47,
49–51, 62, 65–67, 76, 108, 152–53;
French, 19, 49–50, 94–98, 104; fur,
19–21, 42, 47, 49–51, 54, 63–67, 136,
179, 198–99; liquor, 188; New
England, 65–67; Ohio Country, 95–
98, 103–4, 188; Pennsylvania, 54–56,
76, 81, 95–98; Swedish and, 76–77;
Virginia, 76, 97–98, 151–54, 160;
weapons, 19, 21, 77, 98, 117–18,
136–37
Trade, Lords of, 137–39, 144–45
Treaties: Albany (1677), 71–73; Albany
(1722), 85–86; Buffalo Creek (1838),
13–14; Conestoga (1710), 83–87, 153,
186; Easton (1758), 107, 109; Fort
Stanwix (1768), 110–12, 146; Franco-
Iroquois (1665–67), 21, 24, 67; Lancaster (1744), 100; Logstown (1752),
103–5; Three Rivers (1645), 22, 36.
See also Grand Settlement of 1701
Tribe, 89, 184, 187
Tuckaseegee River, 136
Turtle Heart, 191
Tuscaroras, 151–63; American Revolution and, 158–60, 163; Catawbas
and, 118, 162; Cherokees and, 35,
162; English and, 152–57, 160–62;
French and, 157; Lower, 154–55;
Moravians and, 151; New York and,
155; North Carolina and, 151–56,
160–63; Pennsylvania and, 83–84,
151, 153, 156; political organization,
152, 157, 160–63; Protestants and,
156–57; as Sixth Nation, 7, 120, 151,
155–60, 163, 186, 201; South Carolina and, 154, 160–62; Susquehannocks and, 153; trade and, 152–54;
United States and, 163; unity and,
159–60; Upper, 154–55, 160–63; Vir-

Tuscaroras (cont.)
    ginia and, 151–53, 160–62; warfare
    and, 125, 152–55, 162–63; as
    Younger Brother, 34, 159
Tuscarora Valley, 156
Tutelos, 121, 159
Twenty Years' War, 81–82

Uncas, 63
United Colonies, 63–65

Virginia, 33, 38–39, 43–52, 55, 76–79,
    96–98, 101–6, 109, 112, 116–18, 126–
    27, 138–39, 143–44, 151–54, 160–62,
    198

Wabash River, 146
Waccamaws, 120–21
Walking Purchase (1737), 89. See also
    Thomas Penn
Wallace, Paul A. W., 84
Wampanoags, 67, 70–71
Wampum: as currency, 62–63, 66; func-
    tions of, 25, 32–33, 37, 50, 55, 61–
    63, 86, 104–5, 109, 126, 139–41, 145,
    173, 198; sources of, 61–65, 181
Warfare: European view of, 118–19,

Warfare (cont.)
    125–26, 130–31, 137–38, 148–49;
    feuds and, 16, 118–19, 131; intercolo-
    nial, 32, 51, 72–73, 81–82, 97–98,
    105–10, 130, 138, 198; interracial,
    38, 87, 109–11; intertribal, 16, 47–48,
    54, 65–72, 76–77, 83, 115, 120–25,
    130–33, 137–39, 141–43, 148–49,
    152–55, 162–63, 183, 199; native
    American view of, 119–21, 124–26,
    132, 137, 148–49, 193; trade and, 19–
    21. See also Mourning war
Washburn, Wilcomb E., 184–85
Washington, George, 105, 131–32
Webb, Stephen Saunders, 5, 43, 184–85
Weepawaugs, 181
Weiser, Conrad, 89, 95, 122; Mingos
    and, 98–103
Wickmannataughehee, 121
Williams, Roger, 64–65
"Woods Edge" ceremony, 36
Woronoco, 69
Wright, Asher, 12–15, 27
Wyandots: Ohio Country and, 34, 38,
    94, 98; Sandusky, 110
Wyandot (Wyandotte) Town, 34, 95, 188
Wyoming Massacre (1778), 91
Wyoming Valley, 90–91

Yamasees, 162
York, Duke of, 46, 50, 69–70
Younger Brothers, 17, 34, 45, 159

BEYOND THE COVENANT CHAIN

was composed in 10 on 12 Palatino on Digital Compugraphic equipment
by Metricomp;
printed by sheet-fed offset on 55-pound, acid free, Glatfelter Antique Cream,
Smyth sewn and bound over binder's boards in Joanna Arrestox B
by Maple-Vail Book Manufacturing Group, Inc.;
with dust jackets printed in two colors
by Niles and Phipps Lithographers;
designed by Sara L. Eddy;
and published by

SYRACUSE UNIVERSITY PRESS
SYRACUSE, NEW YORK 13244-5160